W0017639

How to Write Poems for Loved Ones and Save a Ton of Money on Gifts!

Including
Wisdom from My Younger Self

(A Memoir)

DON RUTBERG

© Don Rutberg, 2021
All rights reserved

ISBN: 978-1-09838-379-4

Table of Contents

About the Author

Don Rutberg considers it narcissistic to dedicate a page or even a paragraph to detailing the author's background. He is from Philadelphia and has been writing and teaching for 40 years.

INTRODUCTION

I was 16 in the summer of 1972, a waiter/dishwasher at an all-boys ice hockey camp near Philadelphia. There were no girls, almost no time to play ice hockey, and a kitchen supervisor named Wanda who screamed "How many?" in such a shrill voice I still have trouble looking at pancakes. The counselors would take kids they didn't like and tie them to a post, then light a fire around them and pee on the fire to extinguish it just before any flesh burned.

It was still a decent summer. We had beer, music, basketball and naked night swimming. Late at night, we'd climb trees next to the Perkiomen creek and swing on a rope to the other side, then swing halfway back and drop into the middle of the creek the Lenape Indians called Cranberry Place. To us, it was like an E ticket ride at Cranberryland. Occasionally, a drunken counselor would describe a hellish experience in the Vietnam War and scare us half to death but it was still a decent summer. Then my uncle showed up at camp.

"Your grandfather passed away," he told me.

What was my uncle doing at camp? He was my mother's brother, so he had just lost his own father, my Grand pop Lou. He should've been grieving, not driving. Then it hit me: some sons don't get along with their fathers.

My maternal grand pop, Louis Wagner, in the 1920s

"He blew his brains out over at Einstein Hospital," my uncle revealed matter-of-factly. Then he asked, "Approximately how long will it take you to get your stuff? I'm driving you back."

Now it was what you'd probably call a bad summer.

My hard-nosed, Romanian Grand pop Lou, an ex-cop and detective, who used to swim around Steel Pier in Atlantic City in his late-60s and whose own brother (Eddie "The Kid" Wagner) was tough enough to be elected to the Philadelphia Boxing Hall of Fame, decided he

Uncle Eddie "Kid" Wagner in the 1920s. He was a boxer known for defeating the middleweight champ in a non-title fight and for throwing a brick at my Grand pop Lou and breaking his nose.

didn't want to live as a blind or weak man. (Not that he told us what was wrong; all we knew was that he had some health issues, like a detached retina.)

I loved my Grand pop Lou, the man who taught me how to swim as a 4-year-old in a salt-water pool in Atlantic City, NJ. He even taught me how to dive. He picked me up and fired me like a javelin, headfirst into the pool.

"That hurt?" he asked.

"A little," I said.

"Tuck your head next time and it won't hurt."

Grand pop taught me how to walk on the monkey bars (they were shaped like igloos) without using my hands, at all. I had to walk like a trapeze artist and get the middle of my feet onto the middle of the bars. I fell a few times.

"That hurt?"

"A little," I said.

"Keep your balance next time and it won't hurt."

So, my maternal grand pop was gone and I realized I had no grand pops left! How was that possible? What would I do? In the car going home, I wrote a poem about him. It wasn't my first poem. I started writing poems in my early teens. And I didn't write it for anyone in particular. It was a poem I just had to write.

The poem to Grand pop Lou wasn't written on a laptop. This was 1972. It's probably been tossed or lost. I remember writing how he had broken everybody's heart with his suicide but at the end of the poem, I gave him that piece of my heart. My dad said it was very compassionate and I wasn't sure what he meant. I had to look up the word, then reverse engineer my poem to Grand pop Lou. Although it was completed, questions remained in my own head, like what was I trying to say? Was it good that I became misty-eyed while writing it? (By misty-eyed, I mean I cried in violent bursts.)

No one else openly expressed feelings like I had done in the poem, except for my Grand mom Lil, who, at the gravestone, sounded a lot more pissed-off than grief-stricken with the man who made her get a second kitchen (that was kosher enough for him) in their South Philadelphia row house. Our family didn't talk much about Grand pop Lou's death. They did mention that, several times, he said dinner was so good, it would be fitting for a "last meal." I thought, back then, that I may have been able to save him if only I were home that summer night, instead of stacking dishes at camp. I may have noticed his erratic behavior and gallows talk and changed his mind. In theory, at least, it seemed possible.

If you love someone, and you all know you do, you express yourself with generous and gentle actions and words. Maybe you write a heart on the steamy bathroom mirror with your finger every morning. (I haven't done that but I've seen it done.) On special occasions, you buy greeting cards and gift cards for loved ones and take them out to nice dinners. Many of you have bought expensive jewelry or imported cars for your soul mates. You've bought tickets for games or concerts that are so expensive, you can only buy one ticket and you can't even tag along.

Case in point: During the Great Depression, when my Dad was a boy, he and his father went to see a Max Baer fight. The problem was, they only had enough money for one ticket, so my Dad saw the fight and his father, Ike, went home. This did not sit well with my Dad — for 75 years!

"Why didn't we both go home and save up for another fight?" my Dad would ask aloud. It tormented him for a good part of two centuries.

Do you see what happens when you try to give an expensive present? (The fight tickets were a dollar each.) Treating loved ones to nice dinners, jewelry, cars; forget all that. They're nice gestures but, let's face it, they've been done before. Be more original. Write your own poems to loved ones. You'll get the hang of it quickly. You'll be able to express the love inside (it's a feel-good release for you) and save money in the process.

And that's not all. For those of you misunderstood by jealous family members, no matter what kind of trouble you get into next time, there will be at least one person who will come to your defense and say you're not all bad because you wrote them a nice poem. That's a chip you keep in your pocket. Use it when the time is right.

GETTING STARTED

S tart by thinking of a shared experience you've had with your loved one ... and then go ahead and poke fun at it, like the time I was in Beverly Hills, CA and dyed my (gray) hair brown. (Someone actually asked me why I had "that stupid gray hair.") It was in 1999, eight years after I met my girlfriend/soon-to-be-wife, Marcia, when I wrote this to her on her birthday and set the words to a 1960s song I liked.

March 3rd, 1999
I LOVE YOU, MOO

(Listen to Sonny & Cher's, "I Got You, Babe")

Dear M:
They say we're not young
But that's all right,
At least we're young enough
To drive at night.
On your birthday,
Missy Moo,
The joy that moves me is
My love for you.
Moo. I love you, Moo.
Slots and horses
May pay our bills;
But you're the only place
I go for thrills.
No matter how much
We may accrue

The real wealth in my life
Is Missy Moo.
Nu? I love you, Moo.
I love shopping with you for phones.
Where the hell are those dial tones?
And when you wear those sexy clothes.
I lose all sense of calm and repose.
So, let them say
My hair's too gray.
Who likes having
Beige hair anyway?
On your birthday,
Missy Moo,
The joy that moves me is
My love for you.
Moo. I love you, Moo.

WHAT I PROBABLY MEANT TO SAY: You thrill me and bring me joy. You're my treasure.

Marcia signs her love notes to me in the morning with M ... two hearts, which looks like the word Moo. Pet names, like Missy-Moo, are fine. Use them gratuitously.

Take another example of shared experiences you've had with your loved one ... and then go ahead and poke fun at it, like when your spouse gets overbearing. I wrote this to Marcia sometime in the mid-1990s:

I like it when you're acting pretty bossy.
I like it when you order me around.
Although I like it when you're acting pretty bossy –
I'd like it more if you stopped right now.

WHAT I PROBABLY MEANT TO SAY: Just line four.

Soon after Marcia and I met, we were called an unlikely couple by some. But to me, that means we have complementary skills to help us overcome life's challenges. We are a loving team. I truly believe that and told her as much in a birthday poem.

March 3rd, 1996
BIRTHDAYS WITH MARCIA GREES
(Listen to Deep Blue Something's, "Breakfast At Tiffany's")
Dear Marcia:
They said, we were an unlikely tandem,
Thrown together at random;
A senseless spin of fate.
You thought, we'd only last two weeks or so.
I called you "Missy Torso."
Before our second date.
And I love spending the summer with Marcia Grees,
Stay at home, down the shore, at Saratoga.
No matter what time of year, she makes me happy.
Commitment, that unlikely word, enlightens my soul.

Your birthday, brings good vibes, dear, I feel it.
But how can I reveal it
Without the big expense?
It's clear now, we met because fate really loved us;
Together it magically shoved us.
Fate always makes sense.
And I love spending these birthdays with Marcia Grees,
On the way to New Hope, soaring like black hawks.
No matter what time of day she makes me happy.
Even at 3 am, we like to talk.
They said, we were an unlikely tandem,
Thrown together at random;
As senseless as a dream.

> We've got complementary skills, hon.
> Life's challenges – we can win some,
> Because we are a team.
> All my love, D

WHAT I PROBABLY MEANT TO SAY: My fear of commitment is gone; eradicated by her love. And then I reveal a secret:

> Your birthday, brings good vibes, dear, I feel it.
> But how can I reveal it
> Without the big expense?

I'm revealing that I'm trying to save money on her present. No truer words were ever written.

You can even reach multiple targets and touch several generations of loved ones if you follow paradigms of the next poem. Wife, mom, grand mom, all checked.

March 3rd, 2011
THE THIRD GREAT MRS. RUTBERG
(Listen to Bruce Springsteen's, "No Retreat, No Surrender")

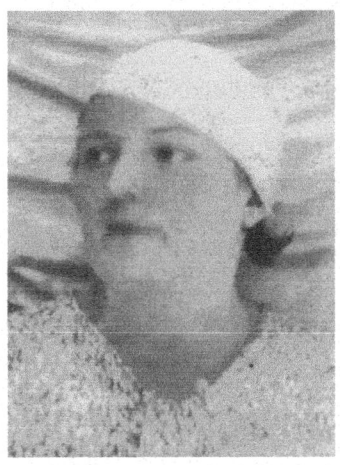

Grand mom Sarah Rutberg,
my Dad's mother

Dear M:
(1- Sarah)
She was born 114 years ago
In a European town;
Her name was Sarah but they pronounced it with
A local, Yiddish sound.
And she dazzled everybody
With her wisdom and allure.
When it came to finding the USA,
For our sake, she made sure.
It was just so simple to love her and trust her,
The first great Mrs. Rutberg.
Beautiful and bright and adored by her man,
The first great Mrs. Rutberg.

My Mom, Bernice,
at age 26

(2- Bernice)

Well, she was famously favored by her Dad
With her little girl, sweetheart aura/theme.
Just a South Philly girl; a breath of fresh air
And the backbone of this or any other team.
A best friend through life storms, with a power to
  soothe;
The building lights up when she opens the door.
Her joy and selflessness will always move
Each one of us to a higher floor.
It is just so simple to love her and trust her,
The second great Mrs. Rutberg.
Beautiful and bright and adored by her man,
The second great Mrs. Rutberg.

(3- Marcia)

Now you were waiting for me in Disneyland;
You're a combo of the other two Mrs. R's best qual-
  ities.
And everything I love in the human heart
And what I dreamed you'd be.
And on your birthday, let me tell you
With straight-up faith, on bended knee,
You're my reason for living
And the greatest gift ever given to me.
It is just so simple, oh how I love you and trust you,
The next great Mrs. Rutberg.
You prove great things come in threes, it's what
  nature likes to do.
You're my very own great Mrs. Rutberg.
Beautiful and bright and adored by her man,
You're my very own great Mrs. Rutberg.
All My Love Forever! D!

WHAT I PROBABLY MEANT TO SAY: Thank you to my Grand
mom Sarah for getting our family out of Europe and securely into the
U.S. before the world wars started. Thank you to my Mom for being such
a breath of fresh air. When I say that Mom was "famously favored by her
Dad," I'm referring to my favorite hard-boiled detective, Grand pop Lou.
Maybe that's why my uncle didn't like his father Lou, because my Mom
was far and away Lou's favorite. Now it's starting to make sense.

Also, in the poem above, when I tell Marcia "You're everything I dreamed you'd be," I mean that when I was a little kid, I dreamed that my future wife would be a good-hearted, smart, pretty and sexy, sports-loving girl like you. And then I go full hanky by saying "You're my reason for living and the greatest gift ever given to me." So, it's not one of those ambiguous love notes. Sometimes a direct approach works best.

What I'm trying to say is that I've noticed similarities in three generations of women called Mrs. Rutberg. And while I didn't have kids, at least I contributed a third generation of great women by marrying Marcia. So, the poem about my three all-time favorite women (grand mom, mom, wife, all named Rutberg) is really about me.

Marcia went with me to Saratoga Springs, NY, throughout the 1990s
We weren't married yet. But it sure looks like we're married.

WRITING POEMS TO LOVED ONES

What Techniques Can You Use?

Write your poems or cards to loved ones like you're talking to them. Figure out what you want to tell them. What important things are happening in your lives? In a recent poem to my wife, who just retired, I ask her all the pertinent questions: How much have ya got for early retirement? Whatcha gonna do in early retirement? Whatcha ever do to deserve early retirement? Who ya gonna hang with? (With me, that's who.)

Let's say you want to write a retirement poem to your spouse. First, brainstorm those pertinent ideas or anecdotes. Ask yourself: is he or she thrilled to retire or not really prepared for it? How will this affect your relationships long-term? Random thoughts are perfect.

Next, select a song that inspires you. The song has a hook. What's your hook?

I was inspired by Joan Jett's "Bad Reputation" and wrote down some notes for a poem to my wife called "Early Retirement." (The poem appears on page 230. It's about bowling, among other passions.) Joan Jett rhymed each verse with reputation, I rhymed each with retirement. Just follow the number of syllables in each verse and end with a rhyme. Funny, honey, bunny, sunny … money; the list goes on. (By the way, there is something called a rhyming dictionary to help you rhyme. It's on the Internet, though I have a paperback copy from 1985.)

Your poems don't even have to rhyme, as Larry The Ice Cream Man claims. (Read more about the war veteran, poet and chipwich peddler on page 85 — and please buy something from him.)

When I write these love poems, I think about a chorus and a rhyme scheme and see if the concepts are meshing with the rhymes. For example, if the poem is about getting drunk and screwing, don't use complicated or snobby words in your rhymes. As Allen Iverson once said, sort of, "We're talkin' about practice." It really is about practice. You just have to keep working on the poem until it feels right. Then you hand it to your loved one and save at least $1,000 on a gift.

By now, you should be thinking of shared experiences. An easy example is a vacation. Isn't it true that whacky stuff happens on vacation? Maybe a butterfly in the Butterfly Museum in Key West, Florida lands on your wife's breast. ("It's a male," Marcia says.) Or when you're ready to swim with the dolphins and you fall off a ledge in a lagoon (while video rolls) and a dolphin is giving you that "Stay on your side of the lagoon" look. ("Are you eye-ballin' me, dolphin?") Or you move her beach chair to a different spot on the beach while she's sound asleep. How about when a Cancun bartender puts a fake tarantula on your spouse's drink or when you feed mosquitoes to fish in a Jamaican pond.

While on vacation, you can take a nighttime picture of a coconut tree and when you look at the print, you see it's been photo-bombed by a playful bat!

Full disclosure: I have not written any poems about these events, all of which are true. But I did write one about a starfish we knew. We met this particularly large starfish in Aruba when Marcia picked it up in the ocean, with both of her feet. See what I mean? Whacky.

A bat photo-bombed my picture of a coconut tree in Jamaica

December 10th, 2010

LUCKIEST GUY IN ARUBA

(Listen to Simon & Garfunkel's, "Only Livin' Boy In NY")
Dear M:
Starfishy under my feet.
You aren't the luckiest fish in the sea.
I'm holding my bride in the equatorial waves
To celebrate our 10th anniversary.
Look at me.
I'm the luckiest guy in Aruba.
I knew I couldn't live without her since the minute we met.
I knew I couldn't live without her since the minute we met.
More than a bissel mazel (little luck) the wise man said.
And now it's our 10th anniversary.
Look at me.
I'm the luckiest guy in Aruba.
I'm just so darned proud of the way she acts
And the way she looks.
I'm just so darned proud of the love she makes
And the love she gives.
Starfishy, swim, go free
And find your special mate in the sea, there.
I wish you the same mazel in love that I've had
And hope you feel the same wave on your 10th anniversary.
Look at me.
I'm the luckiest guy in Aruba.
I'm the luckiest guy anywhere.
All My Love Forever, D

WHAT I PROBABLY MEANT TO SAY: We've got this loving glow between us and I want everyone to have it.

I do buy gifts for my wife every once in a while. This next poem is about that time I actually bought her a gift.

March 3rd, 2005

HAPPILY WED

(Listen to Al Stewart's, "You Should Of Listened To Al")
The clerk asked, "How much do you want to spend?
Are you shopping for your wife or a close friend?"
Then this love-struck buyer, with intentions gone higher,
Pointed over to the Bloomingdale's choir.
Although recently merged
And some choir members purged,
They sang out:
"It's what's written over his face, not what he said.
You can tell from one look; this guy is happily wed."
I told the clerk how you are a real classy mare.
If I bring you one piece of fruit, you say, "What a nice pear!"
And how you're considerate;
Mood – always temperate
If there's stress – you just get rid of it.
"Is there any gift
That would give her a lift
With no doubt?"
It's what's written over my face, not what I buy.
They could tell from one look, I'm a happy-to-be-married guy.
 She showed me some jewels and some carpenter's tools.
Some gold-trimmed pant cuffs and white, fur-lined ear muffs.
But I could attest
To what you would like best –
And that's not for sale.
It's what's written over my face, not what I said.
You can tell from one look; this guy is happily wed.
This guy is happily wed.
Happy Birthday Baby!
All My Love On Your Birthday & Forever & Ever & Ever! D

WHAT I PROBABLY MEANT TO SAY: I'm in love with an unspoiled woman and people can tell how happy I am just by looking at me. When I say "But I could attest to what you would like best – And that's not for sale" I'm implying that she would prefer a love poem (or a pear) to a pair of expensive, white, fur-lined ear muffs.

Apparently, I was intrigued by Bloomingdale's layoffs at the time. Not sure why.

Here is a poem I wrote to my wife on her birthday nine months before we got married. I had already known her for nine years and by that time I was regularly writing love poems to her. We were going to Atlantic City, NJ, to the casinos.

March 3rd, 2000
A TAJ MAHALAN SUNDAY
(Listen to John Dawson Reed's, "Sally Alley Sunday")

Driving to the sea shore
Hoping it won't snow.
Praying that the donut tire
Won't decide to blow.
Get to the apartment,
"Where ya wanna go?"
And how does anybody
Open this screen door?
My love is acting kooky;
Says she had a dream;
Saw it all so clearly,
The details of the scene.
She saw us at the Taj Mahal
Winning lots of green.
But what are all the workers there
So mean for?
It's a Taj Mahalan Sunday
And it's really ecstasy;
We meet horses named for Malta,
New friends from Albany.
Then the Franny horse comes in
Like Mom said, "Have some fun on me."
And we high-jump into bed
Like we're both gymnasts.
Climb down from the mattress
Time to start the day.

Walk into the Taj Mahal –
The dream is holding sway.
We hang out in the horse room;
We can't sit but we can play. Huh?
Oh, how I love being with you
On your birthday.
Then I join you "Let it ride"-ing,
I say, "A flush is nice."
But you set your standards higher;
"The straight flush pays the price."
And the jack of clubs comes winking;
If we're winning, where's the vice?
And we're smiling at each other
Like it's our first date.
Driving back to Philly;
How long were we away?
How long have we been holding
 hands
And eating up buffets?
Let's spend our lives together;
Keep on cherishing each day.
Smiling at each other
Like it's our first date.
All my love on our first date,
our second date (!) And forever, D

WHAT I PROBABLY MEANT TO SAY: We're still smiling at each other like it's our first date. At the very end of the poem, I added an exclamation point after mentioning our second date. Why? Let's just say it's a reference to romance and the laws of physical attraction. My Dad's generation called it "chemistry." More than 15 years later, in 2015, I wrote a poem to Marcia about "chemistry" that began like this:

HOT SEX AT 60 PLUS
(Listen to Bruce Springsteen's, "Held Up, Without A Gun")
Dear M:
I was a newlywed at the turn of the century
And I knew it was love and it was meant to be.
But there's one thing a bride and groom do not discuss:
(Is there)
Hot sex at 60 plus.
Hot sex at 60 plus.

That full poem appears on page 224. And since it's not the 1950s, I didn't have to call it "Chemistry." I called it "Hot Sex At 60 Plus."

In the poem "A Taj Mahalan Sunday" (set in a defunct Atlantic City, NJ casino, not India) about smiling at each other like it's our first date, I give away my intention to ask Marcia to marry me. It was a step short of a genuine marriage proposal, which followed that summer, in August of 2000. I sat my darling down on a boardwalk bench at the Jersey shore, and I popped the question. "Will you …." That was it: "Will you …." I was 44 years old and had never asked anyone to marry me. I was inexperienced and nervous, which led to the ridiculous stammering of a half-sentence that could've meant everything or nothing. When we first met nine years earlier, I told her I was a writer and now she was saying, "You're a writer and that's all you can say? 'Will you….?'" Someday, I'll write her a poem about that clumsy proposal on the boardwalk. I'm saving that idea for the right moment.

IMPORTANT TO REMEMBER:

When you write your own poem to a loved one, make sure it's appropriate and never in any way hurtful. If you think it's clever and then they read it and they look more disgusted and offended than happy and touched, don't give that poem as a present. Your love poems have one goal: to show the recipient how much you love and appreciate them. You want to make them aware of your feelings, like any greeting card. But this card is completely personalized; an inside-straight from the heart.

Think of shared experiences you've had with your loved one. Take an easy example: things you've done together.

August 24th, 2001 (Ten years since we met!)
FOR TEN SWEET YEARS
(Listen to Dire Straits', "On Every Street")

Dear M:
There must've been a lucky star in Memories that night;
Thought I saw some angels runnin' loose.
Or cupid, who'd later take flight
With the smiling moose.
Oh, my life, it had changed.
Look what fate had arranged.
It reached down and pulled us together by our ears.
And it's those ears I've trusted now
For ten sweet years.
Flash it forward to May '94;
All your stuff's moving in.
We gave out water because we happened to have it in stock.
Let the structural changes begin.
I should've married you then,
Downstairs in the den.
Two peas in a pod though our brains use different hemispheres.
And it's your brain I've counted on
For ten sweet years.
A vision of ivory vivaciousness, flanked by Mom and Uncle Irv,
Sniffling toward me down the aisle.
There I saw the angels again and the face of God
In my Mom and Dad's smile.
We laughed like kids, side by side.
Tell the groom – kiss your bride!
In the annals of loving couples, we're creating new frontiers,
But we've been a loving couple now
For ten sweet years.

And the best part: those sweet years
    are just
The first ten years.
Thinking of you
  and the things we could do.
    let's hitch a ride
      with the next butterfly.
What a first kiss
  in the dark, boardwalk mist.
    we didn't care
      we were getting no air.
Wanting you more
  on the PMS floor.
    better stay low
      so the neighbors won't know.

"An unlikely pair."
  horseshoes in the air.
    you gave it two weeks
      but my interest was piqued.
Drive to the spa
  and get splashed in the car.
    my fondest wish
      is peeled olives and fish.
Mt. Diablo,
  yes, I'm driving slow.
    clouds down below,
      dragonflies that we know.

We love the shore;
  there are spots we love more.
    countries to tour
      and the duty-free store.
Drive to Quebec;
  please rub my neck.
    driving too fast,
      almost missed, "Sexy Gas."
Old city wall,
  that's a tall waterfall.
    where's Woody's hair?
      he'll go with us anywhere.
Freezing cold hands
  as we sit with the fans.
    warm up your chin;
      it's our time to win.
I'll be the cook
  never read a cookbook.
    you make it clean
      in the seat where I've been.
Move to the woods
  we got out of the 'hoods.
    there's the Delaware, see?
      why'd they cut down that tree?
Thinking of you
  and the things we could do.
    let's hitch a ride
      with the next butterfly.
All my love forever, D

WHAT I PROBABLY MEANT TO SAY: The first ten years have been wonderful and I expect them to only get better. As a matter of fact, I should've married you sooner.

"Hitch a ride with the next butterfly" refers to our shared experience soon after we met in the late summer of 1991. We were walking along the shoreline near Atlantic City, NJ, and looked up at the blue sky, except it wasn't blue. It was orange and black. Tens of thousands of Monarch butterflies were flapping in formation. They finally landed on the beach, looking exhausted. It was like gazing at an alien or the opening of a time vortex. The greatest navigators on Earth, and they were visiting us. You just had to smile. I began researching monarch butterflies and soon wrote a children's book, *The Traveling Monarchs*. I also mentioned them in this ten-years-since-we-met poem to Marcia because seeing so many butterflies directly above us on the beach was a shared, breathtaking experience; unique to us. When you write to loved ones, refer to those shared, breathtaking moments. It was a good thing we both saw this Monarch migration in progress (they fly from Canada to Mexico) because it was hard to believe unless you were there to see it with your own eyes.

That's not my only reference to something that has to be seen to be believed:

> There I saw the angels again and the face of God
> In my Mom and Dad's smile.

It's true. I have never felt as close to God as when I saw my Mom and Dad's smile at my wedding. It's a heavy concept, for sure, but what I do with a heavy concept is write it down, and then I feel lighter.

We do use different hemispheres of our brains. Marcia is left-brained (organized) and I'm right-brained (creative). Between us, we have one whole brain! Not every couple can claim that, as far as I know.

"I'll be the cook. Never read a cookbook" is my promise to cook dinner for her every night. I won a wok on The Dating Game in 1978 (I was Bachelor #3) and have been cooking ever since. Although it's true I've never read a cookbook, I did write one recently called "We'll All Be Eating In 15 Minutes – No Matter What!" Sales are flagging.

When I say, "It's our time to win," I mean it was time for the Philadelphia Eagles to win the Super Bowl. I was only off by 16 years.

YOU CAN WRITE POEMS TO YOURSELF, AS WELL AS TO FAMILY AND FRIENDS.

I write poems on my birthday whenever possible, to gauge my feelings at the time. Here is one about turning 29 and being ridiculously burned out after seven years in L.A.

November 6th, 1984
YOU'VE GOT A FRIEND IN PENNSYLVANIA

(Listen to Toto's, "Africa.")

I'll tell you how my 29th was spent.
Walking streets carved up with names of Hollywood celebrities.
I left no footprints in cement,
All I left were fingerprints embedded on these typing keys.
I crossed the street and looked around,
Remembering the hope and the excitement clearer than the fear.
Then from behind me came a sound:
Could there be a birthday greeting here?
When I turned a truck was bearing down on me.
Stopped so close the license plate was all that I could see:
YOU'VE GOT A FRIEND IN PENNSYLVANIA!
Then I saw the passenger door open up for me.
I walked down Sunset Boulevard,
To visit my professor and to see what sense that he could make
Of my near-miss with the moving cars,
And reveal to him the ubiquitous advice I was about to take.
He said he didn't believe in fate;
Then we felt the earth begin to shake!
Suddenly, the ceiling caved right in on us.
But I could see a message spelled out in rubble and dust:
YOU'VE GOT A FRIEND IN PENNSYLVANIA!
Then I saw an airplane headed east that I could trust.

WHAT I PROBABLY MEANT TO SAY: I was walking down Sunset Boulevard on my 29th birthday, burned the fuck out. Yes, after writing over 100 books and scripts without cursing (and without getting famous), I am allowing curse words into my work. After what we've all heard on TV, how can crude language offend us? I'd rather hear a cuss than see actual TV news footage of severed heads in an open duffel bag. ("Film at 11.")

The above poem was a milestone for me, written on or about my 29th birthday. It would be my last one in L.A. I had gone to grad school at USC and stayed in town for seven years, trying to be a freelance screenwriter and it was becoming obvious I had to leave for my own peace of mind. I got closer and closer to my goals every year without actually reaching most of them. There were way too many bizarre near-misses. When I heard The Animals singing, "We Gotta Get Out Of This Place, If It's The Last Thing We Ever Do," I sang along with all my heart. My poem supported this theory. Like most poems, it would turn out to be prescient. I did have a friend in Pennsylvania (Marcia) who would marry me and make my life so joyful.

In the above poem, "You've Got A Friend In Pennsylvania" (subtitled "You've Got Very Few In California") I refer to my old professor, A.J. Langguth, who lived near Hollywood and Vine. He'd treat the two of us to dinner and drinks at Musso and Frank's, the oldest restaurant in Hollywood, where they filmed "Ed Wood" with Johnny Depp and "Once Upon A Time In Hollywood" with Brad Pitt. He was there for the turkey a la king but made us order lobster thermidor. I knew he was paying but he kept insisting so we said ok (couldn't be rude) but that was the only time I let somebody treat me to an entrée six times more expensive than his. He was my mentor. You could smoke pot around him. He helped me sell my first movie outline straight out of USC. Then he told me I would probably have to wait five or ten years to make it big in Hollywood. I thought he was kidding. He wasn't.

Sometime in 2014, after hearing that A.J. had passed, through a torrent of tears, I wrote this:

PULITZER PRIZE (for A.J.)

(Listen to Bob Seger's, "Manhattan")
You never had to tell him; he knew what was really going on.
He came from Minnesota, where they named kids Arthur John.
Never said anything about Harvard but back in 1955
A lot of Ivy Leaguers thought he'd win the Pulitzer Prize.
Next thing he knew, he was in the middle of the Vietnam War.

And he was writing about things he was told to ignore.
The NY Times said, "You don't always have to write down when a U.S. soldier
  dies."
When the NY Times don't like you, you don't win the Pulitzer Prize.
He held onto his beliefs.
His time in Saigon was brief.
The Times went out and replaced him
As bureau chief.
They sent him to Brazil where he wrote a book about Macumba,
White and black magic; he once helped me use some.
Then he wrote about the CIA in Brazil and all its mob ties.
When the CIA don't like you, you don't win the Pulitzer Prize.
I can still see him smiling there
In Hollywood, at Musso & Frank's.
I'd do bumps on the table
While AJ drank.
He'd dole out wisdom, tolerance and kindness
Through those war-torn eyes.
Closest I've ever been
To the Pulitzer Prize.

WHAT I PROBABLY MEANT TO SAY: The man did not judge. I had finally come across someone like that, a rarity, almost an impossibility. Also, I learned that talented, hard-working people can get screwed out of credit they deserve so we should get over it quickly when it invariably happens. You can get shafted, all right. Of course it's possible; relax. (See my poem on page 91, "Of Course; Relax!")

Did he use Brazilian magic, called Macumba, on me? This was California in the 1980s. Using Macumba or placing healing crystals on your body or going to psychics was common, like going to breakfast at 1pm. He used a little rice wine to clear my path (according to the legend) and within a month I was back home in Philly. He was more than a mentor; he was a wizard.

This man, Jack Langguth, was my brush with greatness. And they gave the Pulitzer Prize to David Halberstam who replaced him as the New York Times' Bureau chief in Saigon in the mid 1960s. Jack was demoted for telling the truth. But you can't be demoted for writing truthful poems to your loved ones. At least I haven't been yet.

When I write, "I'd do bumps on the table while A.J. drank," I mean I would do *bumps on the table* while he drank martinis. I'm telling you — the man didn't judge. Most adults would tell you to stop doing anything illegal at their table, but not him. My generation's mantra of, "Never trust anyone over 30" melted away that night.

Now I have trouble trusting anyone under 30. And I've met a few thousand college students (I was an adjunct professor) so I'm no stranger to "yoots," as "My Cousin Vinnie" would say. In my experience, the Baby Boomer generation, and I'm the middle child of the Boomers, had more respect for professors than the following generations. And if that offends some young readers who are the sensitive kind, like in a J.J. Cale song, remember my motto: "If I haven't offended you in this book, I didn't do it on purpose." However, in general, I am supportive of sensitive people.

"I was a poet once. I worked my feelings into verse. And took the blessing with the curse." (From my poem, "The Ride," which appears on page 265.)

I make another reference to a table in this next poem, written 30 years earlier. Instead of bumps on the table, I'm looking at the jelly on the table, hoping to eat some because I'm fucking broke and drifting around in the most expensive city in the world, New York City. As I drift, I start to realize that I don't belong in L.A. or NYC. I'm no coastal elite. To me, that's a good sign and confidence booster.

Sometime in the early 1980s:
ONE MORE STOP

West 44th, with a view to the North

In a room where claustrophobia
thrives.
While I reside here, I'll laugh and I'll
cry here;
Knowing only the savvy survive.
From the third floor, I see more
Than the pavement turn neurotic
And once romantic movie houses
Long since turned erotic.
The windows; clean, yet gray
Cannot reflect this sunny day.
New Yorkers, in a rush today,

Decide to hide – I see them stop
Inside of Dumont's barber shop.
They'll shave you for a dollar;
If you want to sit, it's two.
Protection in the mirror
Though they can't improve the view.
A dirty joke, a puff of smoke
That might just be the air.
And you know you'll be late for work
But this time you won't care.
You leave and give your hat
To someone lying on the trash.

You're both the same except that
You've got credit cards and cash.
He hasn't had a haircut
But he'd rather have a meal.
When he wakes up, he'll trade the hat
For food he used to steal.
The people; clean, yet gray
Cannot reflect this sunny day.
As hungry as they're rushed today,
They find the time for one more stop
Down there at Belcrep's coffee shop.
A very normal place to eat
If not positioned on the street
Facing "Association of the Bar."
The waitress doesn't seem to care
That she works here and they work
    there.
A narrow street; to me, it seems so far.
But I can almost taste
The maple syrup on the seat.
And jelly on the table
That turns toast into a treat.
From the third floor, I see more
Than a shop that's worn and shows it.
While New York gamblers bet on
When the Board of Health will close it.
The windows; dirty, gray –
Getting washed now, any day.
As gamblers, rushing all the way,
Find one more familiar stop
And that's the Off-Track betting shop.
It's often called a parlor –
When a long shot winner dies,
His friends will crowd around
To search his coat and eulogize.
Can't you see them rushing
To make bets they'll never win?
Ask about the champ
They could've owned and could've been.
They're looking for some safety –
Betting with no sense or fear,
And if the town starts burning down
They'd like to watch from here.

Imagine cashing tickets
Just as Armageddon nears.
But neither one may happen
For a hundred thousand years.
At windows, people stay.
This could be their lucky day.
Soon, they'll have to turn away,
Past the one, poor, happy cop
And toward the crowded cabbie stop.
From the third floor, I see more
Than cabbies getting drunk.
The yellow mangled steel suggests
The Dodge once had a trunk.
A checkered cab with room for six
But I'd sit on the stool
And hear them curse in languages
I studied once in school.
The windows; up they stay.
The fare is just protection pay
For you or him; either way.
The lights are red – the ride non-stop
Right past the Dumont barber shop.
Closing my shade,
Blocking out the parade
Just as concrete walls block out the
    sun.
I shout out, "I'm staying"
But don't know who's paying
For strangers to sample the fun.
The Dumont prices I can't pay
Unless that's all I do today.
Strong coffee – I could use a sip
From waitresses I couldn't tip.
There's no way I can make a bet.
I haven't had a winner yet.
Sure, I can walk most anywhere.
What else in town is free but air?
What happens when the natives here
Have nothing left to spend?
Does it mean the fun is free
Or coming to an end?
Who cuts Dumont's daughter's hair?
And how much does it cost?

How many stop in Belcrep's
Coffee shop because they're lost?
From the third floor, I see more
Than a town promoting greed.
No one thinks of what they have
While chasing what they need.

Bus windows ... clean today!
Next week I'll be in L.A.
A different pace – the same ballet,
Where everything's a betting shop.
For me, though ... only one more stop.

WHAT I PROBABLY MEANT TO SAY: New York and L.A. have
a different pace ... but it's the same ballet/bullshit, the same cutthroat
rat race. I liked the New Yorkers better because they ran a more open
and honest rat race. It's like what Leonard Cohen was saying: "I will kill
you if I must" is nicer than "I will kill you if I can." In Hollywood, your
competitors will kill you if they can get half a chance. Those movie people,
I'm certain, all voted for an L.A. subway system — so they could push
rivals off the platform. New Yorkers will only kill you in business if they're
forced into it. That's relatively sweet.

They're looking for some safety –
Betting with no sense or fear,
And if the town starts burning down
They'd like to watch from here.
Imagine cashing tickets
Just as Armageddon nears.
But neither one may happen
For a hundred thousand years.

In the snarky paragraph above, I chide gamblers. You know, I grew up
20 minutes from Garden State Park race track in Cherry Hill, NJ. That's
the place that burned the fuck down and people wouldn't leave (and
subsequently died) because they hadn't yet cashed in their winning tickets.

Basically, the poem predicts that I'll leave L.A. in 1982. I did leave
L.A., in 1984, two years too late in hindsight yet I had the foresight to
already know it and write it down in 1982!

"I'll leave Hollywood after I'm rich and famous," while a noble and
popular notion, doesn't usually work out and it didn't work out for me.
However, by not accomplishing much in L.A. for seven years, I lucked
into a situation where a major setback surreptitiously led to greater things,
which I describe in the next poem.

November 6, 2003

48

(Listen to Simon & Garfunkel's, "Dangling Conversation")

There was a message on the voice
    mail
From a university.
The title, "English Professor"
Was waiting there for me.
But I couldn't take the meeting,
Out in California
For at least a dozen days;
They gave the job away.
It was another major setback
That led to even greater things
And now the bell of irony rings.
So, I mailed away a children's book;
The one about the goats.
Typed the addresses clearly;
Personalized the notes.
Seems I submitted two to Viking.

I didn't mean to do it.
But Viking said, "Wow. Great!"
Like a twisted piece of fate.
It was another major setback
That led to even greater things
And now the bell of irony rings.
Driving all around the freeways
Like I did in '84,
When they threw me in the dumpster
And then ran up the score.
But the scars and tears, they sent me
Back to my beloved family,
To the woman of my dreams
To loving, emotional streams.
It was another major setback
That led to even greater things
And now the bell of irony rings

WHAT I PROBABLY MEANT TO SAY: I have scars. And tears. I have scars from the tears. It doesn't make me any tougher than you. Don't pity me, and I mean it this time, because the experiences (rejections like you wouldn't believe) have made me a better and happier man. Harry Truman wanted to own a clothing store. He failed and after that became President of the United States. "It was another major setback that led to even greater things," in other words.

    I had spent seven years in Los Angeles and felt enough disappointment and seen enough foul play to know I had to leave. (Read more about it on page 249, in my poem, "It Was Time To Leave L.A.") Leonard Cohen said that he was sentenced to twenty years of boredom "For trying to change the system from within." Well, I was sentenced to seven years of ambivalence … and I wasn't even in the fucking system! I was like a boat owner: the happiest days of my life were the day I arrived in L.A. and the day I left. At least I was on two legs when I departed. Many of my friends, mainly actresses, were taken to the airport on stretchers. I know because I dropped them off.

Below is a love poem to a place, not a person. (Joni Mitchell did it with her 1971 song, "California.") Saratoga is a race track in upstate New York that was built in the 1860s, on Native American land. New Yorkers must have used some pretty cagey negotiating tactics (firing squads) because the Native American land became our land. The white man didn't adhere to the theory of "take what you need and leave the rest." They took the very best from the original residents of Saratoga Springs (including the natural springs with healing waters). Levon Helm and Joan Baez both sang about it in the classic: "The Night They Drove Poughkeepsie Down."

Saratoga Springs, NY, old-fashioned and quaint, is our happy place. We go there to celebrate the anniversary of the day we met (August 24th) every summer.

Here I am in the dining room at Saratoga Race Track.

Summer, 2008
SARATOGA
(Listen to R.E.M.'s, "Day Sleeper")

North on the thruway –
New York state –
Surrounded by natural spring sources.
We told the Indians,
"Thanks for the land"
And then built a track to race horses.
I'm moving closer to a place in my
    dreams,
Where everyone loves horses
And even horses can dream.
And I look in their eyes
And I see the hope
And the trust in their souls –
And in mine.
At Saratoga.

The man's got a shovel
On the track. Now he cleans it.
He calls himself
The park superintendent and he
    means it.
He smiles as he shovels,
I wave, now I'm sure,
He's happier than most men
And he's lifting manure.

And I look in his eyes
And see the fine line
Between winning and living his life.
He's got a job like mine.
At Saratoga.
I long for this place.
From a past life; one that's fleeting.
I'm up six hours early, at the stables by
    dawn,
Just to watch horses eating.
I know all the people along the main
    street.
"Tell me, in what other life did we meet?"
And I walk in the lobbies of downtown
    hotels:
That's me in this picture from 1912.
Oh, one day I'll stay.

And I sit in the bath house
Where Roosevelts preened,
Then I breeze through the parks;
Just blend into the scene.
Oh, the Mohawk river is whispering.
I can hear it.
I must be near it – Saratoga.

WHAT I PROBABLY MEANT TO SAY: One real-life image stands out to me, that of the track superintendent/shit remover smiling as he did his job. He knew more about horses than a Kentucky Colonel. (My Dad was an honorary Kentucky Colonel, and so was his cousin, Sid Pranikoff, and no one ever knew why.) The track superintendent/ shit remover knew about all kinds of dirt and grass. His duties included and even featured shoveling horseshit away from the racetrack. "He's got a job like mine" is my crack about how much bullshit I've seen in my years in Hollywood.

I blend into the scene at Saratoga, sort of like how Jack Torrance blended into the Overlook Hotel in "The Shining." I can prove it. I have pictures of me standing by a tree. Me and the tree match perfectly. (That was almost the title of this book.) I have photos of me wearing a plaid, summer shirt that matches what the stable hands are wearing. And there I am in 1995, in a video joking with the Crown Prince of Saudi Arabia. He was wearing a $20,000 silk suit (I guessed Harrods) and I was wearing a plaid, summer shirt like Joe The Cable Guy, but I was still blending in with the scenery, if not the Prince.

"Don't I get a hug, too?" Marcia asked the Prince, who had already hugged over 30 men in his entourage, near his limo.

"No, I am married," he told her.

I thought I read somewhere that Saudi princes had many wives. It wasn't the right time for me to ask him, though. I admit to hearing the voices of childhood friends saying, "Hey, Don. It's a fucking prince. Go bullshit him and see what he says." (I was always a good talker.)

Then Marcia half-screamed, "I'm married to him!" as she pointed at me with her little girl charm.

The Prince waved and gave me a look like, "It's that same chatty guy from before, who complimented my suit and asked if I got it at Harrod's."

"I love the America!" he shouted as he went back to pat his horse, Point Given, who had just won the 1995 Travers Stakes, a million-dollar horse race. (That means, as the owner, he earned $600,000 in that one race.)

If I ever win $600,000 on a race, I'll show more emotion than this fellow did, trust me. But I've seen other super-calm, oddly-stoic reactions from folks who just won a million dollars. That summer, Marcia and I were in Bally's casino in Atlantic City, NJ, the town that's riding high in April, shot down in May, every year, until the asteroid hits (and the NYC betting shops start burning down). We suddenly heard loud bells by the slot machines along the wall.

My journalistic instincts were on fire.

"What's the scoop?" I asked a member of the Bally's cleaning crew. He picked up a few empty glasses and pointed to the wall.

"See that guy over there. The one arguing with the waitress over his drink."

"Yeah," I said. "He looks pissed. She must've botched his order."

"That guy just won a million bucks."

He pointed to the man, whose wife was playing a slot machine next to him but not paying any attention to him.

I was told by my sources (the Bally's cleaning crew) that the guy had won $50,000 per year for 20 years and $50,000 apparently wasn't a lot of money to him. He looked like he couldn't care less about winning a million bucks. He was just a gambler with a bad waitress and an apathetic wife. It wasn't his day, I guess.

I saw one fellow at Saratoga get annoyed at the stack of money in his hand. I have witnesses to this odd act (getting mad at your own money). "Sal the Philly barber" hit a Pick-6 at Saratoga, collected at a window near me (I wasn't collecting anything) and started counting hundred-dollar bills. There were plenty of hundreds, like in the movies. Sal mumbled, "Look at all these fucking hundreds."

Now he's pissed. Why? He had to pay off his many partners and pay taxes on the money, most likely more than his fair share.

The Talmud is right: the more you have, the more you have to worry about.

Below is another poem set in Saratoga. It's a love poem to Marcia, on the anniversary of the night we met 23 years earlier.

Marcia took this picture of horses running at Saratoga and gave it to me as a birthday present. She was allowed to stand right next to the starting gate to snap the photo, despite having no credentials or licenses.

August 24th, 2014
ANNIVERSARY AT SARATOGA
(Listen to Kansas', "Miracles Out Of Nowhere")
Dear M:
On an August evening,
Where cicadas buzz outside,
Savoring the summer specials
Like the ocean's warming tides.
The only thing that's on my mind
Is what I'm gonna do
When I get to the Spa with you.
In those early years,
I had my girlfriend by my side,
Stood where Onion beat Big Red
And bet she'd make a stunning bride.
Goose bumps on my flesh
You touched my arm and felt them, too.
Walking 'round the Spa with you.
Spin around with me on the carousel.
Sprinkle me with water, I'll fall under your spell.
It's not a dream.
My favorite scene
Is our anniversary at Saratoga.
Twenty-three years of joy
Since I found your love and light.
Every trip reminds me
Of the luck I had that night.
Every year in August, there's a pilgrimage we make.
To an exit near Saratoga Lake.
Spin around with me on the carousel.
Sprinkle me with water, I'll fall under your spell.
It's not a dream.
My favorite scene
Is our anniversary at Saratoga.
Looking forward to all the Augusts still to come …
All My Love, D

WHAT I PROBABLY MEANT TO SAY: This 2014 poem refers back to 1992, my first full summer with my future wife. I was in my thirties, had met my soul mate and checked off a key box on my bucket list. Another thing on my bucket list was going to Saratoga race course in upstate New

York so we took the five-hour car ride from Philly to Saratoga Springs.

Standing at the rail where they turn for home at the 19th century track (it only closed one day, for a Civil War parade, during the Civil War) I relayed to Marcia one of the most inspirational sports stories of all time. In the 1970s, a cheap, runt of a horse named Onion beat arguably the greatest race horse of all time, Secretariat. It was a win for the little guy. If Onion could beat Secretariat ("Big Red") anything was possible. I wrote a children's book about Onion; how he overcame mighty obstacles but his feelings were often hurt when the crowd yelled, "Onion stinks."

Do you like underdog stories? Saratoga has plenty of them, including the time when the mighty Man O' War was upset by a horse named Upset. That horse's name became a new word in the English language, like getting "Munson-ed" (see the film, "Kingpin.")

What did I mean to say in the poem? I'm dizzy in love with her.

Below is a 2015 poem about how I met Marcia 24 years earlier, on a night when I was supposed to be in Saratoga but wasn't.

August 24th, 2015
GONE TO SARATOGA
(Listen to Queen's, "Barcelona")

Dear M:
I had this lucky day.
In 1991.
It was August 24th.
The Travers was on TV
But no one there could find me
Because I was down the shore in surf
    and sun.
I finally left the beach.
Dad was watching ESPN.
He said, "It doesn't matter
But your horse just won the Travers.
If you had gone, you'd be a rich,
    young man."
Gone to Saratoga?
It was the only year I missed.
Saratoga.
I was shocked and I was pissed.

The horse that I'd been following for
    months
Just paid a couple grand!
Saratoga.
I wasn't at Saratoga.
It turned out I was only following God's
    plan.
I borrowed 20 bucks
And went out to the clubs;
Hit all the Margate pubs.
I started talking to Marcia
But soon ... wanted more.
I'd met the woman I was supposed to
    meet, for sure ...
Just off the dance floor.
Saratoga.
I missed a big payday and that ain't fair.
Saratoga.

Let me tell ya, I didn't care.
I'd found in her a lifetime filled with
    love, respect and joy.
Saratoga. Saratoga.
On August 24th

We celebrate
Our anniversary.
The luckiest day ever.
At Saratoga.
All My Love Forever, D!

WHAT I PROBABLY MEANT TO SAY: In this story, I reveal how I met the love of my life on a night when I had to borrow 20 bucks to get in the club. So I don't buy the excuse from single friends that they don't have enough money to go on dates or go out mingling. This is how our first few dates went after we met at a nightclub.

1st date: I took her out for pizza on South Street near downtown Philly. Then we went to a coffee shop and shared a pastry and espresso. It was not an expensive night out. (This was pre-Starbucks.)

2nd date: Marcia took me out, to a full course dinner and drinks.

After that 2nd date (see "January 10th, 1992. First Poem To Marcia" on page 163) it didn't matter where we went or who paid. We were falling for each other. She thought I had some kind of Romeo complex and I'd be moving on to other women in a matter of weeks. I thought, although built a little like Raquel Welch, she was overly strict about time schedules. But when you're falling in love, you don't care about those red flags. She didn't care about my Romeo complex and I didn't care when my friend saw Marcia for the first time and said, "That's your new girlfriend? With the big, gawky feet?"

"Yeah," I said with a huge smile. "Isn't she great?"

I hadn't noticed her feet up to that point. To be honest, I never looked at Raquel Welch's feet in any of her movies and I watched "Fathom" a dozen times.

What I'm saying in this poem is that I'm most definitely lucky in love. I also mean to say, and this is important, just show up with a smile on your face and you too can find your soul mate.

POEMS TO MOM & DAD

I've been writing poems to my parents since my teens. Maybe I continued writing them because I moved 3,000 miles away from Philadelphia to Los Angeles (long story) when I was 21. It seemed so strange to celebrate milestones without my parents. So, I'd write them poems like the ones below on their birthdays and wedding anniversaries.

My folks, Bernie and Bernice, met in the summer of 1942, when both were working at a beauty supply company in Philadelphia. Dad had almost no competition in the heterosexual dating world (very popular back then) because all the men were away fighting in World War II.

The army wouldn't take Dad because he had scarlet fever and diphtheria as a kid and lost his left ear drum. He tried to give the examining doctor his right ear (drum) twice but that didn't work. It was like how some teenagers lied about their age to get into the U.S. army and fight. Dad went to work for the government in 1943, making sure U.S. weapons were sent to the right places.

Dad was able to choose the nicest, prettiest girl in the city, my mom. Cool.

Mom (Bernice) at 21, Dad (Bernie) at 25. Cute names

Mom and Dad were snow birds who loved Florida. It's become a family tradition.

April 23rd, 2011
FOR 67 YEARS
(Listen to Dan Fogelberg's, "Mornin' Sky")
Dear Mom & Dad:
The two of you are lovers through and through;
There's never me in front of you,
It's "us," a couple.
Of all the successful things you ever did,
Whether it was in business or with kids,
It couldn't be done with one, you needed double
Don't even matter who navigates or steers.
You two know true love – which is the reason why we're here!
Your love is still in its heyday;
If marriage is sunshine, you're sunrays.
You've been shining through for 67 years
Hey, look at the plaques upon the wall,
Some just for walkin' through the mall,
Fingers entwined there.
But your real success is not how you raised kids
Or the business that you did;
Your remarkable success is your marriage
And the love you find there.
Don't even matter which one drives and which one hears.
You two show consideration that inspires heaven's cheers.
Your love is still in its heyday.
If marriage is sunshine, you're sunrays.
You've been shining through for 67 years.
All Our Love & Appreciation, D&M

WHAT I PROBABLY MEANT TO SAY: Dad had lots of plaques on his walls. One claimed he was a Kentucky Colonel, like his cousin, Sid Pranikoff, who was the winner of a significantly greater award, the Distinguished Flying Cross in World War II, and he didn't tell anyone about that for 50 years. (I wrote a book about it, "3 Cousins," that is in The U.S. Memorial Holocaust Museum in Washington, D.C.) Sid lived in Cincinnati, Ohio, right across the river from Kentucky. I'm guessing that Sid had a hilarious story about being named a Kentucky Colonel and Dad said, "I want to be a Kentucky Colonel, too!" Not to be confused with the prestigious Distinguished Flying Cross, this was a joke, like the guy who offered to make me an Indian so I could be part-owner of a casino on Indian land. (He could make me 1/8th Indian, which was all I needed, allegedly.)

Dad as a Mason

Many of my Dad's awards came from the Allied Jewish Appeal, Deborah Heart Hospital and from the Masons. Dad was a past master of his lodge and he said the Masons were not a secret society but a society of secrets. Yeah. "Pass me the paddle, Mister Jones." I didn't relate to some of his Masonic beliefs or the myriad rules he had to follow; heck, he never taught me the Masonic handshake (which I learned recently from a horse racing buddy) but I sensed it helped him make business connections. The Masons may have indirectly helped me get a new bike when I was 11, a Schwinn Apple Crate, sharp as could be, so that's something.

One older Mason, also a horse racing buddy, told me he was surprised that my Dad, a Jew, would be voted into the Masonic Lodge and become master of the lodge.

"My Grand pop Lou got him in," I said, and as soon as the words came out, I saw the bigger picture. Grand pop Lou's brother owned the flower shop next to Philadelphia City Hall. This great uncle of mine, Abe Wagner (the surname in Romania one generation earlier had been Gimbelovich) got some of his brothers, including Grand pop Lou (but not the boxer, Eddie "The Kid" Wagner) jobs as cops in 1929, before the Great Depression and a hiring freeze. That job kept my mother from going hungry in the 1930s.

Lou's brother Abe, in all likelihood, recommended my grandfather and my father (and even my uncle) to the Masons. He had connections to the police and politicians (they were two different groups back then) so his faith was never a factor. The closest comparison to Uncle Abe would be Heshe in "The Sopranos."

On a related note, if my religion, race or gender can hinder my acceptance into a clubhouse, I don't want to join. I may even want to pee recklessly through the window screens, like my camp counselors did in the '60s and '70s.

While not all of Dad's awards impressed me, all of his good deeds did. One special award (from the Allied Jewish Appeal) was handed to me for safe-keeping when I was about eight years old and I guarded it proudly on the night of the ceremony, even turning down big money offers from my Dad's playful friends.

In the previous poem, I give my folks an award just for walking around the malls, fingers entwined. Whenever I walk in a mall with my wife, I wrap my fingers around hers and sing this song in my head, remembering my parents' love for one another. I often get misty-eyed. Other people I see in malls seem to be crying too but that's just buyer's remorse.

How can you write your own poems? Well, think of experiences you've witnessed between your loved ones and other people. For example: my parents would always get soup at their favorite deli near Atlantic City, NJ. But the deli didn't serve soup every night. They knew my parents liked soup so they made it especially for them, for decades. Marcia and I sang this song to my parents, who were in their mid-late 80s in 2009, on their 65th wedding anniversary.

April 23rd, 2009
CELEBRATE 65
(Listen to Simon & Garfunkel's, "Keep The Customer Satisfied")
Dear Mom & Dad:
Isn't it great that you've reached 65!
Think that no one has noticed you
Being married so beautifully,
Showing us what love means
When it's tried and true?
It's a well-known story.
Everywhere you go
They embrace you,
Kiss-face you,

40

They give compliments reserved for the royal
And make soup for you when it's a no-soup day
Let you taste dessert from dessert trays.
We're kvelling (loving it) as we're helping you celebrate 65.
So many people will stop and say,
"Are those your parents over there? My,
How lucky are you to have them?" they ask.
And we say, "We're so lucky we can't count that high."
It's a well-known story.
Everywhere you go
They adore you
Rush toward you
And give compliments reserved for their favorites,
They buy oil for your car on vacation.
Marvel at your classification.
We're kvelling as we're helping you celebrate 65
It's a well-known story.
Everywhere you go,
You delight there
And bring light there.
Your marriage dignifies the human adventure.
That's why they make you soup on no-soup days
And let you taste dessert from dessert trays.
We're kvelling as we're helping you celebrate
65.
All Our Love Forever,
D&M

WHAT I PROBABLY MEANT TO SAY: I'm telling my folks why they get soup on no-soup days: they are kind and generous, loving and regal. It's not just me who sees them as a special pair who brighten every room they enter. The deli owner in Margate, NJ, put my parents' wedding picture from 1944 on the wall. It's still there.

Sometimes, when you write down a nice thought, the recipients think it's the nicest thing anyone ever said about them. My Dad loved the line about how his marriage "dignifies the human adventure." He repeated it constantly when we were together. It made him happier than if I had bought him a new Cadillac, not that he loved Cadillacs but he had a new sedan de Ville every two years for 50 years. I could've written Dad a poem called "Cadillac Fleetwood Brougham de Elegance; rolling at eight miles per gallon." He would've appreciated the thought.

I can still see my parents' reaction to this performance, as Marcia and I sang in unison. This song made them as happy as I had ever seen them, and they were an overtly happy couple. The feeling that I get, what I'll always get, from remembering their smiles is beyond beautiful; way past priceless. It's like a gift that keeps on giving just by thinking about it. ("You only have what you give away," as I'll explain later.) I would not have elicited such a warm reaction from Mom and Dad if I had given them a $250,000 set of his-and-her watches (like NFL players wear during games) instead.

The theme of the poem below, an anniversary poem to my parents, is that the Mayan calendar is ending. It's an end of the world poem; one that inherently reeks of honesty. I mean, why make things up when the world is ending?

April 23rd, 2004

Dear Mom & Dad:
You're still in love; still the greatest of friends,
A few years before the Mayan calendar ends.
That's right, the Mayan calendar ends in 2012.
They may have seen the future; they may have had some help.

It just stops that year, when all the giant asteroids are due.
But I think we'd get an extension, if the Mayans knew about you two.
In a dream, I met a Mayan and said if the Earth is hit by an asteroid,
That turns our little planet into one big, vexing void ...
(I guess we always knew it could be coming our way ...
From what I hear, it's still a few decades away)
Sure hope it doesn't happen on your anniversary (or Kentucky Derby day).
The Mayan nodded, like it made sense, and seemed to concur.
Then he told me not to eat meat and not to wear fur.
I nodded, like it made sense; then the dream started to blur.
No one knows exactly where the Mayans went
Or why they just picked up and packed up their tent.
Maybe they wanted to own, not rent.
Maybe none of us know why we were sent.
These past 60 years – I bet they just flew,
While your love touched so many as it sweetened and grew.

All I know is that what I told the Mayan is true.
There's nothing in the world as special as you.
All Our Love,
D&M

WHAT I PROBABLY MEANT TO SAY: I just wanted to tell my parents that their love has enriched so many of us.

I'm also saying don't wear fur. I only touch fur when I'm in a petting zoo but back in 1965, buying a fur coat for your wife meant that you were well on your way to living the American Dream, like Don Draper. And just like in today's world, owning a luxury car and buying a diamond ring for your wife meant you had "arrived" and were a success. You had to live in a big house and put a big fur coat in one of the many closets. As Randy Newman wrote in "It's Money That Matters," some people took their new money and bought a house with two pools. Well, our modest house didn't have room for even one pool so my Dad went out and bought my Mom a fur coat.

The owner of the fur salon asked for $10,000 so my Dad brought him $10,000 in cash. The owner asked my Dad, "What are you doing?" My Dad said, "I'm giving you the money for the coat." The owner said, "You're the only guy who brought in $10,000. Everybody else brings in $5,000, then we negotiate a price of $7,500."

The real price was $7,500 but Dad didn't want to haggle with the man. He respected a businessman's pricing policies. If he couldn't afford $10,000, he wouldn't have bought the fur coat. Now you know why the Cadillac dealer was always happy to see my Dad in the showroom: "Here comes the guy who doesn't haggle!"

On my Dad's last car lease, the Cadillac salesmen distracted him by singing "Happy Anniversary" and bringing out a cake … while they had him sign a six-year lease deal. (He asked for a three-year deal because he was 87 and didn't want to drive past 90.) On a related note, the New Jersey Better Business Bureau misplaced the paperwork with my complaint against the Cadillac dealer in New Jersey — twice!

Dad wasn't going to bail out with a voluntary repossession. After he stopped driving at age 90, he bought out his lease, had me sell the car, then let me keep the cash.

When I dig deeper into the problem of corporate greed, like when Cadillac fucked one of its best all-time customers (Dad's company bought or leased a half dozen Cadillacs virtually every year for decades), or when the Philadelphia Flyers sent a nasty letter to longtime season ticket holders (us) for cancelling, I think back to a line in the film, "Scarface": "Never underestimate the greed of the other guy!"

Now I have the unenviable job of filing a complaint against the New Jersey Better Business Bureau's Department Of Complaints. ("Hello, complaint department? I have a complaint about you!") I want to send them an email and ask, "Who watches the Watchers?" And my follow-up question would be: "Who's paying the Watchers?" But if I sent an email to the New Jersey Better Business Bureau, they would probably misplace that, too. That's why they're better at business.

So, if you ever see me getting out of a Cadillac to watch a Philadelphia Flyers' home game, call 9-1-1 and tell the police I've been kidnapped.

Because I used to love them. But it's all over now.

POEMS FOR DAD

My dad was beyond 100% supportive of me. He paid for my necessities whenever I needed help, which was practically all the time. My years in L.A. (1977-1984) were sponsored by him and I wanted to tell him how much I appreciated it.

June 19th, (Father's Day) 1983
A STARRING ROLE IN A KNOCKOUT FILM

Dear Mom & Dad: I promised
To return, "Soon as I could."
But who can stay down on the farm
After Hollywood?
Now, guess what? All my patience
Has rewarded me at last.
I just got a starring role
In a knockout film, with an all-star cast.
You were right – my luck is good.
The people treat me kindly;
Signed me in the animal guild,
A giant shark told me to join.
(That's how he got top-billed.)
I also met the deer
That Bob DeNiro liked to hunt.
He said we looked alike
And wondered if I'd do his stunts.
I made friends with a buffalo
(He's got a stampede job on a cowboy
    show.)
He said from 60 million
There are only 20 left
And all but five were slaughtered
On a motion picture set. Wow!
But leave it to this beaver,
Once again, I write too fast.
Let me tell you all about
My starring role

In a knockout film, with an all-star cast
'Cause I'm getting' my paws wet.
My agent, Arv, the aardvark,
Who forced me to persevere,
Only gets me acting jobs
That further my career.
So, once he read the script
He knew exactly what to do;
I limo'd to the studio
To join the cast and crew.
The female star just won
A big contractual dispute.
She tickled me beneath the chin
And told me I was cute!
Her boyfriend is the leading man
But doesn't seem so bright.
He said he ate our cousin Merv
For hors-d'oeuvres Sunday night.
What do you think he meant by that?
I laughed suspiciously.
Merv and I had lunch today –
He looked ok to me.
I got a glimpse of someone
Who wore seven diamond rings.
They called him "Boss" but he didn't
    seem
To work at anything. Hmmm?
How are both the mourning doves?

Send love … oh, if they ask,
Say I've got a starring role
In a knockout film, with an all-star cast
And they can stay with me for free!
I went to work in some sound stage;
Carried all the way in my own dressing
    cage.
Then a man they called "Doc"
Said, "It's time for his shot."
He took out a sharp thing
And stabbed … where I squat. Ouch!

The lights came on; cameras rolled.
The actors took their mark.
Then I felt a sense of change
And everything got dark.
I guess the scene went perfectly.
My memory's inexact.
When I woke up, I saw the Boss
And asked him, "How'd I act?"
He looked at me with great respect,
Then said, "Without a doubt,
You're the best trained animal
I've ever seen knocked out."
The first test of my film career.
I'm proud to say I passed.
What a break – a starring role
In a knockout film, with an all-star cast:
Get those tuxedos out!
Then, they had the screening
Where the critics write reviews.
The Boss was very nice to them –
Kept pouring lots of booze.
Soon, my scene was on the screen.

I rubbed my snout for luck.
I saw me falling to the ground
Like someone had said, "Duck!"
As I fell, the leading gal,
Said, "Oh, poor Tiger's dead."
Sometimes, actors have to change
Their names to get ahead.
When they rolled the credits
(Which can lead to fame and wealth)
There it was, in Panavision:
"Tiger … as himself."
Since today is Father's Day
I thought I'd fill you in,
On who I've met, what I've seen
And done, and where I've been.
And since today is Father's Day,
I'll give it to you straight:
The hardest workers, brightest minds
    –

In this town have to wait.
The top dogs knock the others down;
Have loyalty to none.
Make the safest bets around
Then boast how much they've won.

But I didn't leave the farm
To take a beating or a loss.
The road before me may be wide
But I will get across.
Thank you for your blessings
And your love – infinitive.
Here is where I'm working
But the farm is where I live.
Happy Father's Day!
Enjoy the seaside farm! All my love, D

WHAT I PROBABLY MEANT TO SAY: I wanted Dad to know I was serious about my education/career and he wasn't totally wasting his money by supporting me. It's my version of Albert Hammond's, "It Never Rains in Southern California," where he's hankering for Hollywood stardom but feels under-loved and under-fed. But Hammond is disingenuous when he says he wants folks back home to know he's nearly made it and he's "Had offers but don't know which one to take." In my version, I'm honest about the hardships involved in pursuing a writing career and the preponderance of narcissistic, soulless assholes that I'm forced to deal with. In this poem, I'm assuring my Dad that one day I will make it.

Well, guess what? I didn't make it but Dad loved me unconditionally anyway, like I was a superstar, his pride and joy.

Parents say they will accept their children's choices and love and support them no matter what happens. I tested that theory and my parents came through every time. Albert Hammond was broke and broken because he didn't have parents like I had. How could I not express my appreciation to them on their birthdays or anniversaries?

Dad was a self-made man, as you can tell from the poem below, written for him on his 84th birthday.

August 18th, 2004
NORTH PHILLY BOY
(Listen to Steve Forbert's, "One More Glass Of Beer")

Dear Dad:
There was once a North Philly boy,
Working in a store,
Scrubbing marble, dragging ice.
Now he's 84.
He grew up with some wild kids;
Didn't go to private school.
Didn't gnaw about a sledge or saw;
Gray matter was his tool.
He saw others go to war,
Read letters stained with tears.
Found a pal in a South Philly gal;
Been married 60 years.
Worked for others for a while
But he was born to lead.

He took a chance, flew by the seat of
   his pants
And faith helped him succeed.
Who just entered? You, who named
   Yourself
Jehovah. You can't be seen.
But I know You're near, Your spirit's
   here,
Like it's with the man born 8/18.
You know all about love and joy;
You invented them, to guide.
Your love and joy, well, our North
   Philly boy
Has spread them far and wide.
It must be overwhelming

To savor all you've touched.
Ocean waves and summer days
And dinosaurs and such.
Maybe you can measure
How much a father is loved by his son.
I'll count with you the million or two
Righteous things he's done.
And me, I'm truly grateful that,
In all Your Sacredness,
You've somehow made it possible
For me to show him this.
All Our Love & Joy, D&M

WHAT I PROBABLY MEANT TO SAY: I'm thanking God for keeping us alive so I can give this love poem to him. This poem is at the top of my spirituality scale; telling God that His creations like love and joy are being generously spread around Earth by my Dad. And, hey, if you're mentioning someone in these poems with God and love, you know they will be well received.

I'm not sure why I put "ocean waves and summer days" in the same sentence as dinosaurs. I must love dinosaurs.

My Dad at age 21 at the start of World War II.
Since he had lost his left ear drum to scarlet
fever as a boy, the army wouldn't let him enlist.

My Dad is 19 in the beach picture, standing on the far left. Notice the sign behind him: "George Whites scandals of 1939." The only scandal I can see in that sign is bad punctuation.

June 20th, 2010
HOT-AIR BALLOON

(Listen to James Taylor's, "Sweet Baby James")
Dear Dad:
I was watching a special on the history channel
About old Las Vegas in the mid 1960s.
Of course, I remember Paul Anka at Caesar's.
And the trip where we tossed baseballs on Sid Colin's lawn.
I was watching a special about what happened in Israel
In the Six Day War, in the Golan Heights.
I remember standing in the breeze caused by the retreating Syrian army;
How grateful I felt to be in the big picture
Because these experiences could only enrich.
And how did I get to these places?
Some magic bubble? Or hot-air balloon?
I was breathing that air because you put me there.
Like you knew it would help me throughout life.
So, thanks Dad for putting me there.
I was watching a special about the Pacific Coast Conference.
My USC tuition didn't come from my dishwashing job in '72.

I saw the glamour of L.A. and the backwoods of Georgia;
I saw the NY garment biz up close and a Kentucky Derby or two.
I've hawked books from a booth in a cavernous book expo,
Sailed on yachts with fast women I didn't have to marry.
I've had special moments next to you in the lofty winner's circle
Where I learned that sometimes you can get lucky if you follow your
        dreams.
You guarantee that I follow my dreams.
And how did I get to these places?
Some magic bubble? Or hot-air balloon?
I was breathing that air because you put me there.
Like you knew it would help me throughout life.
So, thanks Dad for putting me there.
All Our Love & Appreciation Forever,
D&M

WHAT I PROBABLY MEANT TO SAY: I refer to my dishwashing job in 1972, when Wanda in the camp kitchen would ask how many pancakes I needed for my table and I would try to avoid looking at Wanda or her scary pancakes. My camp salary in 1972 was about 3% of my USC tuition in 1978. In this poem, I'm thanking Dad for putting me through college because I couldn't have done it alone. Back then, almost no one paid to correct their kids' SAT test answers or claimed they were on the rowing team, then photo-shopped their kids in a rowboat to gain admission. Heck, photo-shop wasn't even invented yet. Yes, rowing was invented and it was a real sport but colleges admitted students who actually rowed in high school. As my Dad used to say about his youth in the 1930s, those (the 1970s) were primitive, innocent times.

Primitive times equate to less expensive times so my bill wasn't too exorbitant and I didn't order the caviar at the USC cafeteria. I ordered from the food trucks. I even worked on a food truck, mainly to meet girls my age. The owner was a race track buddy who claimed that his grandfather was the last man to see Jimmy Hoffa alive. There was no Google at the time, so I had to actually read newspapers and magazines (they were two different things back then) to verify his wild claim. The odd part was, the articles pretty much verified his story. The 2019 film, "The Irishman" does too.

As an undergraduate in the mid-1970s at Penn State University, the tuition for each trimester was only $395. Some of my friends, though, needed outside help to pay for tuition at state colleges. My wife needed a scholarship to attend Temple University, a state school. My Dad was behind me every step of the way, paying the bills, lending emotional support at all times. If I had a problem, he'd help me fix it, and I thanked him many times in poems spanning 40 years.

In "Hot-Air Balloon," when I say I "Sailed on yachts with fast women I didn't have to marry," it's my version of a line in Frank Sinatra's "It Was A Very Good Year" when he was 35 and rode in limousines.

I also refer to standing in the paddock at Atlantic City Race Course in the mid-1980s. We owned Southern Clogger, one of the thoroughbreds running in the $20,000 stakes race. (In the 1980s, $20,000 was considered to be a lot of money.) When I say "We," I mean my Dad owned the colt. I was just tagging along, rubbing elbows with the prettiest and wealthiest young ladies on the East Coast.

"Dad," I said, "keep entering the horse in this kind of race. I don't care where he finishes."

Years earlier, I met singer Kate Smith and her young niece in the dining room at Garden State Park race track. I didn't marry the girl. Come on, I was only 15 at the time. But I had tons of great experiences usually reserved for the upper class. How did I get to these places? Magic carpet? Hot-air balloon? No. Dad put me there, to give me an advantage in life.

In 2019, the Philadelphia Flyers removed the statue of Kate Smith from the sidewalk in front of the Wells Fargo Center. It had something to do with Kate allegedly singing racist songs almost 100 year ago. Kate's niece, the same girl I met as a teenager, defended her aunt in the media and said everyone knew the song was a satire. Kate raised tons of money for the U.S. war effort and was known to speak out against bigotry. She was nice to me even though she was eating dessert when I approached her table — plus, I was trying to get a date with her niece!

Do you remember the lyrics to Randy Newman's song, "Rednecks"? If you do, and if you're offended by satire, which apparently everyone is these days, Randy Newman can say goodbye to his Grammy awards. He belittles the bigots and unmasks the morons by simply letting them talk out loud. (Example: his narrator in "It's Money That Matters" is not a Harvard MBA; he's a professional car washer.) I played Newman's song, "Short People" (about bigotry) for my college students and a student nurse finally spoke up and said, "I don't think this song is about short people." The light bulb had gone off. It was one of the highlights of my career as a college professor.

Randy Newman wrote a satirical song about a guy who's still sore that South America stole our name. Or maybe it wasn't satire.

I mention standing in the lofty winner's circle because that was my Dad's favorite thing to do. He owned two thoroughbreds in the 1980s and when they won, we'd get to take a picture in the winner's circle, with the horse. Those were some very happy horsey pictures because we had just won the purse money and all our bets. When we thought our horse was going to win, which was almost always, I'd bet every dollar in my wallet. I'd bet $87 on him to win, or $123 or, on a super high rush of adrenaline, $155. When the horses won, it was ecstasy. Strangers would hug me for helping them pay their rent or pay for their kid's heart transplant. I got that "Barton Fink" feeling, like I was really improving society. No one ever explained to me why they were gambling with money they needed for their kid's life-saving surgeries.

I wrote a poem about the colt, Southern Clogger. I gave it to Dad to cheer him up after he needed surgery. Dad looked pale in the hospital. I told him he had to perk up because Southern Clogger was running soon. By race day, Dad was so psyched to see his horse run (he won) that he nearly ripped the 10-foot glass door by the paddock at Garden State Park right off in his hand. Dad was 65 at the time, and just past surgery. Yet he was like a supercharged lion, running around the paddock.

Below is a poem about Dad's favorite horse.

Allowance / 5 Furlongs - :58 2/5
Cool As Ice, 2nd
Yankee Affair, 3rd
November 4, 1986

Southern Clogger

Itram Stable, Owner
E. Euster, Trainer
Jeffrey Lloyd, up
PHILADELPHIA PARK

I'm standing behind my parents in the middle of the picture with Southern Clogger. We're left of center in the picture of Molly Lu. Dad enjoyed owning those two horses and we treated them like family.

INTERNATIONAL TECHNOLOGY GROUP
Trophy Presented By Paul & Ethel Goldy And Ivan & Melinda Bloomfield

Itram Stables, Owner
Eugene Euster, Trainer
Rick Wilson, Up

Molly Lu

Purse $11,000
Garden State Park - June 11, 1987

Dave's Kate 2nd
His Ex 3rd
1 1/16 Miles Turf - WTD 1:45 1

Spring, 1985

BORN A FLIER

(Listen to Tom Petty's, "Rebels")
Hey, hey, hey. He was born a flier.
In Kentucky, on a Derby morning.
Yeah, with four legs in the air, nose right on the wire,
He was born a flier.
Well, we worked him out in the morning.
It was still dark and freezing.
And he went about six furlongs
In 1:10, and breezing.
I can still see the eyes of jock Mike Gomez spinning.
But the news this week is Southern Clogger is winning!
Hey, hey, hey. He was born a flier.
In Kentucky, on a Derby morning.
Yeah, with four legs in the air, nose right on the wire,
He was born a flier.
Even before he broke his maiden,
He looked like a winner.
It was one of those times
When we had the luck of a beginner.
I can still see the eyes of jock Mike Gomez spinning.
But the news this week is Southern Clogger is winning!

WHAT I PROBABLY MEANT TO SAY: Get well soon, Dad, because you do not want to miss Southern Clogger's next race! Thankfully, he felt fine by race day so maybe the poem worked.

Incorporating the Frank Sinatra/Paul Anka theme (always a winner with the Greatest Generation), here is a poem for my Dad's 88th birthday.

August 18th, 2008
YOUR WAY

(Listen to Frank Sinatra's, "My Way," written by Paul Anka)
Dear Dad:
You found a perfect spot, there on the lot, at Down Beach Deli.
You got the soup and spilled some on your shirt, some in your belly.
Unwrapped the cracker pack with a stabbing fork – it's the only sure way.
That kind of style, has worked a while; you did it your way.
DQ's, you've had a few; the 2-9-10, is hard to mention.
You bet on Molly Lu, although you knew, she reeked with tension.
You cheered for Clogger too; pulled the paddock door right off the doorway.
And through it all, you made the call, you did it your way.
(And still do.)
Oh, there were times you struggled through.
But so many people believed in you.
And in those days, when you felt stress,
You went and made a better dress.
You beat the clock, head on the block
And did it your way.
Today, it's fair to say, you have a style of life that's winning.
But truth be told, these days of gold, are no sweeter than your beginning.
You've earned so much respect from Hawaii out to Norway.
You stayed the course – didn't know from borscht –
You did it your way.
Those wonderful years, now 88.
Was it just luck or was it fate?
That you'd become the family star;
The one most loved for who you are.
The kid named Rut – you checked your gut
And did it your way.
All Our Love Forever, D&M

WHAT I PROBABLY MEANT TO SAY: In this poem, I tell my Dad how much I admire his guts and determination. And I mention some of his favorite things, like his two thoroughbreds, the dress business and soup. Stick to the basics, people. Even if you write a less-than-perfect poem, go with themes related to your loved one's lifestyle. They'll appreciate it when you tell them you think their hobbies are cool.

I also make fun of the way Dad opened his crackers when he was telling a story about his adversaries. He'd complain about the union guy who'd come to his factory and just steal a bunch of dresses. He'd seethe about the contractor who constantly lied about delivery dates, even though Dad was in danger of losing his house if those dresses were not delivered on time. And as he told the stories, his fork would demolish the plastic around the crackers, like he was stabbing the union guy (who was probably dead for 50 years) and the contractor (dead 60 years) in the gut.

The term "didn't know from borscht" must have originated in Eastern Europe hundreds of years ago. It means you don't care that it's an impossible task, you're doing it anyway. This amusing saying loses much in translation from Yiddish to English. You know, the worst thing you can say to someone in Yiddish, "Gai kocken offen yam," roughly translated, is "Go take a dump in the ocean." I spent many nights thinking about the acrimony associated with this term. Imagine despising someone so much, you want them to get away from you, go to the ocean, and take a dump.

I wish I had thought of it.

Here is another poem about Dad's favorite hobby, horse racing.

The only photographic evidence that Dad ever had a drink. This picture was taken at his dress company's office party, which looks similar to Don Draper's office parties in the TV show, "Mad Men."

June 18th, 2000
DO WHAT YOU DO

(Listen to Harry Chapin's, "On The Way To Kingdom Com")

Dear Dad:
And the three just beat the two.
'Cause the favorite threw a shoe.
It was an outcome that you knew.
So do what you do.
The stock market is volatile.
Golf means walking in the sun.
Roller skating at your age;
It's already been done.
Checkers is for country folks
And bridge is just no fun.
Now you could spend time
Telling stories;
I bet you'd make
A buck or two.
But you should figure out
The simulcasts
And do what you do.
You're working your muscles of
   concentration
While moving your spirit of participa-
   tion.
And the five just beat the two.
It was 5-2-4, you knew.

Got the superfecta, too!
So do what you do.
Traveling is tedious.
You're at the airport by dawn.
Photography is technical;
Where have the easy-loaders gone?
And you're not about to garden,
The condo tower has no lawn.
Now you could spend time
Writing stories;
I bet you'd sell
A script or two.
But you should figure out
The simulcasts
And do what you do.
You're exercising – to and from the
   tellers
While you're bonding with the fellas.
And the three just beat the two.
It was an outcome that you knew.
And if the day is fun for you,
Then do what you do.
All my love on the joyous weeks be-
   fore your 80th!

WHAT I PROBABLY MEANT TO SAY: Enjoy yourself at all times, Dad. If people think you're gambling too much, who cares? Do what you like to do. You've earned it.

Years ago, in the late 1970s, a cousin asked me, "Do you know how much money your Dad has lost at the track?"

I didn't know. I called Dad that night from Los Gatos, California and encouraged him to go to the track the next day.

"The three will beat the two," he said.

That much, we knew.

When I say:

> Roller skating at your age;
> It's already been done.

I'm referring to the time one of his 80-year-old buddies went skating; actually, bike riding. His doctor said it was too dangerous to ride a bike at 80 so he stopped riding a bike. He was walking on the Atlantic City boardwalk a week later and got run over by a bike.

The month of August, 2000 was joyous for two reasons: Dad's big 80th birthday party and my engagement to Marcia! Dad threw a first-class party for himself at the Ram's Head Inn near Atlantic City and at the end of the day, Marcia and I announced we were getting married within a year.

On a car ride the next day, Dad was driving down Pacific Avenue near the ancient Convention Hall and casually mentioned that we didn't have to wait a whole year to get married; we could probably do it before the new year (2001). Mom, uncharacteristically, chimed in from the front seat and said, "Bernie, they're in their 40s, let them make their own decision!"

As usual, Dad had a good point. Marcia and I had been living together for more than six years and were madly in love for nine years. We couldn't live without each other. Why wait? So, we got married four months later, on December 10th, 2000. That's "The Best Day On Earth" as my poem "December The Ten" on page 190 explains. But that day would've come six months later if it weren't for Dad's good advice. That's one of the reasons why he's the greatest of Dads.

August 18th, 2006

YOU'RE THE GREATEST OF DADS

(Listen to Johnny Rivers', "It Wouldn't Happen With Me")
Dear Dad:
You thought you were the best at playing handball.
You claimed you could hit the factory's upper floor.
But someone came along after the invention of the half-ball
And hit that thing all the way to the Jersey shore.
Well, you were great at 40-yard dashes
And skating in roller boots,
But there were other North Philly cowboys
Who could throw Stetson hats down a chute.

Were you the best at making milkshakes
And scooping those ice cream cones?
No, there was a fellow in St. Louis
Who scooped two-handed in two time zones.
But of all the titles you've had,
The one I know is ironclad
Is you're the greatest of Dads.
Oh yes, you are.
Oh, were you the greatest lodge boy
Ever elected master or president?
Well, you memorized 10 million secrets
And that didn't even make a dent.
But of all the titles you've had,
The one I know is ironclad
Is you're the greatest of Dads.
Oh yes, you are.
It's true these folks have shown some talent through their deeds;
They've won medals in a war or Olympiad.
But they can only watch and wonder as you increase your lead;
They'll never, never, never, never catch you as a Dad.
Oh, some say you are the very best dress manufacturer around.
I looked in Wanamaker's recently; none of your dresses could be found.
But of all the titles you've had,
The one I know is ironclad
Is you're the greatest of Dads.
Oh yes, you are.
These folks I mentioned have some talent, it's true;
They're known as whiz kids or as Harvard grads.

But they can only watch and wonder and take lessons from you;

They'll never, never, never, never match you as a Dad.
So, you think you're the best handicapper who sometimes makes a bet?
Well, I know some people at the Spa who say they haven't lost one yet.
But of all the titles you've had,
The one I know is ironclad
Is you're the greatest of Dads.
Oh yes, you are.
(And you're the greatest Father-in-law, too!)
All Our Love & Appreciation Forever! D&M

WHAT I PROBABLY MEANT TO SAY: If you have a great Dad, tell him that directly. In this poem, I say the hell with the Kentucky Colonel award or the Friend of Israel Award or the Masonic Super-Secret Award, his top prize is the Greatest of Dad's Award. I wander outside the safety zone here when I poke fun at one of his passions, the Masons:

Oh, were you the greatest lodge boy
Ever elected master or president?
Well, you memorized 10 million secrets
And that didn't even make a dent.

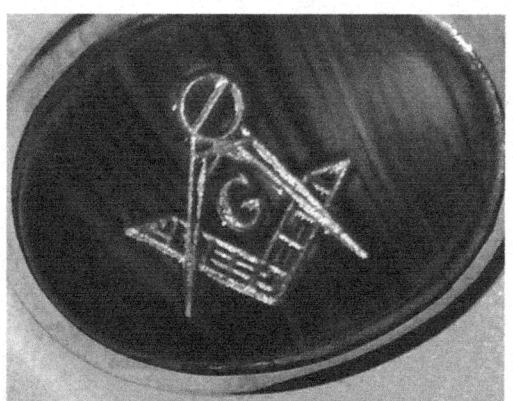

Dad's Masonic cuff link. Oh, the stories it could tell. Dad was a Mason and Past Master of his lodge but that's all we knew about his activities and/or antics. When asked about the Masons, he would change the subject or speak in riddles.

In my family, you weren't allowed to poke fun at certain things. If Dad loved, let's say the president, then you were expected to love him, too. But the beauty of writing these poems to loved ones is that you get to make your point if you don't love the president. (The last president I truly loved was JFK, who was assassinated by a crazed, lone weirdo, not some secret organization. And that weirdo was shot by another crazed, lone weirdo, not some secret organization, if you believe that.)

Go ahead and mention the unmentionable in your poems. If your loved ones are raging alcoholics, you can write them love notes filled with hints about AA meetings and their starting times. Without being preachy, you can lovingly bring up matters in your poem that you wouldn't necessarily bring up at Thanksgiving dinner.

It's like the scene in the old movie, "My Favorite Year," when they all warn their uncle not to mention the legal troubles of a pompous, yet wildly popular actor (played by Peter O'Toole, who swore, "I'm not an actor, I'm a movie star!") in connection with a pregnant hooker in New Jersey.

"Don't bring it up at dinner!" they say over and over again to him … yet he brings it up for public discussion almost immediately and gets scolded. ("What did I say?" asks the uncle.) You can bring up touchy subjects in your love poems. It's worked well for me.

Here's what I wrote on Father's Day, 2007, instead of buying Dad a card at the dollar store.

THEME ALERT! The repeated theme is whenever I have a problem, he helps me fix it.

June 17th, 2007

THE GO-TO GUY

(Listen to Cat Stevens', "Father & Son")

Dear Dad:
In most songs about fathers and sons
There are common themes that prevail.
The father gives advice to his son
About women, mostly, but to no avail.
The father says something like,
"Settle down. See the big picture.
Hold onto your dreams, son.
Marry someone you love completely, just like I have done."
But this isn't the usual song
Because in those others, the son won't listen;
And neither father nor son really expresses himself to one another.
There's a distance between them;
A separation because they're prideful and too much the same.
In those other songs, they wish they had what we have in so many ways.
Here's what I know about Father's Day.
You define it by your actions.
You set the example.
It's a lofty plan which we should follow to the letter.
Father's Day, to all of us
Is what you have made it mean to us,
It means that a father is the go-to guy
Who lives his life to help our lives get better.
One day each year
I get to act a little bit like the father;
Taking you out to eat, helping you get a TV or anything you might need.
It's a responsibility that feels great,
It's truly life affirming; makes me shine.
And you get to feel that way all the time!
All Our Love & Appreciation, D&M

WHAT I PROBABLY MEANT TO SAY: Dad, you're the team captain, the go-to guy. And since you're the one who mentors us and who picks up every check, you receive all kinds of rewards. Everyone thanks you, hugs you and sings your praises. Well, where is my "Barton Fink" feeling? Not to come across like Freddo in "The Godfather" or anything but when can I shine and be happy? Answer: on Father's Day, one of the few days per year when Dad let me treat him.

A woman I met on the boardwalk, a Holocaust survivor, once told me, "You only have what you give away." I knew she was right but I'm still reverse engineering the quote to find out what she really meant to say. If anyone already knew that, it was my Dad.

There is something else going on here. I think I was unconsciously referring to the relationship between Grand Pop Lou and his only son, my uncle, when I wrote:

> The father gives advice to his son
> About women, mostly, but to no avail.

(My uncle usually listened to his father's advice, then did the opposite.)

> But this isn't the usual song
> Because in those others, the son won't listen;
> And neither father nor son really expresses himself to one another.

There was hardly any communication between Grand Pop Lou and my uncle. Their pride got in the way. Newsflash! All fathers and sons fight periodically. Often, they make up and have a shot of whiskey together and watch a game. Grand pop did both. My uncle did neither. Grand pop was macho; my uncle was mild. Grand pop was a pious Jew; my uncle hated religion. I should've made them both watch Arthur Miller's play, "Death of a Salesman" or at least make an appearance on "The Jerry Springer Show," not that I'm comparing the two. I prefer Miller's play. That's just me.

> It means that a father is the go-to guy
> Who lives his life to help our lives get better.

Maybe my uncle didn't believe that his father, Lou, lived his life mainly to help his kids. Or he believed Lou wanted to help one kid (my Mom) and not the other (him). I'm thanking my Dad in this poem for his unconditional love. If my Dad wasn't such a loving father, I couldn't have written the poem, which demonstrates how your loved ones actually help you write these poems. My uncle, to the best of my knowledge, never wrote a poem to his father, my Grand pop Lou. If he did (the odds are low that he did) it would've happened between 1938 and 1955, before my time.

My Dad's advice helped me survive and I'd tell him that in my poems. But not everyone listened. Some close relatives would go against my Dad's advice just to show him how smart they were. They always regretted it.

No one ever discussed it after the fact. So, on Father's Day, 2005, I wanted to let Dad know I would welcome his advice (like when we moved up our wedding day at his suggestion) and it would always be important to me.

June 19th, 2005

Dear Dad:
I heard you say, the other day,
That you couldn't give advice
To certain individuals,
Who rebuffed you once or twice.
"I'm done trying," I heard you say.
"They don't want to hear it from me,
    anyway."
And I thought, "How could someone's
    outlook be so dim,
As to refuse advice and wisdom from
    him?"
It's like ignoring the doctor
When he tries to soothe all your aches.
Or shrugging off the mechanic
When he says, "You really need
    brakes."
Or paying no heed to the sign,
"Watch out for snakes."
Or not listening to the farmer
Who says, "Don't stand on those
    rakes."
Or discounting the geologist
Who says, "Good chance of earth-
    quakes."
Or dispensing with the prediction
Of mounting snowflakes.
Or snubbing the suggestion
That the sun bakes your skin.
Or paying no attention
When the coach says, "Do this to win."

We solicit your advice in
Everything we undertake.
By doing so, we reap rewards
Instead of reeling from mistakes.
Look, I've heard more of your advice
Than anyone alive.
I let others speak in business meetings
And don't let anyone dictate how I
    drive.
I know they can't cheat an honest man;
Only take temporary advantage with
    their jive.
The only things I've learned without
    your guidance
Were how to swim and how to dive.
(When I was four, Grand pop Lou
Threw me headfirst in a pool;
He was less subtle than you are,
In giving advice, as a rule.)
No matter where I'm headed
Or what I find when I arrive,
It's your advice inside my head and
    heart
That will help me to survive.
I've lost track of just how many times
You've helped us with advice in this
    past week!
And we're here on Father's Day to tell
    you
To keep up that winning streak.
All Our Love & Appreciation, D&M

WHAT I PROBABLY MEANT TO SAY: I'm saying that Dad was such a great mentor that there were just a couple things he didn't teach me, like how to dive and swim. (Reminder: my Dad didn't learn to swim because he had no left ear drum and couldn't get his ear wet.) Grand pop Lou taught me how to do those things, as well as how to eat a lemon like it was an orange.

"Just bite right into it. Don't spit it out!" Grand pop Lou told me when I was 10.

I chewed on lemons to prove my grit, like I did when climbing the monkey bars without using my hands and diving when I didn't really know how to dive. So, these few things that my Dad didn't teach me, I had to learn from others. My Dad taught me virtually everything else, like how to be a stand-up person, how to treat women, drive a car, hit a baseball, handicap a horse race and tip for better service.

He also revealed that people can't cheat an honest man, they can only take temporary advantage of you (see Cadillac, NJ dealers).

What did I mean to say? He's the greatest of dads.

The next poem has two dates: the day my Dad turned 85 in 2005 and the day he passed away almost seven years later. Dad was ready to go by 2012 when he was in his early 90s. If he had thought of it, he would've put a special rider in his will forbidding all measures to keep him alive in case of an accident, even things like Bactine and band aids. He hadn't checked his pacemaker battery for years. He wanted it to suddenly fail and kill him on the spot. For the most part, Dad's plans worked really well. This was a terrible plan, just slightly better than Grand pop Lou's pull-the-trigger-and-aim-for-your-own-head plan.

Dad went to a diabetes doctor who was, to be kind, preoccupied. (This doctor was accused of ordering his wife's murder and selling opiates to motorcycle gangs. He hung himself in jail. ABC's "20-20" produced a special on the murder in June, 2018.) Dad was forced by worsening health in 2011 to move with my mother from a high-rise beach-front condo in Ventnor, New Jersey to a retirement community in Philadelphia. He was pissed at the battery company for keeping his pacemaker turned on. Now he had to put up with bad food and service, in a place where he couldn't really tip. The "No tipping" policy, I believe, weakened his will to live.

Dad was not himself and didn't want to live that way. I now see the connection to my Grand pop Lou. Grand pop used a handgun. Dad used bad medical care. Know what I learned from my Dad and my maternal Grand pop, Lou? Pick your poison but wait until you're very old and sick.

My paternal Grand pop, Ike, admitted on his death bed that his real name wasn't Isaac, it was Abraham, and he wasn't born in July, he was actually born (in Vilnius, Poland; now Lithuania) in September, 1888. Ike was so loveable that a banker, in 1929, purposely insulted him and told him to take his "stupid immigrant" money out of that bank right away, saving my grand pop his entire life savings because the bank closed forever the next day. Ike taught us all to be nice to people. He was even nice to a hateful neighbor who was trying to break down the door to his store with his shoulder, because Ike was Jewish. My grand pop said to his son (my dad, Bernie), "Poor John. He's gonna hurt himself."

My paternal Grand pop, Ike, never boxed like Grand pop Lou and his brothers. Ike worried about money. He ran a luncheonette but had debts, as Bruce Springsteen wrote, "That no honest man could pay." During the Depression, though, his landlord bailed him out.

Ike rented the store from a 90-year-old German woman, Mrs. Josephine Bong. Dad said she was a wonderful woman who would tell him stories about the 1800s, when people would promenade on Broad Street in Philadelphia. She was short, on the stocky side, and lived privately, four blocks from the store. Dad always walked her home and she would always tell him one thing: "When a man is down, you don't kick him, you give him a helping hand."

Things were so bad during the Depression that Ike couldn't pay the rent. Mrs. Bong would take a note from him, agreeing that he owed her the rent every month. This went on for years. Finally, when the store turned around, when Ike started to make a profit from the luncheonette (converted from a tobacco store), he went to repay Mrs. Bong for all the times she let him off the hook.

According to Ike, who told this story to Dad, who told it to me, Mrs. Bong went to her attorney's office.

"Am I of sound mind?" she asked him.

The attorney said, "Yes, you are."

"The give me your waste basket."

He looked at her oddly and gave her the waste basket. One by one, she started to tear up the notes and throw them into the basket.

"Do you know what you're doing?" the attorney asked.

"Yes, absolutely. I told them for many years: 'When a man is down, you don't kick him, you give him a helping hand.' Well, I'm giving this man a helping hand. I don't need the money and he needs it badly."

She just tore up all those IOU's. That impressed my Dad. He saw a woman who preached something and then actually lived that way. Mrs. Bong's kindness inspired my Dad to pay it forward all his life. He also learned human values from his parents, Ike (Abraham) and Sarah Rutberg, who were known for their integrity and kindness, even to harsh neighbors who brought old-school antisemitism to their door.

Therefore, if one of my neighbors tries to break down my door while yelling slurs of any kind, including but not limited to race, religion or hair color ("Why do you have that stupid gray hair?") I will not pee out the window onto their heads, like my former camp counselors. I'll remember the words of Abraham Lincoln, who said, "I hate that man. I must get to know him better."

Unfortunately for Lincoln, James Wilkes Booth never got that memo. Not a lot of people did. My Grand pop Ike did, making him Lincolnesque.

For my Dad as a child, there were two worlds: the harsh streets of North Philadelphia during the Depression and his home life, where he saw, as he told me, "A different world, a beautiful world; a world of two people working day and night, who were so honest and nice that people couldn't say no to them."

A lot of that went into this next poem about my Dad, the one I read at his funeral. I tried to capture the essence of a wonderful man, my hero. Only I could have written this because I was close enough to him to really understand the way his mind worked. This poem, if nothing else, proves that I paid close attention to his stories. It's like when we were kids and wanted our parents to watch us on the baseball field or on stage at school. "Hey, pay attention!" Dad always paid great attention to what I did. This poem is my way of saying that I paid attention, too.

August 18th, 2005

March 19th, 2012

NO ONE ELSE COULD WRITE THIS

(Listen to Queen's, "Too Much Love")

Dear Dad:
You don't play hardball catcher at age
   91.
But you're more valuable to us than
   anyone.
I've never heard you lie;
You're a guy who identifies
With a VIP or waiter.
Your wife never had to wonder where
   you'd been.
You tell her she's the prettiest gal
   you've ever seen.
You've just got that special knack
To provide what we all lack,
Sooner, not later.

You know I couldn't write this
If I hadn't seen what I have seen.
I can't adjust the brightness
On the life-sized, movie screen.
The life that you were living,
It was second, Dad, to none.
No one else could write this
But your son.
Oh, I could act like we're two sides of
   the same coin
But it's a role I'd have to pilfer or
   purloin.

I'm just so glad you wrought me
So I can tell everyone what you have
   taught me.
"Ya had to have been dair, Chal-ly," to
   know what I mean.
91 years of sparkle have gone into that
   good-guy sheen.
And the love that's in your heart, I
   know
It's there for me to find deep in my
   genes.
No one else has noticed
As I've watched in bliss and awe;
Dignity through the struggle –
That was what I saw.
You're always clutch when under
   pressure
Like the pressure just adds to the fun.
No one else could write this
But your son.
No one else has noticed
How hard it is to fill your shoes.
The things that we're most proud of
Aren't broadcast in the news.
When your loved ones miss the curve-
   ball,
You take the heat and pay the tab.
And no one else has noticed …
I think everyone has noticed
Like I have.

All Our Love Forever,
D&M

WHAT I PROBABLY MEANT TO SAY: When I say:

> You know I couldn't write this
> If I hadn't seen what I have seen.
> I can't adjust the brightness
> On the life-sized, movie screen

It's my way of telling him it's not just my opinion. I mean, look at the review on the big screen. It's bright because you made it bright. No one could adjust the light you've created for loved ones and, sometimes, for complete strangers.

When I say:

> Oh, I could act like we're two sides of the same coin
> But it's a role I'd have to pilfer or purloin

It's my way of telling him that I'm not as accomplished as him. But that's all right. Dad would agree that his father, Ike, was more accomplished than any of us. Ike achieved more because he got himself and his future family out of a desperately poor situation in Poland and into the U.S. (He did so legally, which was considered normal in 1904.)

When I say:

> "Ya had to have been dair, Chal-ly," to know what I mean.
> 91 years of sparkle have gone into that good-guy sheen.
> And the love that's in your heart, I know
> It's there for me to find deep in my genes.

It's my way of telling him I remember his stories of growing up in a tough neighborhood during the Depression. Whenever someone told a story in Dad's old hood, a guy would look at the storyteller with a raised eyebrow and say, "Was you dair, Chal-ly?" Like, "What are you talkin' about? We all know you're just repeating senseless rumors from dead-end kids on the corner."

I also tell him that I've inherited some of his good traits and I hope to put them to good use. What I'm really trying to say is: I'm proud to be your son.

My Mom in the kitchen, circa 1966

POEMS TO MOM

I'm also wildly proud of my sweet mother, Bernice (my parents' names were Bernie and Bernice, also known as B&B). I'm telling you, she never, in 91 years, pissed anyone off. (See a related poem, "In All This Time," on page 82.) In most of the poems that I wrote to my Mom, I call her a breath of fresh air. In one poem that was handwritten and lost, I even refer to the breeze coming in from the ocean and then the breeze talks about how my Mom was more of a breath of fresh air than fresh air! She liked sweet and gentle poems. I never gave her little digs about her behavior, mainly because her behavior was so wonderful.

May 11th, 2008
MOM HANDLED THAT JUST RIGHT

Dear Mom:
You know, it happens all the time. It's extra-sensory.
A reflection or a nod; a favorite memory.
"Mom taught me that.
Mom gave me that.
Mom helped with that.
Mom knew that.
Turned out, Mom was right about that.
Mom handled that just right.
Mom smiled her loving smile tonight.
Mom is there for us, all right."

It's a feeling that stays with me
Like a present from the past.
Real beauty, which defines you,
Well, that always lasts.
All our love & appreciation forever,
D&M

WHAT I PROBABLY MEANT TO SAY: You're a real beauty.

May 9th, 2004

NO WAY TO THANK YOU ENOUGH

Dear Mom:
Love always favors
Substance above style.
Love, above all,
Makes existence worthwhile.
This is all relevant to you, Mother dear,
Because love is the greatest whenever you're near.
A bastion of unselfish love without peer,
You keep the love train on track; in fact, you're the engineer.
There is no way to thank you enough for what you do.
There is no way for all my grateful feelings to get through.
But the next time I hug you, try to sense beyond the touch
And you'll understand instinctively how I love you so much.
All Our Love And Appreciation Forever, D&M

WHAT I PROBABLY MEANT TO SAY: You're a bastion of unselfish love. And love makes our lives worthwhile. (Leonard Cohen said "Love's the only engine of survival"; same thing.)

May 14th, 2006

AND THAT PERSON WAS YOU

(Listen to Neil Diamond's, "If You Know What I Mean")

Dear Mom:
When I think of my earliest memories,
When emotional commotion was the
  norm,
I knew I didn't have to travel far to find
Comfort in the storm.
Some people told me to be strong
Others said, "Just try to get along."
But only you could ease my troubled
  soul while you
Taught me right from wrong.
How can I thank you, Mom?
How can I thank you, Mom?
From the time I was born

To this Mother's Day;
You always know what to say.
And I started to cry
When they told me to stay
In the principal's office
The rest of the day.
But I knew I'd be fine
'Cause when the school day was done
Someone would be waiting in line.
And that person was you.
Thank God it was you, Mom.
Here's to the trust we've always known,
From birth to forever; from forever to
  now.

Having you as a mother, with perfect
    talent to soothe,
Got me through the grind, somehow.
How can I thank you, Mom?
How can I thank you, Mom?
From the time I was born
To this Mother's Day;
You always know what to say.
And I started to cry

When they told me to stay
In the principal's office
The rest of the day.
But I knew I'd be fine
'Cause at the end of the day
Someone would be waiting in line.
And that person was you.
Thank God it was you, Mom.
All our love, Mother dear! D&M

WHAT I PROBABLY MEANT TO SAY: Trusting my mother "From birth to forever; from forever to now" is so deep that I must admit I don't understand it. (It's from the heart so I left it in the poem. It could mean that time is circular.) But the general theme of trust is clear. Mom was known for her trustworthiness, and I was her favorite, so that generated quite a nice feeling inside me and I wanted her to know. Also, according to this poem, my first day of kindergarten was troubling. I remember being put in a room with a bunch of strangers, then complaining about it, then getting sent to a quieter room, then seeing my Mom and feeling better. She never let me down. Dad never let me or any of us down, either. Through their actions, my parents instilled in me the notion that you do not ever let down anyone you love. You remain trustworthy. My poems to Mom and Dad are simply recycling concepts that they taught me.

Mom is behind the scenes, taking this photo of me, Dad and Grand pop Ike at camp in 1965.

May 16th, 2010
IT'S MOM BEHIND THE SCENES

Dear Mom:
Found some "good-old-days'" pictures
Taken on a bus painted Smithsonian
    green.
Seems like every special moment
It's Mom behind the scenes.
There's one with me and Dad,
And Grand-pop Ike is in-between.
Seems like every special moment
It's Mom behind the scenes.
I had just finished swimming
You gave me a towel to wipe off the
    chlorine.
Seems like every special moment
It's Mom behind the scenes.
You took me for eyeglasses.
They were the gawkiest I've ever seen.
Seems like every special moment
It's Mom behind the scenes.
You defend your family
Like a mother tigress or wolverine.
Seems like every special moment
It's Mom behind the scenes.
In this pic, you look exactly
Like a model 1960s mother figurine.
Seems like every special moment
It's Mom behind the scenes.
It's amazing how the years have treat-
    ed you
You're beautiful, with an added tint of
    carotene.

Seems like every special moment
It's Mom behind the scenes.
The picture shows your innocence,
Like you are always age 18.
Seems like every special moment
It's Mom behind the scenes.
When I came home hungry from
    school
You had lunch waiting behind the
    kitchen screen.
Seems like every special moment
It's Mom behind the scenes.
Any family issues
Are solved when you intervene.
Seems like every special moment
It's Mom behind the scenes.
When I need some comfort
You always have the "Mom vaccine."
Seems like in every special moment
It's Mom behind the scenes.
The pic of you embodies
The grace and elegance of a Queen.
Seems like a very special moment
When Mom steps in the scene.
You bring out the sunshine
From Ocean City to Brigantine.
Seems like every special moment
It's Mom behind the scenes.
All Our Love Forever,
D&M

WHAT I PROBABLY MEANT TO SAY: You've got the "Mom vaccine." You never let us down. You nourish us. I'm thanking Mom for wrapping me in giant, comforting, nautically themed towels on the beach in Atlantic City, NJ when I was young. Not only do I have wonderful memories and pictures, I still have the towels!

This is the beach towel that my Mom would use to dry me off when I crawled out of the ocean as a toddler. The towel was already old in the 1950s but it's still in working order.

July 30th, 2003
REMINDS ME OF YOU

Dear Mom:
Do you know how often I think of you?
It isn't once in a while or out of the blue.
It's always and it's everywhere
And it's forever coupled with,
"Thank God she's there."
Everywhere we went on our West Coast trip,
I was reminded of things you introduced me to
Or nurtured in me;
You know, that special nurturing you do.
When we drove past the Getty Museum,
I thought of you.
When I walked to Louise's front door,
You were with me, too.
I videotaped the animals at the safari and zoo,
So I could show them to you.
(When I'm at Del Mar, I think of Dad,
But you already knew.)
When I'm in the ocean I think of your father, Lou.
When I dry off, I use the boat-themed towels,
Green and blue,
That you wrapped over me in 1962,
Long after they were new.
It doesn't matter what I do.
Or what I see.
I'm reminded of the love
You've showered on me.
I remember how you gently explained to me everything I didn't understand
When I had to reach up high to grab your hand.
What a gift it was to experience the sweet things in life for the first time,
With the sweetest person of all time.
Your influence is the reason why
I'll pet a deer or chase a butterfly.
Whatever I see in nature or in human nature;
The arts, sciences, or what I read in the paper.
Wherever I go, whatever I do …
I see beauty because it reminds me of you.
Love, Love, Love … … … D & M

WHAT I PROBABLY MEANT TO SAY: Thank you, Mom, for introducing me to some of the sweetest things in life. Also, thanks for instilling in me a love of nature. I'm the first one to suggest going to wild animal parks and I'm known for getting down in the dirt to play-wrestle with young gnus.

> Your influence is the reason why
> I'll pet a deer or chase a butterfly.

When I go the race track, I bring carrots and sweet potatoes so the horses (not the ones who are about to race) can enjoy a healthy snack and I can pet their noses. I wrote a children's book (middle-grade fiction) about a horse who loved his snacks. His name was Seefood. The kids' book about the loveable Seefood, like my kids' book about Onion (who beat Secretariat) was never published. To my surprise, long after I'd written about Seefood the fictional horse, I read a true story about a loveable rascal of a race horse who did all the quirky things my fictional horse had done in my book. That's called life imitating art. The closest comparison would be how the moon landing imitated "Star Trek."

My parents' wedding picture. April, 1944. This is the family's inner circle; what we call the whole Mishpoocha

July 30th, 2009

THE CORE

Dear Mom:
The apple has just a few sections:
The stem, the skin and a few more.
But most important is the core.
And the core is named for you.
The earth has a few continents:
North and South America and a few more.
But most important is the core.
And the core is named for you.

The solar system has a few planets:
Mercury, Venus and Mars and a few more.
But most important is the sun, the system's core.
And the sun, at its core, is named for you.
The apple. The earth. The sun.
All have a core.
And each is named for you.
It's just a few of us in the family, really.
A handful of loved ones, maybe more.
But the most important member is you, the family's core.
There wouldn't be a family without you.
Have the happiest of birthdays!
All our love forever, D&M

WHAT I PROBABLY MEANT TO SAY: You're the centerpiece of the family.

This poem below is one of my saddest. Dad had passed in early 2012 and left Mom alone after nearly 68 years. The old song, "Alone Again, Naturally" by Gilbert O'Sullivan had the same theme in one verse and was very melodic and touching … and I couldn't listen to it. It was too sad. Of course, I won't stop listening to a beautiful song because it's too beautiful or turn off a funny song because it's too funny. But if a song is too sad, I'm leaving.

If you are a theater or film director and you need a middle-age man to cry on command, you can trust me to do it. Just play that song for me. You won't even have to get to the verse about his mother being "alone again, naturally." I'll know it's coming and start to cry, whenever you need it (or even if you don't).

In the same vein, I will turn on the spickets if you show me a picture of my beloved childhood dog, a basset hound named Snooper, and play "Mr. Bojangles" at the same time.

The Greatest Generation mothers were usually overly dependent on their husbands. I think Mom would've been ok with the Native American

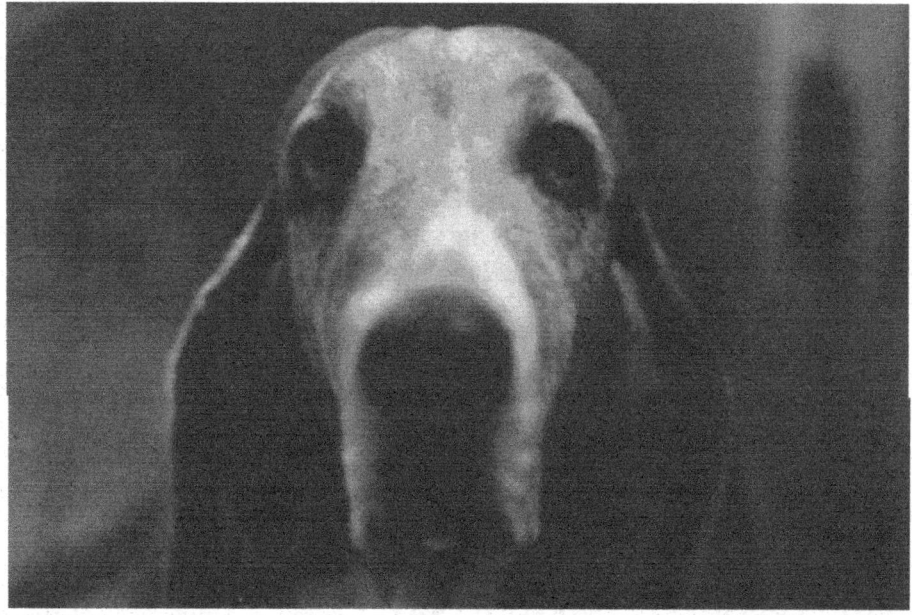

Our family's only pet, a basset hound named Snooper, seen here in her golden years

custom of strangling widows of important men. (Close family members, all men, would do the actual strangling so it's not as bad as it sounds.) Or Mom could've chosen the popular "Ride the ice raft out into the middle of the warm lake" option after Dad left us, with Dad on the raft with her, of course. ("Take your pills, Bernie," she'd tell him.) The odds of her surviving more than a year without her lifelong partner were not very high but Marcia and I took care of her and kept her spirits up for another four years.

That was my "Barton Fink" feeling. Marcia had it, too. Far better than picking up checks, we had kept our word to Dad and taken care of Mom exactly like he would have done.

July 30th, 2012
WE'LL GO TWO FOR TWO
(Listen to John Prine's, "Hello In There")
Dear Mom:
We've finally got you living local.
Minutes away, right place to be.
You and Dad in the picture frames,
Poems on doors with both your names,
Both in our Hall of Fame.

Dinner is now served in your building.
Your heartbeat's regular, nice and strong.
Your 88th birthday, in a new frontier,
Where your smile lights up the atmosphere;
We're so blessed to have you here.
Yeah, it's true there have been many changes
And as you say, nothing ever stays the same.
These days, whenever I call you two
I get twice the good advice
And a double shot of love
From you.
Last week I was standing on the sand near Resorts.
Didn't the Breakers Hotel used to be around here?
That was where the valet smashed Dad's new car;
Salt water baths, then you'd wrap me in a giant towel.
Now there's a beachside tiki bar.
I think I know what Dad would've wanted.
That we remember him with love and take care of you.
We know so well that the first is true.
And as far as giving joy to you
We'll go two for two.
All Our Love Forever! D&M

WHAT I PROBABLY MEANT TO SAY: Mom, you're so comforting, it's beyond belief. I re-imagine her wrapping me in a giant nautical-themed towel on the beach in Atlantic City, NJ when I was very young. Call me sentimental for mentioning those towels over and over again in poems to my mother but they were a real source of comfort, provided by her, the best source of comfort. (I never mentioned the towels in poems to Dad; the towels were strictly a motherly device.) This was about the time when her father, Grand pop Lou, taught me to dive by throwing me into the pool headfirst. I saw on a TV movie that billionaire John Paul Getty supposedly taught his grandson the same way. Old school Grand Pops; you had to love them … or you'd drown by age four.

I'm also saying that we'll take care of you, like Dad wanted us to do.

May 11th, 2014

WHAT MOTHER'S DAY MEANS TO ME

(Listen to John Prine's, "Standin' By Peaceful Waters")

Dear Mom:
I'm so lucky.
Raised by a gentle mother.
Peaceful, like no other.
That's what Mother's Day means to me.
I'm so grateful.
For all your love and attention,
And non-stop, umbrella protection.
That's what Mother's Day means to me.

WHAT I PROBABLY MEANT TO SAY: I'm lucky to be your son. No need to get overly complicated when your mother is about to turn 90. Mom made it to her 91st birthday. It would be her final one. I was able to thank her in writing one more time.

July 30th, 2015

IN ALL THIS TIME

(Listen to UFO's, "Love To Love")

Dear Mom:
Yeah, I can't believe
In all this time
I have never seen you piss somebody off.
You have a way that is so sweet and soft.
And you're the best thing still around from 1924.
Yeah, it's a repeated theme
When people say to me:
"You know, your Mother is just beautiful and wonderful."
Hard to get a total consensus anymore …
Except that you're the best thing still around from 1924.
Yeah, so what's in store
For your 91st tour?

We hope it's filled with love, good health, laughter, joy and more.
Since the day I was born, I've been sure
That you're the best thing still around from 1924.
All Our Love & Appreciation, D&M

WHAT I PROBABLY MEANT TO SAY: Mom, I love you. You stand alone as the only person who has never pissed anyone off. I got pissed at Dad a few times, usually right after he got pissed at me for doing something reckless. But Mom? She never pissed anybody off. That's a record that may never be broken.

My Mom passed away in the Spring of 2016. She lived four years as a widow, surprising everyone and outliving the widow in the old song, "Alone Again, Naturally." Mom was lost without her man and she kept her emotions locked inside, making things even tougher. But she lasted just long enough to help me through trying times. When my wife, Marcia, was diagnosed with uterine cancer in March of 2016, hearing my Mom's voice and her advice every night was the only thing that kept my spirits up. She'd say odd things that inspired me, too, like "Daddy's working on it." Days later, Marcia was miraculously saved, then Mom fell ill and went peacefully.

July 12th, 2016 (my last poem to Mom)
ONE MORE THING I HAVE TO DO
(Listen to John Mellencamp's, "Rain On The Scarecrow")

Mom was always close to God.
We'd see her near the stairs
With folded hands and trembling lips,
Whispering her prayers.
Her lust for life was languishing
After Daddy passed.
Life's a burden after 90
But she swore she'd save her best for
    last.
Mom's always praying.
She won't say why.
She'll sweetly say, "You only have
What you give away."

"There's one more thing I have to do
Before I leave this fray."
Mom's always praying.
She won't say why.
My wife was Mom's favorite
And one day the doctors said,
They'd studied my wife's CAT scan
And found a "suspicious mass."
"We'll put a scope inside her
To ease your fear and doubt.
But we're not sure what we'll find
Or if we can get it out."
I said, "I don't care how you find it,
You've got to get it out of her quick."

They said they'd try —and then I
    learned
That Mom was really sick.
I rushed to another hospital
To be by my Mom's side.
I said, "I've tried to make you happy
As if Dad were here inside."
She said, "Donny, you did everything"
And then she closed her eyes.
Mom's always praying.
Now we know why.
Doctors found me in the waiting room
To keep me well apprised
About my wife's successful surgery
And how they were pleasantly
    surprised.
I think God moved those tumors
So doctors could get inside.

Mom told us she had one more thing
To do after she died.
I couldn't get God to hear me
No matter how hard I tried.
I couldn't get any counsel
From my so-called spirit guides.
But Mom, she got it done with prayer,
From the other side.
Mom's always praying.
Now we know why.
You may not believe in miracles, per
    se.
You may not believe that spirit guides
    are sent our way.
Even if you don't believe in science,
You know, it's true anyway.
Mom's always praying.
Now we know why.

WHAT I PROBABLY MEANT TO SAY: I'm saying that my mother helped me, somehow, in her dying days. She was unselfish to the end and even beyond the end.

POEMS I JUST HAD TO WRITE

I was talking to Larry the ice cream vendor on the beach in Atlantic City, NJ, about poetry, mostly. Larry is a war veteran (beach vendors in A.C. have to be veterans) and chipwich peddler who enters all kinds of poetry contests.

"I entered a writing contest, back in Bucks County, PA," I told him.

Larry put his frozen burden down on the sand.

"What kind of contest?" he asked.

"It's actually a competition to be the Bucks County poet laureate."

"Is this your first-time submitting poems to be poet laureate?"

"No, I tried in Philly. But I didn't win. If I did, you would know it because I would've gotten a big tattoo right here on my chest —"

I was quoting Charles Van Doren, the guy from the 1950s quiz show scandal who died in 2019. But, in fact, I'm not a tattoo guy and here's why. A famous rock climber died in 2018 and his widow claimed that it was from Hepatitis C, the result of a tattoo he had gotten 30 years earlier from a headhunter in Borneo. And that's just one of the reasons I'm not a tattoo guy.

Larry asked me, "Do your poems rhyme?"

I thought of a Thin Lizzy song: "Ohh-oh, Poor Romeo. Headhunter in Borneo. All, all, on his own-eo."

"Sure," I replied. "Some have uneven rhyme schemes that I don't even think about, they just sort of arrange themselves...."

Larry was already shaking his head.

"You'll never win that way," Larry said unswervingly.

"What way?"

"They don't like rhyming."

"Poems ... shouldn't rhyme?" I asked.

"Not if you want to be poet laureate."

But I've written dozens of poems out of the blue sky and they often rhyme. I'm motivated by a feeling or an idea. Sometimes I'll write one because it's my birthday or I'm breaking up with a girlfriend.

I always thought that when a relationship ended, I should at least try to get a good poem or story out of it. I was trapped once on a balcony in Pittsburgh, not knowing if the angry boyfriend of my new lady (she claimed he was an ex-boyfriend) was going to hurt anyone. I was ready to jump off the balcony onto a lawn to save my life and just as importantly, write about the experience. (I wrote about it in an unpublished novel called "Summer at Saratoga.")

Full disclosure: I was going to jump off that balcony in Pittsburgh because the jealous ex-boyfriend had been in a coma and (allegedly) awoke with telepathic, telekinetic powers and I didn't have either of them. In a related disclosure, the girl in the middle of all this, while very nice, was in all likelihood a witch. Maybe it's better that my novel was never published.

But there was something spooky about my affair with the girl from Pittsburgh. Magnetic forces were at work, or magic potions. It felt naughty and nice. We met again in New York City in the mid-1980s, a few months after I almost had to leap from her balcony in Pittsburgh to avoid a teed-off telepath with telekinetic powers. Her long hair was tickling my thighs as she sat on my lap in the hotel room. Her perfume was sinking into my skin. Somehow, hers was the only perfume that didn't bother me. Ever.

I played a Gordon Lightfoot tape, featuring the song "Affair On 8th Avenue." (My hotel room was next to 8th Avenue.) As we explored each other, I heard Gordon Lightfoot singing about his lady's long, flowing hair and how "The perfume that she wore, was from some little store, on the downside of town. And it lingered on, long after she'd gone. I remember it well."

I wondered how long a moment like this could belong to someone. Then I heard Gordon sing on cue: "'How long,' said she, 'could a moment like this, belong to someone?'"

I made a conscious effort to keep my thoughts to myself concerning the spooky connection to the song playing in my old cassette player. One reason was that the Pittsburgh girl claimed to possess some telepathic powers, too. Have you ever made love to a telepath? It's complicated. I've done it, in two states, though you won't find it on my resume.

Gordon Lightfoot wrote "If You Could Read My Mind," not "You Can Read My Mind."

Then Gordon sang, "And if you should ask me what secrets I hide, well I'm only your lover, don't make me decide."

I know I'm not alone in feelings of déjà vu. Bob Dylan wrote about it in "Tangled Up In Blue," when he picked up a book written by an Italian poet from the 15th century and "Every one of those words rang true ... like it was written in my soul, from me to you."

How could a book written centuries earlier have anything to do with Bob Dylan's relationship? How could Gordon Lightfoot's song ring so true about my time in New York City with the Pittsburgh girl and her non-allergen perfume? The only way to prove this correlation is for someone to read this book in 600 years and say, "Yup! Don knew exactly what was goin' on with the two of us in 2620."

I won't be around in 2620 but maybe you will. Check it out, Mr. and Mrs. Robot.

A year before my affair with the good witch in Pittsburgh, I was romantically involved with my literary agent in L.A. The poem below is one I just had to write; actually, it's a combination of two poems I wrote to my (soon to be ex-) girlfriend/agent months apart in 1984 to express my feelings.

THE BOTTOM LINE/ EVEN IF IT'S WRONG

I'm just another player
In the exhibition game.
Out there on the field
Between rejection and acclaim.
And this, like any movie,
Has a message in each frame:
The bottom line is money
And under it is fame.
Throw away the rules
And other tools of desperation.
Leave out in-betweens
And other means of arbitration.
Like a barroom brawl, get out or fight
    until you win.
Losing's not a crime but never trying is
    a sin.
We've had the feeling for so long,
Let's do it even if it's wrong.

Like I've been saying all along,
Let's do it even if it's wrong.
Even if it's wrong
I have to see you one more time.
Break out of this social jail
For one more social crime.
Even if there's no one home
Or nothing left to say,
Let me make the last mistake;
Then let me walk away.
Sacrifice the ones you love;
Success must be to blame.
We may be a part of
Everything you overcame.
Hardly an original,
Your message is the same:
The bottom line is money
And under it is fame.

87

Here I am in January, 1988, reviewing the shooting script for a very low budget movie, shot mostly outdoors in Philadelphia during a great freeze.

WHAT I PROBABLY MEANT TO SAY: The bottom line isn't money. Almost everyone thinks it is, though. And there are plenty of people who would betray their best friend or do something worse to procure a new house or boat. (Personally, I'd rather get a tattoo than a boat.) But when they say the bottom line is money, it's not true. Most people want fame more than money. With fame, they figure they'll get money and power.

Why can't everybody just stick to the wise, old saying: "If I am not for myself, who will be? If I am only for myself, what am I?" If you go around saying that type of thing in Hollywood, the local famished-for-fame gang will eat you alive. (Watch the film, "Sunset Boulevard.")

"Even If It's Wrong" is about love gone bad. I've been through this a few times and I bet you have, too. Mine was the typical love story: boy meets woman in Hollywood, you can redact the rest. It really was like "Sunset Boulevard" except I wrote myself out before they found me face down in a pool, like William Holden, narrating.

But I had to see her (the agent) one more time and "Break out of this social jail for one more social crime." I wanted to tell her my side of the story, I wanted to set a few things straight, I wanted ... sex! I was in my 20s and my career was not going as well as I expected. Thanks to my Dad's help, I could afford to rent an apartment near the beach, a decent car, food and ... sex.

Game show question: What do poor people do for fun? I'd say right off the bat: the answer is they have sex.

What if you could combine a game show with a sitcom. I wrote an original script for such a sitcom in the 1980s called "Finders Keepers." I included scenes in my proposed game show/sitcom about people facing their fears ("Face Your Phobia!") that were almost identical to "Fear Factor" twenty years later. I wrote another script called "Boardwalk" that was nearly identical to the hit show, "The Jersey Shore." Everyone thought I was crazy to come up with those concepts in the 1980s. Everyone thought I'd never make a dime on those shows. They were only half right.

There is more to "The Bottom Line" poem. I suggest that she cared more about business success than anything else (not the first time I noticed that in a girlfriend).

I wrote about a businesswoman bird who was hyper-serious in "A Leprechaun Named Levity" (learn more about the poem on page 154). And I wrote this to another businesswoman I was involved with in the mid-1980s:

> Hey, Amway girl, there's two ways to advance,
> Who likes business better than romance?

These girls did!

What I'm trying to say in "The Bottom Line" poem is that my ex-girlfriend/ex-agent's win-at-all-costs behavior is not my style, sort of like when Bob Dylan says, "Don't think twice, it's all right" but really means it's all wrong.

The inspiration for this poem came from two sources: my agent, a desperate, single mother in L.A. in 1984, my only friend, it should be noted, and from an old-time baseball manager, who looked around the dugout in disgust at his losing team and muttered, "Let's do somethin'. Even if it's wrong."

Try it sometime. Believe me, you'll know when the time is right.

I wrote this one below sometime in the early 1980s, after a night of God-knows-what.

AND I KNEW, THEN ....

I was talking to a child
And the look on his face said, "Amuse me."
And I knew, then, that he'd be all right.
I didn't worry; that kid was all right.
I was talking to a woman
And the look on her face said, "Abuse me."
And I knew, then, I'd wait for a wife.
Shouldn't hurry when choosing a wife.
I was talking to a maniac
And the look on his face said, "Attack me."
And I knew, then, that wasn't my fight.
Got to have a good reason to fight.
I was talking to a senior citizen
And the look on his face said, "Give it back to me!"
And I knew, then, the meaning of life.

I knew, then, the meaning of life.

WHAT I PROBABLY MEANT TO SAY: The meaning of life is "Give it back to me!" Full disclosure: I am not a philosopher but I did read "How Real Is Real" in college so I may be right about this. I mean, is the secret to life abuse or attack me? That better not be the secret to my life. Is it "amuse me"? That's close. But as a young man, I guessed it was "Give it back to me!" As I get older, I see how that idea could be considered Wisdom From My Younger Self.

This is an example of a poem that I didn't understand at first, even though I wrote it, like my early poem to my late Grand pop Lou. I wrote the poems and then had to go back and reverse engineer them, to see what I had done with the rhyming scheme and overall message.

In this one, I liked the pacing and the existential shit, but what was happening with the uneven rhyme scheme? The spirit guides who had taken over my brain to write that poem had to explain the crisscrossing action of the rhymes.

Rhyme schemes should come naturally to you. If they don't, then don't use rhymes. This no-rhyming tactic has been successful for poet laureates throughout the nation. I don't know why. Ask Larry the ice cream man on the Atlantic City beach. And buy something from him.

If you're a beginner, keep the rhyme schemes simple, like in the one below where I rhyme the first line with the second line, then repeat the chorus.

OF COURSE; RELAX!

Years from now when we're fallin' apart,
We'll look back on these days with only fondness of heart.
Of course; relax!
I live at night 'cause I'm havin' too much fun
To go to sleep while I'm still full of run.
Of course; relax!
Can't resent someone's good fortune. There's got
To be a good reason; or maybe there's not.
Of course, relax!
There's a guy who took the easiest path and the easiest wife.
He's making thousands a week and really hating his life.
Of course; relax!
I see the studio door, but when I get there they shut it.
I've got deadlines: Do they just wanna see how close I can cut it?

Of course; relax!
I've got inventive friends; they help my wheelin' and dealin'.
But if they spark a new song I write, they cry about stealin'.
Of course; relax!
It was always my goal: to be a writer's guild member.
If they want me, it's just for the dues that I'll tender.
Of course; relax!
The worries, the burdens, the doubts and the fear
Abate when the plane lands and loved ones appear.
Of course; relax!
I got something published and shouted, "Hooray!"
Years from now, I'll ask myself, "That made my day?"
Of course; relax!
There are songs that I sing in my head for no reason.
And they're always in synch with my mood and the season.
Of course; relax!
You're looking ok but obsessed with success.
Strike it rich; looking good will have you obsessed.
Of course; relax!
A college professor; well, he gets respect.
While a writer gets to crawl through a hellish neglect.
Of course; relax!
Guess I'm resting on the laurels I believe I deserve.
But there aren't any laurels I receive or reserve.
Of course; relax!
The wisest all tell me I must take a side.
In the flowers or garbage … and I can't decide.
Of course, relax.

WHAT I PROBABLY MEANT TO SAY: There is no date attached to these random notes to myself because this poem is ongoing. I'll write a new verse every few years. (I should rewrite the line about college professors getting respect; they don't.)

But the theme of this living, breathing poem that I began writing in the 1970s never changes: of course, these things are true. What can you do about it? Why don't you just relax. Earlier in the book, I gave away the title of this poem in reference to my mentor, Jack Langguth, who got screwed out of a Pulitzer Prize. (It had something to do with the Vietnam War and the New York Times not letting him tell the whole truth.) Sometimes we all deserve a prize, but it goes to somebody else for reasons no one can explain or defend. Take a deep breath, then say to yourself: "Of Course; Relax!"

I say "Of Course; Relax!" to myself all the time, prefaced with:

Guess I'm resting on the laurels I believe I deserve.
But there aren't any laurels I receive or reserve.

When writing about yourself, it's ok to be unnecessarily cruel. That's called progress. Some call it self-deprecating humor. And it sells! Charlie Daniels used that kind of humor in his songs. So Did Harry Chapin. Tom Petty admitted that he went to the "Zombie Zoo," for crying out loud. Meat Loaf, in one song, actually cried out loud.

In this next poem, the main character finds a way to relax. He drinks.

1984
A DECENT MAN

He had a drink or two to toast the ending of the war.
He had a drink or three to start a life with his new bride.
He had a drink or four to welcome twins he couldn't afford.
He had a drink or five to mourn the friendships that had died.
He had a drink or six while watching games he used to play.
He had a drink or seven when the welfare check would come.
He had a drink or eight for pain that wouldn't go away.
He had a drink or nine because it almost made him numb.
He had a drink or ten when he felt helpless as a man.
He had a drink or twenty when he voted; or bet wrong.
He had a drink or thirty when another war began.
They told him that his problem was his drinking all along.
He checked into a hospital; ashamed of what he'd done.
He drove out with a bottle in his hand and then was jailed.
He died a short time later in the company of none.
So I had a drink to mourn a decent man who failed.

WHAT I PROBABLY MEANT TO SAY: Don't do drugs. Don't be a drunk. This is a repeated theme of mine. It's a repeated theme in many books and films. For example, remember when everybody was getting high in "Trainspotting" and the unattended baby almost fell down the steps? That's an anti-drug scene written by someone who was fervently anti-drugs (or anti-babies). Artists write about their own experiences so "Don't Do Drugs" could be the subtitle of many books, films, songs (see Pop, Iggy and spiders, smoked), paintings and more. In the song, "Cocaine Blues," sung by Johnny Cash, George Thorogood and others, they advise us to "Lay off the whiskey and let that cocaine be," while I'm saying you don't have to punish yourself and drink yourself to death but if you do, don't drink and drive.

In my poem, the main character's drinking wasn't the problem; it was a reaction to his problems and his human failures. The problems he faced were overwhelming (again, refer to Bruce Springsteen singing about having "Debts that no honest man can pay") and he needed help coping with them. And then I had to admit I was so shaken by this guy's alcohol problem, and the troubled society in which he lived, the same one you and I live in, incidentally, that by the time I finished the poem, I needed a fucking drink! ("Son of a Bitch," Nathaniel Rateliff would say.) I could relate to this guy trying to numb himself. That's why I wrote it. I didn't realize it until the last line was written but that's what I meant to say.

(Listen to John Lennon's, "Working Class Hero," where he sings about self-numbing with the line, "Till the pain is so big that you feel nothing at all.")

I'm hinting that automatic writing could be involved here and in other poems when I did not realize what I was trying to say until I went back and re-read them.

At Starbucks, before they kick me out for asking if I can use the rest room, people say to me, "Don, you've been writing for 45 years, does automatic writing actually occur?"

Wait. Listen.

That's the air conditioning. Ignore it. Ok, the answer I'm getting telepathically is "Yes."

The voices (automatic writing partners) are saying that the readers will want proof. Fair enough. I can prove it, sort of.

I was leaving L.A. in 1984. There was a feeling of urgency, of impending doom, of self-loathing for not being a millionaire at 29. I experimented with automatic writing and scribbled away on a yellow legal pad in a dark room. Nothing was legible. It was gibberish.

Seven years later, I wrote a script about the only lawyer in heaven, based on the research I had done on a book about life after death. I called it, "When Angels Speak … They Argue." (Debate is very popular in heaven, according to my research.)

A few years after that, I looked at all my old papers from Playa del Rey, California. I guess the post-traumatic stress from my time in L.A. had subsided. I began opening boxes in the garage that were untouched for years and found a two-bulb table lamp that I use to this day. (It can double as a heat lamp in winter.) I also found the yellow legal pad with the failed automatic writing experiment/gibberish. And when I tilted the writing pad, I could make out the title: "When Angels Speak." It was my handwriting on my legal pad. I had somehow written down the title of my script that I wouldn't conceive of until seven years later!

Anyway, I imagine that was a successful attempt at automatic writing. I haven't tried it again and who could blame me.

A few pages ago, I describe the art of numbing yourself in "A Decent Man." I wrote a children's story, called "A Leprechaun Named Levity" entirely in verse, about a leprechaun who had blurred the line between apathy and neurotic concern. (Read more about "Levity" on page 154.) It took one night to write it, 28 pages, all in verse. Come to think of it, that was probably another example of automatic writing.

Maybe all writing is automatic writing, with help from outside influences. That's why you can write poems to loved ones. You (and your spirit guides, etc.) can do it. Just sit down and write on a yellow legal pad, if they still make them.

THEME ALERT! "Levity" and "A Decent Man" liked to numb themselves to escape their troubles. In this next poem, the main character finds a way to relax: he drinks.

(1978)

SPORTS REPORT-OR

(Listen to Charlie Daniels' Band, "El Toreador")

He was totally pissed when the quarterback's fist
Broke more bones in his battered face.
He got over that, got revenge in this spat
In a column of newspaper space.
Seems the girls of L.A., tonight wouldn't play
And tomorrow, he must write once more.
When he left the bar, he would smash up his car,
For he was a Sports Report-or.
The game of the day was just four meals away
When he met bail the following morn.
The waitress asked, "More? Weren't you in here before?
No, I'm sorry, we don't have popcorn."
He went to the park, then made a remark
About wanting free press, nothing more.
He said, "If it's ok, whatever happens today,
Let me write like a Sports Report-or."
The press box de Ramos smelled like cheap wine
As the press box boys dealt out some cards.
The game would go on, as did betting, till dawn,
All the refs wanted extra armed guards.
On and on, on and on ....
The shouts of "Oh No" told him it's time to go
To the locker of the losing home team.
As he thought what to ask, he just took out a flask
And guzzled the rest of Jim Beam
Seems he missed the big game; he drank and didn't feel the same
But his boss said he must write once more.
So he took out a pen, asked why, who, where and when?
Took words out of context, twisted 'em 'round twice again.
And he was heard to say, "You guys sure sucked today!"
Now he's fired like a Sports Report-or.

WHAT I PROBABLY MEANT TO SAY: Sure, I was mocking sports journalists for behaving badly but some, like O.J., deserved it. I'm also defending the First Amendment. Without that, I'd be in trouble for some of the ideas expressed in this book. But remember my mantra and, please, use it yourselves amongst your peers:

**If I haven't offended you in this book,
I didn't do it on purpose.**

THEME ALERT! In this next poem, the main character finds a way to relax: he gets high. Heck, it's a Hollywood story so what else could I write about? The twist in this one is that the action takes place while wearing red shoes.

I wrote this poem in the early 1980s, when I was in my 20s. My original research for this poem is sketchy but it's about getting wasted in red shoes. How many Baby Boomers can remember that far back? Not many, believe me.

Here are a few verses from my "Red Shoes" poem:

> There's gonna be a riot up in Hollywood tonight.
> My shoes are red, my sleeves are cut, my armpits smell just right.
> There's nothing I will do or say I'll ever recollect.
> I'm driving slow and waiting for the drugs to take effect.
> Hey, I finally got here, guess I'll park on someone's lawn.
> Ooops, I rammed a pigeon. I'll clean it up at dawn.
> Are people at this party straight? No way! Just askin' is dumb.
> Hold on. It's true. My wait is through. My hands and teeth are numb.
> Ha. I went up to this snobby chick and shouted out my name.
> And told her all about myself. She muttered, "What a shame." Bitch!
> Throw me out? I'd punch you if you weren't six feet four.
> Why get pissed because I missed and threw up on your door?
> Tell that sleaze who took three hits, she owes me 15 bucks.
> And don't invite me back here. In fact, this party sucks!
> This is weird, I'm in my car. Some senses have returned,
> To focus on my pants and all the holes in them I've burned.
> If paranoia gets much worse, I swear I'll have to swear off.
> OK, two more, while I wait for, these drugs to just wear off.

WHAT I PROBABLY MEANT TO SAY: Don't do drugs.

Below is a rare item: a published poem.

(1983)
NORWEGIAN SOIL

I was just a young man in a century gone by,
Where young men turned old if they dared blink an eye.
So we kept our eyes open and one day we found
Immortal treasures in the Norwegian ground.
Near the north pole, where so few chose to live,
Was a gift that saint nick never knew he could give.
Everyone living; the common, the royal,
Lived longer because of the Norwegian soil.
This dirt held a substance which helped man accept
Synthetic chambers and valves, so adept
At pumping our blood, thus prolonging our lives.
Organs we would've rejected, revived.
The number one killer – wiped out overnight.
Infections: they too lost a long-standing fight.
All people grew older but few grew much wiser.
More time than we dreamed of; more than we desired.
In school for three decades, we built up our minds.
Worked 'till retirement – at age 99.
A man in his eighties was still in his prime,
Trying his best to fill his spare time.
Everyone living; the common, the royal,
Lived longer because of the Norwegian soil.
Oh, yes, we were bored – so little was new –
So we fought with our neighbors, like we always do.
With time, we found patience; so little we feared.
Our enemies' weak sisters soon disappeared.
In 2060, in the Norwegian war,
The country – and soil – weren't there anymore.
What man creates, he is destined to spoil,
Including the treasure of Norwegian soil.
Everyone dying; the common, the royal,
Was helpless without the Norwegian soil.
Me, I've seen 105 years go by.
The first few stand out, though I can't recall why.
My medicine gone now; it hurts so to cry.
But I must, for I've waited too long just to die.

WHAT I PROBABLY MEANT TO SAY: I had a lot to say. That's why I wrote an entire screenplay about it, called "Dirty Rats." In the story, young medical researchers discover the fountain of youth in the Norwegian soil, but Big Pharma takes it off the market. Then, it turns out the soil can also be used as an undetectable weapon, and it's suddenly in demand and being sold to every asshole with a checkbook. The script and poem, written in 1983, predicted that greed could destroy our natural assets. I was right. (See Amazon, burning.)

In fact, in the 80s, I wrote a novel and comic book about a futuristic sports society, "Superfan," and named the Atlantic Ocean of the future "The salty, fluidic garbage dump." I just read that the Atlantic Ocean currently has a section of piled up plastic that is actually called "The Garbage Dump"! I was right again (unfortunately) about how greed would eventually destroy our natural assets.

Don't ask what else I predicted in the 80s about the Earth's pollution and climate change challenges in the near future. I can tell you to run for the hills. (I apologize for using a cliché but in this case it will probably save your life.) Bring scuba gear, gas masks, eye drops, cough drops, canned foods, banned foods, etc. with you to the hills.

I can't help but notice that in the final verse I talk about being old and ready to die. Yikes! I was 27 years old when I wrote this! I was predicting how I'd feel almost 80 years later, when, like my Grand pop Lou and my Dad, I'd be ready to pull the trigger and blow off my own head or pull the pacemaker battery out of my own chest. To be perfectly honest, I'm hoping technology will offer me more choices in 2060.

Sometime in the 1990s.
JUST TALKIN' TO YOURSELF

You can hide but you can't run.
You can try to have some fun.
But it's never any fun
When you're just talkin' to yourself.
You can cry throughout the joint.
You can try to make your point.
But there's never any point
When you're just talkin' to yourself.

You can play "psychology."
You can pay yourself the fee.
But there's never any fee
When you're just talkin' to yourself.
You can hurt the ones who care.
You can squirt paint in their hair.
But there's nothing you can share
When you're just talkin' to yourself.

WHAT I PROBABLY MEANT TO SAY: You can't run from yourself. Sometimes you have to drop problems or at least not pay them so much rent. Gandhi said, "A wise man learns to forget."

Use the above quote to start your own poem to a loved one. I know Gandhi would approve and even if he didn't, he would eventually forget about it. This poem gives a shout-out to my wife's late cousin, Sharon, for squirting paint in Marcia's hair when they were both kids. I couldn't have written that last verse without hearing about their summertime adventures (paint squirting) in the Catskills, circa 1962.

In the next few poems, I write about time and space. I didn't set out to write about time and space but, time and again, wherever I was, I did.

Sometime in the late 1970s, in Playa del Rey, California:

> Time will heal your wounded flesh and heart.
> You need it just to finish what you start.
> Promptly, time pays all outstanding debts.
> And when it goes, it kills you, no regrets.
>
> Don't mumble that nonsense
> 'bout time running out.
> Time has no time for complaints.
> Our days are determined.
> If time has you burdened
> You'll waste it on self-made restraints.

WHAT I PROBABLY MEANT TO SAY: Don't worry about time because that will only handcuff you. In the past 40 years, I've changed my perception on this subject quite a bit. Now, I don't think time really exists. It's like a phonograph record and everything is on the record, at different times, or at different spots on the record. Look for my upcoming book, "Time's Up … But Not Really." It will be published in another 40 years, one way or another.

Sometime in the 1980s, after a night of God-knows-what, I wrote this:

SPIRITS

Many depend upon me;
Some who were born long ago.
Others who wait to be born;
Spirits I don't even know.
They cheer me on in silence.
They've given and they'll take.
Funny, they seem distant
In the hours I'm awake.

WHAT I PROBABLY MEANT TO SAY: My spirit guides are out there but I can't really connect with them unless I'm dreaming. That's why I wrote down my dreams for decades. My first novel was about a man who self-hypnotizes himself in dreams. My latest book was originally going to be my interpretations of dreams from 1977 to the present but I seem to have misplaced one of my two lifetime dream diaries. That's why you're reading this.

(1982)
P.I.T.

P is for the pleasure
In creating forms of art.
I includes ideas to give
Creative forms a start.
T should be tenacity
To swing until I hit.
When I run out of P.I.T.
I'll dig out from this pit.

WHAT I PROBABLY MEANT TO SAY: I'll leave L.A. when I run out of ideas and tenacity and when the writing life is no longer fun. I did just that, two years after I wrote this. The ideas and tenacity were still alive but pleasure had been squeezed out of me, like the L.A. showbiz scene was an attacking alligator with one purpose in life: to spin me around underwater and make the writing life I had chosen seem repugnant and dangerous to my health.

While it would have been nicer to leave L.A. under a glow of success and to the roar of accolades, it was a worthwhile experience (surviving repeated hits below the belt). The "P.I.T." poem really is *Wisdom From My Younger Self.*

POEMS I WROTE TO (WHAT TURNED OUT TO BE) EX-GIRLFRIENDS

I've written most of my love poems to attractive woman with dark hair, a few years older than me. That's my type. How do I know my type? Once, when I was single and in my mid-thirties, I stopped in for a drink ("Son of a bitch!" Nathaniel Rateliff would say) in an Atlantic City beach bar. I greeted a young lady and she said almost immediately, "You came up to me last year." Hmmm. I did?

If you're like me, you've got a type. And you've shared a first kiss with her/him. Try to capture the initial spark of passion in your poem. I dated a nurse in the late 1980s. Our initial sparks reminded me of the summer solstice. This first date took first prize in the Young Adult division of wild kissing on the couch.

I called her the next day. She was suddenly cool, like Billy Joel warned. Reverting to my inner journalist, I pressed on with direct questioning.

"What the fuck happened?" (I was no Walter Cronkite.)

She told me she had gone back with her ex-boyfriend.

"That guy?" I asked. "The guy who forced you to shoot heroin?"

Now you know why I write so many anti-drug poems.

Like any young man, I suffered the heartbreak of broken love affairs. I'd write poems to express the howling grief but ... huh? What was I thinking — that breaking up with girlfriends were some of the most painful moments in my life? No. Going through that was a breeze. Hell, most of my girlfriends said they were doing me a favor when they broke up with me, and they were always right. But as an adult, I know that serious heartaches come along with living a full life. The ordeal of almost losing my wife, then losing my mother in the same couple of weeks was not anything like breaking up with a girlfriend I had known for a year or two. It wasn't on the same scale, like comparing a milestone in your life with a mustard burp. "Momentarily tangy but quickly forgotten" the old man said about mustard burps in the film "Things To Do In Denver When You're Dead." In that film, Andy Garcia played the character known as "Jimmy the Saint." I don't believe that's the same "Jimmy the Saint" from Bruce Springsteen's song, "Lost In The Flood." Springsteen's Jimmy would've been older.

Below is one of my break-up poems written when I was young and didn't know any better. I had known the woman, who was a college student (at Vallejo Junior College, not Cal Berkeley like she claimed the night I met her) for just 16 months.

1981
ILLUSIONS
(Listen to Juice Newton's, "Angel Of The Morning")

There is no bridge to cross back on.
As a matter of fact, there's nothing there.
The dynamite has done its job.
I've got empty space, tryin' not to care.
Crossing that bridge as if on cue.
I may have loved it more than you.
I'm not the villain who has misconducted.
I want that next bridge, not ours reconstructed.
My path leads elsewhere, just as you've instructed.
But through the darkness and fear,
I wonder, is your mind clear?
An aging man can look away from illusions rooted deep in youth.
We must be children if we stay long after we have learned the truth.
And I'm afraid I stayed too long,
Inventing reasons to be strong.
I'm not the villain who has misconducted.
I want that next bridge, not ours reconstructed.
My path leads elsewhere, just as you've instructed.
But through the darkness and fear,
I wonder, is your mind clear?
Who now to guide you through the fog?
Who will hold you through the darkest night?
If freedom shines in lieu of love
It will soon become your only light.
You fell in love with feeling free.
What if it walks away, like me?

WHAT I PROBABLY MEANT TO SAY: We all do it. We stay too long, inventing reasons to be strong, believing we can fix whatever is broken. But in this case, as in most cases, it was a lost cause. In retrospect, it was ridiculous to feel so heartbroken. I eventually saw through my own charade (and her Cal Berkeley charade) and wrote a poem about all the women who had broken my heart … and how, on one particular night, years later, they had all reconsidered and were coming right over! All of them!

> They can't wait to see me, and to be seen with me …
> I hope I remember their names.

I'm admitting that I won't even remember their names in a year or two. I'll look at the pictures of women I loved and think, "Did I date her?" It's Wisdom From My Younger Self and it's telling me to check my ego.

Of course, it took decades before I heeded my own advice. I figured, who's gonna believe a guy like me?

I wrote these next few poems to a woman who was (predictably) attractive, with dark hair, and a few years older than me.

Summer, 1985
STRANGERS IN THE WAWA
(Note: Wawa is a convenience store.)
(Listen to Frank Sinatra's, "Strangers In The Night")
Strangers in the Wawa
Exchanging smiles.
Wandering in the Wawa.
All through the aisles.
We didn't go to bars because they closed at twooooooo.
Strangers in the Wawa.
You liked my gray hair.
Talking in the Wawa.
We could've stayed there.
Love was underneath the full moon.
Love was on the beach before noon.

WHAT I PROBABLY MEANT TO SAY: I was trying to get laid so I wrote this poem to a prospective girlfriend (who, as it turned out, was also trying to get laid). Flash forward a few years when I wrote this to her:

1990

I'm a baby boomer, yesiree.
Too young for Vietnam, too old for World War III.
The sexual revolution – it was invented for me.
But now I look at it with irony.
Cause my life was saved by monogamy.

(Soon after I wrote that poem to my girlfriend, we broke up and I wrote this:)

You've got my luggage on the lawn;
Whatever could that mean?
You've got my laundry on the street;
Why send it out if it's all clean?

WHAT I PROBABLY MEANT TO SAY: I get it: you're kicking me out because I won't marry you. Fair Enuf.

Sometimes, you start out loving someone and wind up not loving that person. A prime example would be my uncle, who shortly after his own birth stopped loving or respecting his father, my Grand pop Lou. I say go ahead — use that emotion to write a terrific goodbye poem. Here is what I wrote in 1990 to the ex-girlfriend who practically put my luggage on the lawn (see above) when I wouldn't marry her. This actually explains why I wouldn't marry her.

1990
THE ROAD

The road is a lonely
And desperate place.
Unsettled like the sea;
Unforgiving like space.
It's rattled the soul of men
Stronger than me.
If you're lookin' to find me, girl,
That's where I'll be.
I'm writin' this song from the road.
You can ask why I'm leavin'
Three hours before dawn.
But don't ask me what highway
I'm travelin' on.
I'm lookin' for a lover
With a touch of ingénue.

And I'm not gonna find her
If I stay there with you.
I'm lookin' for her on the road.
So I open the moon roof
And boost up the torque.
Miles up the road
I ride up to a fork.
I know one road is white light
And one fades to black
But there's no way in hell
That I'll ever turn back.
'Cause I'm lookin' for her,
I'm lookin' for her.
And I'll find her somewhere on the road.

WHAT I PROBABLY MEANT TO SAY: I predict I'll marry someone with a touch of ingénue; a happy person with an upbeat attitude and that's exactly what I did. It's as if these poems describe your path in life, whether you know it or not or believe it or not. It's all about visualization and psycho-cybernetics, which was very popular in the 1970s, before people started doing cocaine in hot tub clubs.

"The Road" was set to music and recorded by a friend of mine, before his arrest. But he and his drunken band-mates insisted on a change to the lyrics. They wanted to sing about a lover "who will always be true" instead of "with a touch of ingénue." John Prine once changed a lyric because Johnny Cash asked him to do it. But normally, when you write poems to loved ones, never change the words at the insistence of others who think they can write the poem better. I mean, if Elvis returned from the dead and asked you to change a lyric, maybe you'd do it. Otherwise, ignore the third party and write it your way.

Incidentally, the country-sounding CD version of "The Road" is available and features the line, "I'm lookin' for a lover who will always be true." That line sucks but the rest of the song is performed pretty well. You know, it's true: musicians really do play better when they're drunk. "Son of a bitch!"

In 1980, I wrote to an ex-girlfriend:

"Can I get in?" she asked, "maybe go for a ride?"
"No, you keep your distance and I'll keep my pride."

WHAT I PROBABLY MEANT TO SAY: My ego was bruised, again.

This one below is from 1980, when I was 24 and living in Playa del Rey, CA with the ex-Vallejo Junior College student, who was now supposedly attending UCLA.

In 1979, I was a USC student, living in Playa del Rey, California, a few feet from the beach. I didn't live on Montague Street, like Bob Dylan, but I did live in a basement down the stairs.

DINNER

(Listen to Al Stewart's, "A Small Fruit Song")
Said the chicken
To the duck sauce,
"Come on out or let me in.
You're frosty but can warm me
To the bone.
We may not last forever
But we won't go down
Alone."

WHAT I PROBABLY MEANT TO SAY: I wanted to continue having sex with her.

Below is a poem about a lost weekend. I was supposed to drive from L.A. to Berkeley to visit my girlfriend but decided to go to Las Vegas with my friends, instead. A minute after my arrival in Vegas, I went about losing my sense of time and space, my roll-on and my soul. I also lost a Quaalude when it fell from my pocket onto the casino floor. Don't try looking for it because the building burned down decades ago.

Below, like in a Steve Forbert song, I'm asking, "Hey, what'd I miss? What went down?"

Spring, 1980
I'LL SEE THAT GIRL REAL SOON
(A TRIP TO LAS VEGAS)

(Listen to Tom Waits', "The One That Got Away")

I'm sittin' here at Caesars. There ain't a King in sight.
Except for the red one, I hit with a 12 and it kept me up all night.
I can't think about horses, the real sport of kings don't run till the after-
    noon.
So I'm breakin' ludes and actin' crude. I'll see that girl real soon.
My heart is out at Berkeley but my ass is on the bar.
I tell myself to cool it, no one's messing with my car.
Now there's sugar in my gas tank. I'll be out of here by noon.
While I break a lude, no time for food, I'll see that girl real soon.
Well I've lost my sense of time and space, my roll-on and my soul.
Talkin' to a drunk who thinks that I've lost all control.
I'm tired of watching couples lose cash gifts on their honeymoon.
So I'll break a lude, and then conclude, I'll see that girl real soon.

WHAT I PROBABLY MEANT TO SAY: Don't do drugs. And don't go to Las Vegas with your friends every time they ask you to go. You could wind up like the guys in "The Hangover," with a tiger in your suite, along with Mike Tyson. You know what they say: "Everybody has a plan in Vegas, until a tiger claws you in the face."

In October, 2019, a woman at the Bronx Zoo walked into the lions' play area and started dancing, as the lions, a few feet away, looked on impassively. Watching that scene has inspired the TV writer in me (somebody get that woman's agent on the phone!) and sparked an idea for a reality show (working title: "Paws Up or Down?").

When I say "I'll see that girl real soon" I'm simply justifying my decision to go to Vegas. That decision was made with a clear mind so it's not just about drugs leading me into bad decisions. It's more about me choosing vexing vices in Vegas over a busty brunette in Berkeley.

> The wisest all tell me I must take a side.
> In the flowers or garbage … and I can't decide.
> Of course, relax.

This one below was written during a visit to Philadelphia from L.A. I was terribly homesick after seven years of living away. I was also in a new relationship with a young lady I had met at our ten-year high school reunion.

November, 1984

BRUSH ME OFF?

(Listen to Graham Parker's, "Stick To Me")

I've spent my last dime.
But the fun never ends here.
I have more than friends here.
I'm on Pacific time.
Sure, I'm sorry to wake ya
But where can I take ya?
What?
You wanna brush me off?
Don't even bother.
You'll never brush me off
Like a child does to father.
How's the white dog?
I'm allergic to Pokey.
Too late to get jokey?

I only wanna talk.
You've got desires, I know it.
Why don't you maul me to show it?
You wanna brush me off?
Don't even bother.
You'll never brush me off
Like a child does to father.
Don't you know I got used to the
 brush-off's?
Some I'm proud of when I consider the
 source.
But if you just wanna slow down my
 rush-offs,
Kindness is much more persuasive
 than force.

WHAT I PROBABLY MEANT TO SAY: I had just spent seven years in L.A. getting the brush-off, "the ol' high hat" as the late Jon Polito said in "Miller's Crossing." I wasn't going to take the brushoffs anymore. In a recurring theme, I was hinting I wanted sex.

I wrote poems to the "Brush Me Off" woman that were more sentimental, like this one below:

(1985)

Tears

One day it occurred to me
That nothing good comes easily.
Tears of boredom on my face
Felt just like mud.
While I wondered what to do
I stumbled onto something new.
Tears of discovery on my face
Felt just like rain.

Soon, I started to suspect
That precious few cared 'bout respect.
Tears of sadness on my face
Felt just like blood.
Now, I see you by my side
And, unlike other times I've cried,
Tears of joy upon my face
Rinse off the pain.

WHAT I PROBABLY MEANT TO SAY: This was an uneven rhyme scheme that, honestly, I had to reverse engineer to see what I had done. In each verse, I rhymed lines one and two, then lines three and four ended with "face/mud," then "face/rain," then "face/blood," then "face/pain." I was mostly a bystander in this arrangement, leading me to believe that automatic writing was involved. I was analyzing a rhyme scheme that I was seeing for the first time, even though I wrote it.

This was a poem that had a happy ending you could see from a mile away. My girlfriend read it and started smiling at the beginning of the final verse. I had raised her spirits by thanking her for healing me … and in the process saved a few thousand dollars on a gift. Why so much? She was very successful. As my Dad pointed out many years earlier, you can't buy a wealthy woman a cheap gift. If you're dating a woman who lives near the train tracks, a $50 necklace is fine. If she lives in a penthouse next to an NBA big shot (example: Pat Riley's place in Miami) you have to spend more. Both the poor woman and the rich woman will love a personalized poem, however. That's my point and my guarantee.

I moved back to Philly from L.A. in 1985 because I thought I might want to marry the "Brush Me Off" woman. I told her exactly what was on my mind.

(1985)
FIRES IN THE RAIN
(Listen to Bob Dylan's, "Sweetheart Like You")

Well, the script's complete, on its way
   'cross town
Only more to be done.
It seems, today, I'm no further from 45
Than I am from 21.
I can add up the numbers
But I can't begin to explain
How it could ever be done –
Buildin' fires in the rain.
You know, I once built a fire inside the
   fog.
It took courage, and its toll.

It was the kind of a love that needed
   outside support.
The fire grew out of control.
I had to learn from mistakes, it was not
   my intent
To ever get used to the pain.
There are prices to pay
Buildin' fires in the rain.
It wasn't that long ago or too far away
When these things were all pre-
   ordained.
That was your husband and that was
   your wife

And that was the way it remained.
How many of them ever asked for
    divorce?
Just the idea was insane.
Maybe they'd have preferred
Buildin' fires in the rain.
We can dance with propriety.
We can do just what we're told.
Remaining intimate strangers on
    opposite shores
In need of things we can't acquire with
    our gold.
It seems the best in life comes back
    to us
To show what we've missed, how
    we've grown.
When we met again, in just an instant,
I loved a woman I never had known.
But be realistic! Emotions restrained;
We have enough challenge – there are

things we must maintain!
Things we'd have to surrender
Buildin' fires in the rain.
I'm obsessed with a vague and elusive
    career
Sacrificed my share of friends
Tryin' to prove that I'm worthy of
    blessings bestowed;
I play a cold-hearted game as if it soon
    ends.
Just for the sake of religion we choose
    a mate
Our families will condone.
Set our standards low, we live in
    regret.
Set 'em high, maybe die alone.
I'm not denying the love that I'm
    feeling.
But I try not to think love's in vain.
Only with you would I ever attempt
Buildin' fires in the rain.

WHAT I PROBABLY MEANT TO SAY: In this poem to my inter-faith girlfriend in 1985, I'm hoping religion isn't going to be a problem. I admit that I wouldn't go through this with just anybody. I tell her how special she is; also, it's probably all going to be in vain and who are we kidding? It's like building fires in the rain. The fire may not last.

It's the "I don't want to live in regret but I don't want to die alone" conundrum and me admitting to playing a cold-hearted game as if it soon ends. It was a hint to myself about leaving L.A. and I took it. The main reason I left L.A. was to be with her and she lived in Philadelphia. The other reason was that L.A. was making me a nervous wreck. Since I had a steady job waiting for me in Philly (in my Dad's dress business) and had no job in L.A., "It was time to leave L.A.," as I wrote in a poem 33 years later (see it on page 249) when my nerves had calmed down.

When I question the sense in "Remaining intimate strangers on opposite shores," I'm basically saying I'd like to get cozier with her. But this attractive brunette (no surprise) and high school classmate was genuinely touched by that line, like my Dad was touched by the line about his marriage dignifying the human adventure. Both times, I thought, "That's your favorite line?" Who knows why some phrases really connect and others don't? Like in baseball, try to go one-out-of-three.

Bob Dylan often saves his big-picture message for the last verse. For example, "Rubin Carter was falsely tried" or "You just kinda wasted my precious time." If you're just starting out in the writing business, like me (well, 40 years ago) or if you want acceptance at any level, conjure up a strong ending to your song or book. Sometimes they just pop into your mind as you're writing them, like what happened when I was trying to finish a poem called "Josh, The Young Magician," which appears on page 142. I save the main point for the very end of "Fires In The Rain" when I say, "Only with you would I ever attempt buildin' fires in the rain." It's another example of saying things in a poem that you wouldn't really say around the Thanksgiving table.

Not all of your poems to girlfriends will be fully appreciated. I wrote a poem to my literary agent girlfriend in 1983: "Burning holes through people who abuse you burns a hole through you. The only crime you'll ever do. Let my water comfort you."

She shrugged indifferently as she read it. I don't think she understood it, and I didn't care. I cared about her ability to get my scripts to producers. Love was running a distant second to ambition. That's why you should never get romantically involved with a business partner, not even the girl or guy who delivers your pizza.

Also, I've discovered over time that some poems have a different meaning than originally intended. For instance, the "Burning holes through people who abuse you burns a hole through you" poem was more likely written to myself.

BIRTHDAY FILE
POEMS FROM NOVEMBER 6TH

O n my birthday, November 6th, I usually write poems about what's going on in my life. They are poems I just have to write, to get clarity, if not closure.

November 6th, 1980
AND NOW MY TEETH ARE FALLIN' OUT

Well, they tell me I've seen 25
As if a calendar decides
If me and 25, in terms of living,
Coincide.
I vacillate concurrently
From uncertainty to doubt.
Last night I had a dream
And all my teeth were fallin' out.
Interpretation's guesswork
But I chose not to abstain.
I like to get advice from
Hidden levels of my brain.
So, what's the use in wondering
What dreams are all about?
It seems I've dreamt a couple times
My teeth were fallin' out.

Learning from the future
Should not be deemed demanding.
To me, a vacuum doesn't roll,
It's where I'm always standing.
And why is it that all attempts
To learn are roundabout?

I try to dream of flying
But my teeth always fall out.
I doubt the industry's need for me.
And I doubt my need for it.
The script I was proud of for being
    mature
Seems too juvenile to submit.
Peer approval's not substantive
But how long can I go without?
And how long will I go on dreaming
That my teeth are fallin' out?
So I'm 25 and dreaming like I did at
    24.
Wondering about damage, and how I
    still manage
To live in a city that's proudly a whore.
But when I turn 50 – and it's not far
    away –
Whether I've burned through or slow-
    ly worn out,
I'll be better off dreaming about los-
    ing my teeth
Than let time make my dreams all run
    out.

WHAT I PROBABLY MEANT TO SAY: In this birthday drama, I'm feeling helpless. You don't need a degree in psychology, which some claim isn't even a science, but scientists say is a science (and there are good people on both sides of that argument) to connect the dots. I'm hoping to learn from the future (Wisdom From My Future Self) but I'm in a vacuum, and my life and career are filled with uncertainty.

> I doubt the industry's need for me
> And I doubt my need for it.
> (Those were both true.)
> Peer approval's not substantive
> But how long can I go without?
> (Forever, as it turned out.)
> And how long will I go on dreaming
> That my teeth are fallin' out?

(Those dreams faded after I left L.A. which was no surprise. It did put me in the select group of millions of people whose nightmares ended when they left showbiz.)

> So I'm 25 and dreaming like I did at 24.
> Wondering about damage, and how I still manage
> To live in a city that's proudly a whore.
> (What did that make me?)

I end the poem by saying I don't want my dreams to wither and die. Hey, Hollywood, California is THE PLACE where dreams wither and, in most cases, die.

(Ask William Holden in "Sunset Boulevard.")

As I like to say, "Of course; relax!"

I remember my 25th birthday (1980) clearly because my girlfriend (who was attending UCLA, supposedly) threw me a surprise party and I heard the guests entering our apartment while I was in the shower. I dried off, put a towel around me, and went into the living room to surprise my party guests.

I later wrote a poem about how I surprised my own guests at my surprise party. I listened to Dan Fogelberg's, "Same Old Lange Syne" and began with:

> Why on my birthday must I add a year?
> Four turns to five behind the two.
> I heard these birthdays come quite rapidly
> But I hoped it wasn't true.

As the poem continues, I reference my surprise party in 1980, when I wore only a towel, and saw friends hugging each other, bonded by their love for me. That's something I had never been in touch with; how I derive joy from spreading love amongst my friends when I'm the common denominator. I should have been a professional matchmaker. I would've enjoyed that kind of work.

The poem I set to Dan Fogelberg's "Same Old Lange Syne" ends with:

> I know how others see their dreams fulfilled
> With dancing girls and kegs of beer.
> If that were me, I'd have to dance and drink enough
> To get me through the year.
> So many things right now to celebrate.
> I'll only see then when they fade.
> These birthday wishes that we dream about,
> We only get through trade.

WHAT I PROBABLY MEANT TO SAY: I'm saying that I'm just like the New Yorkers I mocked in my poem, "One More Stop." I'm inadvertently imitating them, chasing fame and fortune without noticing the good things around me.

It's *Wisdom From My Younger Self*, imploring me to focus on the doughnut, not the hole.

The poem below is about me chasing fame and fortune without noticing the good things around me, again.

November 6th, 1981
ACCIDENTS HAVE TO WAIT
(Listen to Pat Benatar's, "Promises In The Dark")

Patience they say as you lunge at the door.
You've been trying so long to belong that you don't know what for.
Tell us, what you're trying to prove.
No, you can't always win right away but you can always improve.
Just 'cause you feel it getting late.

You can't negotiate with fate.
Remember, accidents have to wait.
Poised and pretty you smile at the people that you meet.
And they hide from your eyes and decide that you're working the street.
Thinkin' how they would love you if you were a star.
Thinkin' of people in mirrors who know who they are.
Sometimes it's so hard to relate.
And harder still to imitate.
You know those accidents have to wait.
An accident, you can't estimate
They don't give you tickets, with a place and a date.
Move cautiously but don't hesitate.
Cause when you're throwin' the dice
You should be payin' the price:
Go on, smile at things you hate.
You don't have to pay for a thrill that puts you to sleep.
Don't give it away if someday you'll want it to keep.
You'll easily pass all of those who think through their nose.
They know to take profits but have no idea where it goes.
One day you're gonna celebrate.
Let's hope before you detonate.
Remember, accidents have to wait.

WHAT I PROBABLY MEANT TO SAY: On this birthday, 26, I'm already warning myself that it's getting late and I'm not staying in L.A. forever. I'm telling myself that success is like a car accident. It'll happen to you sooner or later, without warning. They don't hand out tickets with a place and a date.

Other themes from the "Accidents" poem above include:

- I'm sick of being an apprentice.
- People think I'm a model or hooker. (Not a compliment.)
- Everyone is a frontrunner and bandwagon jumper.
- Don't give it away if someday you'll want it to keep. (This one is important.)
- Celebrating is preferable to detonating. (Both were possible scenarios for me in 1981.) In other words, try not to have a complete breakdown on your way to a respectable career. I had neither; could've had both. Call it a tie. In hockey, that gets you a point.

Sixteen years later, on my 42nd birthday in 1997, I wrote about how some of my old friends were changing for the worse. This qualifies as a poem I just had to write, to get closure, if not clarity.

November 6th, 1997
SAY GOODNIGHT

(Listen to Eagle Eye Cherry's, "Save Tonight")
I was feeling sentimental
Called a friend from long ago.
We had often saved each other's lives,
Or at least it sure seemed so.
I told him I had called because
Of shocking news that I'd just heard:
That somehow, he was a homeless man,
Eating from a garbage can.
Say goodnight
And just hang up the phone,
Oh, the truth, I guess I should've known.
He laughed and told his life story;
All the prizes he had won.
He put a spotlight on his self-glory
And how his money made him have more fun.
He was sorry he couldn't talk, you see,
Time was more important to him than me.
He had to buy his wife some pearls.
And spend some time with golfing girls.
Say goodnight
And just hang up the phone,
Oh, the truth, I guess I should've known.
I see you've gone and found new, old friends.
In five more years, you'll do it again.
I would've helped a homeless man
But rich guy get help where you can.
Yeah, say goodnight, and just hang up the phone,
Oh, the truth, I guess I should've known.

WHAT I PROBABLY MEANT TO SAY: I'm referring to old pals who had become, maybe, elite. This poem was inspired by a comment I heard about a good friend from my high school days becoming a janitor. I called his mother and she said her son wasn't a janitor. He was a well-respected

… something; I guessed somewhere between The Kinks' "Well-Respected Man" and The Rolling Stones' "You're So Respectable."

What I'm really saying is people change.

The poem below was written in 1982 and has the same theme.

WITCHES

The town that I live in has more than one witch.
They get what they want with a nod or a twitch.
They have all they need yet they need to have more.
They're looking for something, but what and what for?
I felt kind of sorry for witches I knew.
They all seemed to like me so I liked them, too.
People in town asked if I were a witch.
I just have a lot of witch fwends.

WHAT I PROBABLY MEANT TO SAY: This poem is not about witches, although there were plenty of them living in L.A. in the 70s and 80s. It's about the rich and creepy Gatsby-esque crowd and how I saw myself as an outsider.

I had a few rich friends in Southern California. They accepted me occasionally, maybe because I was a good talker.

"Don, there goes (anyone famous). Go bullshit him and see what he says."

Bullshit him. Schmooze him. Same thing.

Summer, 1994

I'M A SCHMOOZER

(Listen to the Beatles', "I'm A Loser")

I'm a schmoozer
And I don't know what I'm schmoozing for.
I'm a schmoozer
Try to stop me and you'll lose that war.
Maybe my schmoozing won't give you a thrill.
Give me a chance to schmooze you and I will.
You may not like it if I schmooze all night.
But watch me schmooze, win or lose, when we fight.
I'm a schmoozer
And I don't know what I'm schmoozing for.
I'm a schmoozer
Try to stop me and you'll lose that war.
Once knew a girl, wish I still knew her name.
I'd know exactly which woman to blame.
She said to me, as she walked out the door,
"You never schmooze me and that that's such a bore."

WHAT I PROBABLY MEANT TO SAY: I'm admitting that I like to talk to strangers, called "schmoozing." And I reveal the origin of such behavior. A woman must have criticized me at a young age for being too much of an introvert. Now I'm an extrovert and I'll tell you why: extroverts, much like astronauts, attract the girls.

Here is something else I wrote in the early 1980s, about a friend who was marrying a cold, humorless woman. This was one of those times, and we've all had them, when we should just throw our friend into the trunk of a car, lock the trunk, hide the car, and have an Uber take us far away. (OK, Uber didn't exist in the 1980s but taxi cabs did.) I should've done that and then waited to retrieve him until his wedding day had come and gone.

REPRIMANDS
(Listen to Fleetwood Mac's, "Landslide")
Go ahead, take a chance.
Walk down the aisle and throw a glance,
Like a friend who's got fire near a volatile fuse
Near a pack of power plants.
Oh, friend in rented suit, what'd ya rent?
Besides a wife and bewilderment?
Has your youth been a classroom, teacher's jewel?
Or did spring bring a greeting, April Fool?
Oh, it seems like you've been planning
For a life of uncertain plans.
Yeah, these steps you've taken,
Unsure and mistaken,
Collapse onto reprimands.
Oh well, go ahead, you know best.
Go honeymoon, I'll go back West.
Never thinking of women who are safe, near and wrong,
As I wonder about the rest.

WHAT I PROBABLY MEANT TO SAY: They'll be divorced in ten years. (They were.)

I believe everyone should write birthday poems to themselves to see where they stand on their own birthdays (it doesn't have to be November 6th) every year. This one below is from 1978. I was turning 23, still a newcomer to showbiz. In later years, I would make a steady transition from new to estranged.

SHOWBIZ
The first year in showbiz is always the best.
The next year in showbiz you go without rest.
The third year in showbiz is bound to improve.
The fourth year in showbiz means you're on the move.
The last year in showbiz will strongly suggest
The first year in showbiz is always the best.

WHAT I PROBABLY MEANT TO SAY: The theme of this poem from the disco era is that I felt like I was making tons of progress in my career without going anywhere. It had been fun earlier but the deeper I got into the showbiz life, the more I wanted to get out. Like the man sang in the song, "On Broadway," in those commercials for Radio Free Europe in the 1960s: "The glitter rubs off and you're nowhere."

I think any gravestone with the inscription, "Show Biz Is My Life" also has an inscription that reads something like: "Born, 1970. Died, 1997."

As Bob Dylan told us in the song, "Idiot Wind": "You'll find out when you've reached the top ... you're on the bottom."

I was saying to myself, "It's no fun anymore."

I rewrote my "Showbiz" poem 27 years later, in 2005, for a poet laureate contest, which Larry the ice cream man insisted I would never win (he was right) because the verse rhymed. (Counterpoint to Larry the ice cream man: the 1960s song "On Broadway" rhymed and it was a commercial hit. In the 1970s, Emerson, Lake and Palmer rhymed "Queen/Vaseline/Guillotine" in the same verse and they had a hit record.) But there are subtle changes in the poem's second draft, which isn't even about showbiz anymore.

THE FIRST LINE
The first line is often the best.
The next line's a much harder test.
The third line is bound to improve.
The fourth line means I'm in the groove.
The final line seems to suggest
The first line is often the best.

WHAT I PROBABLY MEANT TO SAY: My point here is don't fuck up your own work by going on too long. It began to resonate, 27 years later, that my very minor rewrite of the 1978 poem changed the meaning completely. I'm as surprised as you are, in other words.

I changed "The first year in showbiz is always the best" to "The first line is often the best." I changed "You go without rest" to "A much harder test" on line two. I also changed "on the move" to "in the groove" on line four. It took 27 years of subconscious thought to arrive at those changes.

That's almost three years of subconscious thought per word. No one can say I'm unmindful about these poems.

November 6th, 1987
32

(Listen to Dire Straits', "Brothers In Arms")
It snows in November. I still miss the sun.
But I'd rather miss one star than miss everyone.
My 32nd birthday – it's starting to be fun.
And the job seems so easy right after it's done.
There, off in the distance, my apprenticeship.
Driven off by this salesman more than workmanship.
But when the struggle seems gone, another one has begun.
And the last took a decade before it was done.
There were days I could've hid.
Some days I really cried.
If they asked me what I did;
I could just say what I tried.
Now I've taken a step. No, it wasn't for free.
I believe in my plan. Though it don't come from me.
I will keep to this writing 'cause there's a fight to be won.
Won't it all seem so easy right after it's done.

WHAT I PROBABLY MEANT TO SAY: It's one of my apprenticeship poems, like the "Showbiz" poem. I'm the perennial apprentice. But it's no big deal. After all, when I finally get to the top, I'll be on the bottom.

"I believe in my plan. Though it don't come from me" means I'm following someone else's plan. What? That's not a soothing thought. My homeless buddy, Otis, said he listened to voices in his head and everybody agreed he was a psycho. When a black, homeless guy with bulging eyes and false teeth like Otis hears voices, he's a psycho. When a white guy like me in a sports car hears voices, I'm an author.

Yes, we had sports cars back in the 1980s. James Dean's fatal car wreck in 1955 didn't stop baby boomers from buying fast cars. I drove a 1985 Nissan 300zx, but never in the rain. Only psychos drove that car in the rain.

Later in this book, on page 168, I mention Otis in a poem to Marcia:

> Tra la la la la la la
> I was hangin' out on Arch Street, with an old-fashioned girl –
> Marcia G; she had a friend named Otis,
> Who was a bug eyed wealthy, homeless person.

Ever want to just be left alone? Walk around town with someone like Otis. You will be ignored by all socio-economic levels, rich, poor and in-between. When I walked with Otis, crowds would part on the sidewalks of Philadelphia. Rich folks, especially, didn't want to be anywhere near us.

Another way to be left alone is to have a personal conversation about raisins with a Charles Manson-type character in a Marina del Rey Laundromat. No one will engage you or even look at you. (It's a proven fact, as I mention on page 140 in "Don't wake up the raisins.")

To recap, people tend to avoid you when you walk around with social outcasts. It's great if you like privacy.

November 6th, 2004
49
Brothers

Can't stomach mayo.
Forget sour cream.
"Waiter, please bring me
a pitcher of steam."
My 49-year-old belly
Is holding up fine,
As long as I dump in
No vodka or wine.
But I'll tell you what really can't be digested –
Friends treating me like a stranger,
Despite the good energy I've invested.
Some of my brothers are gone
And I didn't see them leaving.
Nobody died
But here I am, grieving.
With some people, kindness and respect, or even love, just don't work,
But those things comprise the essence of who I want to be.
So, before my next birthday, I'll be adding a few more friends,
And they'll spin the good stuff back to me.

WHAT I PROBABLY MEANT TO SAY: This poem has the recurring theme of old friendships dying. (See "A Decent Man" on page 93.)

> Some of my brothers are gone
> And I didn't see them leaving.
> Nobody died
> But here I am, grieving.

This keeps happening, unfortunately. I grieve, not because my friends are dead but because our friendships have gone kaput. Why do old friendships die? In my experience, it's often because one friend makes a ton of money and doesn't want to associate with middle class or poor friends, or deal with their jealousy. I tell friends, "Don't make more than $250,000 per year, because if you do, you'll want new, old friends." Other times, I believe we lose friends when we test them for the first time and they fail the test. Think of George Thorogood's line when he tests his buddy and asks about staying overnight ("I'm outdoors, you know") but his buddy says he has to ask his wife before he makes any promises.

"Uh, I don't know, man. She kinda funny."

George's response is, "I know. Everybody funny. Now you funny, too."

The buddy in that song probably made more than $250,000, or his wife did.

I also reference my stomach problems; the same digestive issues that forced my early retirement from street hockey (goalie) at age 50. I was telling myself in this birthday poem to see a doctor and/or change my diet. (Changing my diet helped. Look for my new book, "No Greasy Food, No Fucking Migraines.")

In the late 1970s, I wrote that some of my friends were turning into snobs.

> I don't know why he talked to me about his many friends.
> I remember thinking, "He tries to uplift but he only condescends."

The poem was written like it was a rant from me to an unknown person, complaining about all of my friends. I mention all their flaws to this other person but the other guy turns out to be me looking into a mirror. I now realize, to some degree, I was complaining about myself.

That's me, Don the Goalie, playing street hockey at age 50 in 2005. In the other photo, taken with a Brownie camera in 1975, I'm the goalie, way over on the right side, facing 80 MPH slap shots with hardly any padding.

In 1999, I wrote a 44th birthday poem, revealing (to myself) what I had subconsciously learned about some of my old friends.

November 6th, 1999
44

You are your friends;
You take a piece from each imperfect one.
And then you find out later
They weren't friends and it wasn't fun.
So, you've got your own flaws,
And the flaws of your ex-friends;
Twenty years, hopelessly, ahead of the trends.
You're aiming high but not on target,
Getting by without the market;
It's the apprenticeship that never ends.

WHAT I PROBABLY MEANT TO SAY: "You are your friends; you take a piece from each imperfect one." Holy shit! You take a piece of your flawed friends with you, fucking everywhere.

I wrote a poem about one such friend, Jordi, the mime. Sometime in the late 1980s, I worked with actor Dom DeLuise on my children's TV show called "Jordi's Place." Jordi was the world's only talking mime and the only one who couldn't remember his lines when we taped the show. He had trouble getting along with his girlfriend and argued bitterly with her while we were taping. He couldn't focus on his lines or get into character. He was ten minutes away from having a total meltdown; that's when he told me wanted to be the director.

Kids love mimes until they're about seven years old. I don't understand why.

Kids hate mimes after the age of seven. That, I can see.

This poem was written for Jordi's act at The Showboat, one of Atlantic City's boardwalk hotels in the 1980s.

JORDI'S THEME SONG

(or "Singing To Strangers In The Showboat Lobby")
(Listen to Willie Nelson's, "To All The Girls I've Loved Before")

To all the girls I've loved before;
I've had a lot, so what's one more?
I gotta sing this song,
Called, "Where did I go wrong?"
With all the girls I've loved before.
To all the girls I've loved before;
Who never let me past their door.
But you think I can sing –
Wait here, I'll get the ring
I gave to girls I've loved before.
(pause dramatically)
Buena que sedan de ville.
Jorge, aqua, if you will.
(makes a gesture like he wants a
glass of water)

We can gamble for rewards,
Or tango on the boards;
Forget those girls I've loved before.
Of all the girls I've loved before,
You're the one I can't ignore.
So, expect a jealous tone
And a tap upon your phone
When you talk to girls I've loved
before.
Of all the girls I've loved before,
You are the one I most adore.
But if you say, "No thanks,"
Then you'll have joined the ranks
Of all the girls I loved before.

WHAT I PROBABLY MEANT TO SAY: He was a strange dude who should have his own theme song.

Some of my friends are very nice. One such friend, Mark, whom we'd met in Saratoga Springs, NY, was flying from Greensboro, NC to Atlantic City, N.J., to visit his Northern buddies. I wanted to make him feel welcomed and appreciated so I wrote and performed this for him (with my sidekick, Marcia) at a Preakness party.

Nice friends are hard to find. But we found two in Kentucky Mark, to my left and Anthony to my right. We found them and they found beer.

May 18th, 2019
KENTUCKY MARK
(Listen to Elvis Presley's, "Kentucky Rain")

A couple years ago
Up in Saratoga Springs,
We looked up one night and you were
    gone.
We'd seen you at the track
And later, at the Shake Shack.
But you left early and flew off on that
    plane.
So we're driving down the shore,
Sunroof open wide
On this bumpy AC expressway.
We've loved you much too long.
Our love's too strong
To miss seeing you when you're back in
    town again.
Kentucky Mark is comin' in.
And we both know it'd be a sin
If we didn't see you here
With the Preakness goin' on.
Writin' this song
'Bout ol' Kentucky Mark.

Showed your photograph
To an old grey, bearded man
On the boardwalk just off the ocean
    tides.
He said, "Yes," you were here,
"He's with Anthony, drinking beer."
And he pointed to a balcony way up
    high.
Finally got a ride
On an elevator where
We met a guy who asked,
"Whatcha gonna do?"
We said, "Mark is back in town."
He said, "Really? 'Foot's' around?"
And he left us with a prayer that we'd
    find you.
Kentucky Mark is comin' in.
And we both know it'd be a sin
If we didn't see you here
With the Preakness goin' on.
Singin' this song
'Bout ol' Kentucky Mark.

WHAT I PROBABLY MEANT TO SAY: Everybody likes it when Mark comes to visit, even near-strangers out on the street. I refer to his beer drinking buddy, Anthony, his nickname "Foot" and his home state of Kentucky to make it personal. This is an example of writing a poem to guarantee that, no matter what kind of trouble you get into next time, there will always be at least one friend who will come to your defense and say you're not all bad because you wrote him or her a nice poem. Kentucky Mark is that friend.

My 46th birthday poem is below. It's about accepting the idea that I'm not famous.

November 6th, 2001
46
I don't need fame and fortune.
I need my loved ones close by me.
I've been given the latter
While the former has been denied me.
As Robert Deutch would say, "Fair enuf."
The other way around would be too tough.

WHAT I PROBABLY MEANT TO SAY: The "Fair enuf" line is a tribute to my late, great poetry professor at California State University, Northridge, Robert Deutsch. (His brother became wealthy by inventing Adolf's Meat Tenderizer!) He would write "Fair enuf" on my homework in class. He'd fix me up with gorgeous (even by California standards) female students in his poetry classes. My first date with one of those girls ended up on the third row of Dodger Stadium at a 1977 World Series game. She drank two bottles of wine before I drove to the stadium, then she fast-talked our way inside by acquiring ticket stubs from a couple leaving the game early (for the birth of their grandchild). I helped by bribing a one-eyed guard $25 to open the stadium gate. Once inside, we had those ticket stubs and sat on the third row. Fun Fact: After I bribed the guard, about 1,000 fans tried to push their way through that same gate and almost started a riot, complete with growling police dogs. But we saw a World Series game; my first ever despite being a diehard baseball fan. (I almost went in 1964 as an 8-year-old but the Phillies lost 10 in a row late and blew the pennant.) Once inside the stadium, my date drank 10 beers and cried about her father. "Strike three!"

Anyway, in the "Fair enuf" poem, I'm not sweating the fact that I failed to make it big in Hollywood. (See the poem on page 23, "You've got a friend in Pennsylvania.")

But I'm not sweating a little too much. It's like that bachelor friend of yours who frequently claims he's not lonely. But I'm ok with my lack of fame and here's why: fans would take the fork out of Wilt Chamberlain's hand and demand his autograph. The guy couldn't even eat his dinner because he was so rich and famous.

I saw Wilt Chamberlain play for the 76ers in the mid 1960s in Philadelphia. My Dad took me to see some very exciting games against Bill Russell and the Boston Celtics, although it was hard to see through the cigar smoke.

November 6th, 2002
47

If I don't have it,
I don't need it.
I'll try to attract it;
Never impede it.
Lovingly grab it
And then try to feed it.
But if I don't have it,
I don't need it.
Oh, my ambition's still there;
For recognition, I care.
If they hired me for steady work,
I wouldn't shrug it off or shirk.
But if I don't have it
Then I don't need it.
At 47
I concede it.
I'm immersed in love,
More than I ever could have dreamed.
Being lucky in love is better than it
seemed
When I schemed for success so madly
And wanted it so badly.
Now I don't have it.
And no, I don't need it.
Though I'll keep trying to attract it.
Find the right fuel to feed it.
At 47, what I have mostly is freedom
and joy.
Is that what I hoped for when I was a
boy?
That's what I needed and it's what I've
been given.
And that, after all, is the wonder of livin'.

WHAT I PROBABLY MEANT TO SAY: It's heavy but hopeful. I've got freedom and joy; isn't that what I hoped for when I was a boy? Definitely.

THEME ALERT! "Being lucky in love is better than it seemed" is a repeated theme in my poems to loved ones and here's why: being lucky in love is always good. It's far better than being lucky with money. Having luck with money can sometimes be worse than it seems. I can point to that gambler who won a million bucks on a slot machine at Bally's in A.C. and all he knew was that he had a bad waitress and an apathetic wife. He couldn't have cared less about winning a million bucks. On the other hand, no one ever said they couldn't care less about being lucky in love.

The above poem is about gratitude. I was in a good place on my 47th birthday in 2002. Of course, I hadn't yet started teaching in college.

Twenty years earlier, on my 27th birthday, the "If I don't have it, I don't need it" mentality was not yet born. As you can see in the poem below, I was sick of being an apprentice on my birthday.

November 6th, 1982
ON THIS BIRTHDAY EVE
(Listen to Joe Jackson's, "Steppin' Out")

Fall:
A time to rise and scrutinize my deeds.
To redefine accomplishment my will exceeds.
Separate the wants from needs
On this birthday eve.
No:
November dreams are not the same in May.
The change precludes abandonment about halfway.
Wonder what my dreams will say
On this birthday eve.
Here:
So far from love and all I still defend.
But close enough to those with credit to extend.
Waitin' for the dividend
On this birthday eve.
Hope:
The hesitant messiah I've seen twice
Comes and goes consistent with the sacrifice.
Hope itself may well suffice
On this birthday eve.

WHAT I PROBABLY MEANT TO SAY: At least I had high hopes. That would have to be enough to keep me focused. A few years later, I wrote the poem below, and my hopes were wavering, if not quivering.

January 19, 1988

AGENDA: JANUARY 19, 1988

Seems every five minutes I'm changing the date.
The projects done early are flirting with late.
I look out the window – the seasons have changed.
And I'd better get this agenda arranged.
I've sent out the novel; the outline, as well.
Who will ignore them – I never could tell.
I'm rewriting something that turned ten years old.
Thinkin' it's time that I got somethin' sold.
I've listened enough to, "I'll take care of ya."
The struggle, while bold, was like malaria.
It's ok to see it in the mirror's rear view.
But there's nothing like looking at dreams coming true.

WHAT I PROBABLY MEANT TO SAY: Hope itself was enough to keep me happy at age 27 but not at 32.

It's not a good sign when (a) you barely realize the seasons have changed in January or (b) you compare your career struggles to contracting malaria. But why not toss in an exaggeration if it helps make your point. Many of my birthday poems have the same theme: I'm struggling in my five-year plan for overnight success. As of today, it's looking more like a fifty-year plan. And I'm afraid to ask if any 50-year plan actually worked. Don't say it was the moon landing. That took less than a decade. Some people claim the moon landing was staged. That's nonsense. The moon, in all likelihood, is an alien-built sphere. I think about that every time I ride an ocean wave and hear the song by R.E.M. in my head about the recklessness of water. No matter what the moon looks like or who built it, I am grateful to the nearby satellite for supplying the ocean waves, which I've enjoyed all my life and find even more delightful than the wave machine at the Margaritaville hotel in Hollywood, Florida.

I became better acquainted with the moon and the Apollo 11 mission when I wrote a book about the first man to walk on the moon, called "Neil Armstrong … Did What?!" Armstrong and I were both USC alumni and back in the 20th century no one had to pay to correct their kids' SAT test answers or claimed they were an astronaut before they actually became one. Neil Armstrong never photo-shopped himself inside a tent lined with aluminum foil to hoodwink the admissions board at USC.

I was desperate (in the writing biz, one must always be desperate to make connections) so I sent the first-man-to-land-on-an-alien-sphere-orbiting-Earth a letter, asking him to read my children's book and, if he liked it, maybe he could write the intro. He agreed to read it, then said he would not write the intro because my "research was wrong" and he did not take Life Savers and a comb with him to the moon/alien sphere. (I had several sources that said he did.) I said I'd cut out that **ONE SENTENCE** but he never got back to me. I learned that if you get a degree from a prestigious university, don't expect any help from the school or the school's alumni, who all make more than $250,000 a year, proving my earlier point.

November 6th, 1983
YOUTH THAT'S GONE ASTRAY

(Listen to Frank Sinatra's, "Cycles")
I have tried to overcome
The burdens – self-imposed.
And I have thrived in reaching for
Doors out of bounds or closed.
Locked inside ambition –
My decision, all the way.
So I won't mourn or hunger for
The youth that's gone astray.
When I came to prove myself
I wasn't used to losing.
Now I know the secret to
Success lies in the choosing.
Others see perfection
In reflections of their fame.

I will trade all accolades
For one well-respected name.
Now, some of you, if here, might ask
How I feel today.
Look all around, you'll know I feel
    committed –
To something more than child's play.
Someday I may even try
To calculate the cost.
We spend our lives regaining
Some small part of what we've lost.
It's gone but it stays with me
In a private kind of way.
So, with pride, I'll kiss goodbye
The youth that's gone astray.

WHAT I PROBABLY MEANT TO SAY: "We spend our lives regaining some small part of what we've lost" is a line that gets more relevant every year. "Give it back to me!" the senior citizen screamed in my earlier poem, "And I knew, then." Bob Seger wrote that he wished he "Didn't know now what I didn't know then." Maybe the Michigan rocker ached for his lost innocence, as I did. Rock stars lose their innocence earlier than the general population, so it could be that Bob wrote that line when he was 14.

When I say "Now I know the secret to success lies in the choosing," I'm saying it's good to challenge yourself.

November 6th, 2020
ELECTION DAY
(Listen to Bob Dylan's, "Highway 61")

I joined up with Medicare, at age 65.
I asked the doc, "What can you do, to keep me alive?"
Doc said, "Don't … eat these things."
I didn't hear the whole list, but it ended with onion rings.
So I resolved to cut out the crab bisque and crème broulet.
I said, "Doc, I'll do whatever you say.
Just give me a good report on election day."
Well, I went to see the rabbi about my spiritual health.
I said, "Hey Rabbi, at this age, what can I do for myself?"
He told me I could start by being studious, and pray
Every single minute of each and every day.
"You've got room for improvement … wouldn't you say?"
We all do, Rabbi, but I can do it your way.
Just say a prayer for me on election day.
I ran into the bartender at the vaping store.
He gave me a wink 'cause he knew what I was lookin' for.
He said, "Didn't I see you drinkin' hard the night before?
And stumbling around the parking lot at quarter to four?
Why don't you take a break; give it up from November to May?"
I can easily do whatever you say.
Just toast to my side on election day.
I was driving along at what I thought to be a modest pace
When a cop pulled me over and he got in my face.
He said the speed I was going was stupid and frightening;
Much worse than "Hot Rod Lincoln" or even "Grease Lightning."
"Slow down or here's a ticket you'll have to pay."
All right, I'll do whatever you say.
Just protect our rights on election day.
I was standing on a rock near the river bed
With the same ol' Lenni Lenape ghosts in my head.
And I know what they always tell me about living peacefully
But I wind up getting angry at the images I see on TV.
I know it's best to live the peaceful, Lenni Lenape way.
Lenape ghosts, I'll do whatever you say.
Just help me out on election day.

WHAT I PROBABLY MEANT TO SAY: I'll give up almost anything except breathing and coffee if it helps my side win the election.

END PART ONE

PART TWO

How to write your own poems to loved ones
Getting ideas for poems from everyday life

When you take time to write a heartfelt note or card to a loved one, it's inherently better than handing out a shiny toy. (NBA stars may disagree.) At the very least, a love note complements the shiny toy. If you give them the dream car and the love note, they won't know what hit them.

But how do you do it?

You could be sitting around watching the History Channel and get an idea for a poem, like I did when I saw a special on old Las Vegas. My Dad took me there in 1967 (when I was 11) and there was no way I could ever repay him for that thrill. (He let me reach over a railing and pull a slot machine, which paid 2-1 on a quarter.) I could've just called him to say "thanks" but instead I started outlining my next poem to him. You could be in the grocery store or the car wash, thinking about your loved ones, and you're halfway to writing a love poem.

In 2005, I wrote a children's book, "In Here, Somewhere." It included various poems I had started writing back in the 1970s. The theme was that we're always searching for something. I was getting ideas for poems from everyday life and adding them to (the still unpublished) "In Here, Somewhere." A few sample verses are:

> When you find it, don't expect
> It to have the same effect
> As when you first discovered it was gone.
> It isn't cheap. It isn't fair.
> It's gonna change but it's in here, somewhere.
> Fading when the night becomes the dawn.
> We think we're searching, but we're not.
> We attract the things we've got.

WHAT I PROBABLY MEANT TO SAY: Everything we're looking for is "In Here, Somewhere." We think we're looking for something but it's more likely we're attracting it.

It's possible that I channeled these thoughts but if I were to guess the meaning of the thoughts I channeled, which is a reasonable thing to do because I'm naturally curious, I'd say it means look inside yourself.

"In Here, Somewhere" continued with what I imagined were everyday scenes in a town, a forest and a desert.

IN A TOWN, SOMEWHERE ...

The poem below was written in a Laundromat in Marina del Rey, CA (a great place to meet actresses and write poems) in 1979. I was inspired to write it when a barefooted guy looked at my carrot/raisin salad a little too closely.

DON'T WAKE UP THE RAISINS
Climb out of bed and tip-toe past your toys.
Don't brush your teeth 'cause it makes too much noise.
Say "Shh" to goldfish if they're acting coy.
But, please, don't wake up the raisins.
Your parents are sleeping; they don't rise at dawn.
K.C., the cat, all curled up, starts to yawn.
Is that your best shirt he's curling up on?
It is, but don't wake up the raisins.
Go in the kitchen and open a drawer.
Empty? My goodness, rush right to the store.
Tomorrow you'll probably go back for more.
Unless someone wakes up the raisins.
Walk up the aisle next to the ice cream.
Pass by the soap; you're unusually clean.
Smile at the dried fruit and casually scream:
"Wake up! Time to eat you, you raisins!"

WHAT I PROBABLY MEANT TO SAY: Since this was a children's poem, I couldn't reveal the whole story about a scary, barefooted guy who entered the Marina del Rey, CA, Laundromat and reminded everybody of Charles Manson. He had a posse. This guy made everyone in the place nervous when he opened with a bold announcement about insects inheriting the planet. "Don't eat bugs," he told a young woman — while she was folding her laundry. (She eventually ran out.) This was decades before they made the film, "Men In Black."

"Trees will become intelligent," he added.

I had been in the Laundromat for hours (I did a ton of laundry about once a month, telling people I'd lost a bet) and was in no mood for his antics. I had been in Manson's old house near USC's campus and seen the murals he drew of naked redheads. This guy was no Manson. He was a Manson wannabe; exactly what Leonard Cohen warned us about in "The Future." It's even possible that Leonard met this Manson wannabe (they both spent time in Los Angeles) and inspired him to write the song.

There I was, in the Laundromat, circa 1979, eating a corned beef sandwich and carrot/raisin salad I'd procured next door at the Boys Market. The market sold certain items in bulk, like Racing Forms, razor blades and straws. I swear, there could be ten people in a line buying the same three items. Where's the oversight, L.A.?

Anyway, I called him over, in-between the washers and dryers.

"Chuck," I said.

He tilted his head at me.

"Shh."

He twitched twice. I had his attention.

"Ya gotta be quiet," I told him as his posse closed in on me.

"Why?" he asked.

I pointed to the carrot/raisin salad.

"You're gonna wake up the raisins."

This mucky, freak of a man nodded in agreement, then asked if I was, "Maybe not finishing" my corned beef sandwich. I gave him half the sandwich and he ate it in two bites, then crawled into a corner of the Laundromat and fell asleep.

The crowd looked suspiciously at ME, for some reason, as if to say, "That crazy man listens to you!"

Since that day in the Marina del Rey shopping center where the stars (Bo Derek) shopped, it's been my custom to look at raisins whenever they're in my hand and scream, "Wake up! Time to eat you, you raisins!"

Try it sometime.

WHAT I PROBABLY MEANT TO SAY (PART TWO): This is the second time I wrote a poem about enjoying something special immediately or saving it for later. In the first one, written in the late 1970s, I started it like this:

> Eastbound in the desert on a highway all alone.
> When sand turns into farmland, then to woodland I'll be home.

Driving home, for me, involved crossing the desert, driving past farmland, then arriving at the woodlands of Pennsylvania (Penn's Woods). The poem continued with me finding a box of chocolates over on the side of the California desert road, in 100-degree heat.

> This box of chocolates from life's candy store
> Is asking some questions I'd rather ignore.
> Is this fragile treat only here for today?
> Do I eat it now or let it melt away?

In the four lines above, similar to the "Raisins" poem, I'm saying you can't have your cake and eat it, too.

Below is another example of why I believe automatic writing is real.

JOSH, THE YOUNG MAGICIAN

> The bag of magic tricks was full
> But none were working right.
> Josh, the young magician feared
> A short career – one night!
> Less than calm, he prepped a trick,
> He hadn't yet refined it.
> The bag of tricks said, "Josh! Think quick!
> It's in here, somewhere, find it."

WHAT I PROBABLY MEANT TO SAY: This is one of those automatic writing experiments where I had to read it back to myself to understand it. ("Oh, now I get it.") I had to read it a third time to recognize that it was, indeed, an automatic writing experiment.

The punch line for this, occurring when the bag of tricks (an inanimate object) magically starts talking, popped into my head as though another voice was instructing me on how to finish the poem, sort of like my automatic writing experiment in 1983 when I wrote down the title of a story ("When Angels Speak") I had not yet written or thought about. Only after I had written down the punch line to "Josh, The Young Magician" did I completely understand that the bag had bailed him out, magically.

It qualifies as an, "Oh, now I get it" moment or a "See what I did there?" moment except I didn't really see it until later. The closest comparison would be to Danny Torrance, the boy in the Overlook Hotel in "The Shining."

I saw "The Shining" in L.A. and immediately put a sign on my wall that was related to the film: "All Work And No Play Makes Donny A Very Dull Boy." My girlfriend read it and moved out that day. It sounds funny now but back then I was hurt. I wrote plenty of breakup poems to her in the following weeks and that's when I knew for sure that if you ever get your heart broken, you must get a good poem out of it.

Here's a poem that was inspired by frustrations of everyday life … and ducks.

(1980)
I WISH THAT IT WOULD RAIN

"Sitting by this man-made lake
How much sunshine can I take?
There are no clouds, for goodness sake.
I wish that it would rain.
I splash around to help stay cool.
Why don't they let us in the pool?
It's stupid but a rule's a rule.
I wish that it would rain.
Maybe I'll go 'cross the lawn
And turn the sprinkler system on.
If they found out I'd soon be gone.
I wish that it would rain.
It's still too hot to eat the food.
I'm really not quite in the mood.
(Be hotter if I wasn't nude.)
I wish that it would rain. Go ahead,
    Donna."

"I dunk my head to look for fish.
Sole would make a tasty dish.
But if I had just one more wish,
I'd wish that it would rain."
"Very good, Donna. Don't eat that
    bottle-cap!
Where was I? Oh. I guess I'm imitating
    man.
Lying down to get a tan.
This grass feels like a frying pan.
I wish that it would rain.
I now decide the sun is stuck.
My wife and I are out of luck.
You think it's fun to be a duck?
I wish that it would rain."

143

WHAT I PROBABLY MEANT TO SAY: I was trying to say that animals have feelings, too, and they should be able to express them. (This was before Facebook.)

The duck poem was my mother's favorite and it wasn't even about her. That was so her. (Dad's favorite was the oft-mentioned, "Your marriage dignifies the human adventure.") You don't know why or when someone will be genuinely touched by what you've written for them. Just be happy that it worked. (See "one-out-of-three" above.) If whatever you wrote made them feel happy and loved (even if they didn't quite understand what you meant) that means you've reached your goal.

A book I had written uncharacteristically got published and the dedication page was a loving nod to my parents. It read: "For B&B, who shine light on me."

Easy to understand, right? Well, not really.

Dad said to me, "I got a lump in my throat," when he read the dedication.

But he didn't understand it.

He told me, "You sure do shine light on us."

"No, Dad. I didn't mean it that way. I meant the other way; that you shine your love on me, it's such a gift from you. From you."

If Dad were right in his interpretation, that would mean I was complimenting myself and, even worse, doing it on my own dedication page. It would be like saying, "This is my book. I shine light on lots of people" instead of "Thank you."

That would be an awkward and inappropriate dedication page, even if the book was on narcissism. Besides, a book on narcissism wouldn't even have a dedication page; it would start off with "Meet The Author."

Dad was so happy about my book getting published that the dedication page didn't really matter.

WHAT I PROBABLY MEANT TO SAY (PART TWO): It was dry in Los Angeles, California in 1980, when I wrote "I Wish That It Would Rain." The duck wanted it wet and the conditions were dry. He couldn't catch a break in his chosen profession (being a duck), just like I couldn't catch a break in showbiz. It's a frustration poem (not to be confused with frustration dreams). I'm the duck in this story and I want everyone to know my line of work is not easy or fun.

THEME ALERT! This is the same theme (work is not easy or fun) that appears in my 1983 Father's Day poem to my Dad, "A Starring Role In A Knockout Film."

It's true: the 1980s were kind of a blur for many baby boomers. The death of disco left us all in shock. There were some who self-medicated, many times in my company. However, out of respect for poetry, journalism and anthropology, I managed to stay relatively sober and write some things down.

You can invent your own greeting cards and give them to loved ones, like the one below about staying strong.

IN A DESERT, SOMEWHERE ... EXTRA EFFORT

"Don't be sad," this camel says,
"Because you're in a slump.
Give that extra effort
And you'll soon get past the hump.
Set your goals realistically;
Take a steady course.
Look at all I overcame –
I used to be a horse."

WHAT I PROBABLY MEANT TO SAY: Don't give up. You can do it!

In the 1980s poem below, about a flying horse, my Mom encouraged me to change the ending. Since she asked very few favors, I complied.

SHALOM, YOU FLYING HORSE

Shalom, you flying horse
You're all alone up in the sky.
People in the middle east
Know you're a peaceful guy.
Every now and then
When you spot fighting down below,
You land on sand to lend a hand
Or just to say, "Hello."
But now, Shalom, you flying horse,

You're joined up in the sky
By radar planes and fighter squads
Who think you are a spy.
They have their anti-air horse guns
And airspace to enforce.
You've had your fun – turn 'round and run.
Shalom ... you fleeing horse.

WHAT I PROBABLY MEANT TO SAY: Like Bob Dylan sang in "Shelter From The Storm," the flying horse offered up his innocence and got repaid with scorn. Almost everyone can relate to this theme, or is it just me (and Bob) being too sensitive?

Why did my Mom encourage me to change the ending to the flying horse poem? She was upset that the original flying horse had gotten his wings shot off and she didn't like how the poem ended with "Shalom, you falling horse." Shalom, of course, means hello, goodbye or peace in Hebrew. In this horse's story, it meant goodbye.

My Mom was an animal lover and instilled that spirit in me. I remember being in Muir Woods in northern California in 1967, when I was 11, and we found ourselves adjacent to a nature reserve. I went over to a fence and touched a young deer's nose. A wild fucking animal! And I touched it. We had a connection. It was beautiful and was one of the factors that influenced my children's book writing career. I've written more than a few stories about kids saving endangered animals during summer vacation. My young characters help save butterflies, whales, goats, horses, baby bears, sloth bears, homing pigeons, rabbits, wolf dogs and others. The kids in those books are all based on me; what I'd want to do to save the endangered creatures. My book, "Running Through Kenya" was published in the 1990s. Yes, it was a rare event and a very small success but if I saved one sloth bear or wart hog, I'm satisfied.

Mom wanted Shalom the flying horse to survive in my poem, and he did. I changed the ending and even created a back story to tell Mom; how Shalom made it back to Tel Aviv and lived a happy and heroic life and found peace.

TAKE AN UNCOMFY RIDE ON A RHINO

There are lots of ways to get around.
Up high in an airplane; a car underground.
Neither compare to a new way I've found.
Take an uncomfy ride
On a rhino.
Don't worry 'bout traffic. Believe me there's none.
No taxis are rhinos? You're lookin' at one.
Getting to school can be easy and fun.
Take an uncomfy ride
On a rhino.
I won't make you carsick. I don't have five gears.
Strap on my seatbelt, you'll lose all your fears.
That is, if you realize my seatbelts are ears.
Take an uncomfy ride
On a rhino.
Sit on my forehead. Hold onto my horn.
Now that you're ready I just have to warn
About all the stockings and pants that I've torn.
Take an uncomfy ride
On a rhino.

WHAT I PROBABLY MEANT TO SAY: There was no moralistic or didactic intent to this story. I just wanted to see a drawing of a rhino dressed as a taxi, or at least driving a taxi.

This next poem has a surprise ending.

THE NEW NEIGHBORS

I took my lifetime savings
From the bank, to buy some land.
I noticed a "For Sale" sign
Sinking quickly in the sand.
They told me it was safe here
For an eager speculator.
I'll ask this kindly gentleman
If he'll watch out for 'gators.

WHAT I PROBABLY MEANT TO SAY: You may think that's a kindly gentleman, but that's a killer alligator! This is my version of the late Shel Silverstein's style of verse. I would read Shel's books in book stores and practically gasp because I had already written poems with the same themes. In one of his children's books, a headless guy was sitting on a stump, and the stump turned out to be his lost head. Shel Silverstein's character couldn't find his own head and he was sitting on it the whole time. My character couldn't tell that his new buddy was an alligator. The stump is the head. The new buddy is the alligator. Follow this formula and you can write children's books. Shel wrote them and spent his free time at the Playboy mansion. I wrote them and spent my free time writing some more.

I was never invited to the Playboy mansion. But I was invited to take a picture with the Lombardi trophy after the Eagles won the Super Bowl

The Super Bowl trophy finally came to Philadelphia, a milestone in my life, comparable to hitting the lottery or learning that an asteroid is not going to destroy Earth. In my hand is an early 1960s autographed football that was a birthday present from my parents.

in 2018. That's what I call a fair trade-off. I'd seen plenty of topless girls around the pool (Las Vegas) by 2018 but I'd never seen my team win the Super Bowl.

THE NATURAL

(Imagine a close up of a snake)
"I haven't got a resume.
Divorce forced me to work.
They tell me I'm a natural for
Complaint department clerk."

WHAT I PROBABLY MEANT TO SAY: This story about a lady snake looking for an appropriate job was written in the late 1970s to show support for divorced women, many of whom struggled to get good jobs. In fact, I wrote a poem with a feminist theme at that same time, about a squirrel named Sally.

SALLY THE SQUIRREL

"Dinner for one," said Sally the Squirrel.
"Boys won't eat with me because I'm a girl.
They said I was weak and couldn't find mood.
Girls can do anything when we're in the
    mood.
So, set up a booth for this so-called 'begin-
    ner'.
Boys, be nice to girls or go hungry this win-
    ter."

WHAT I PROBABLY MEANT TO SAY: Girls are highly qualified and, guess what, so are squirrels. In 2003, 25 years after I wrote about Sally, squirrels moved into the walls of our apartment near the Delaware river. They were smarter than the maintenance men who tried to trap them. I wrote a children's book about it,

A squirrel photo-bombed my picture of a palm tree in Florida.

called "What Time Do The Squirrels Go To Work?"

You never heard of that book because (a) nobody wanted to publish it and (b) the artist I wanted to work with, who was an expert at painting squirrels, had a problem. He worked at a high security installation and reported something that went off track, then felt like he was being watched and micro-waved! He thought the Deep State was conspiring against him, along with his neighbor, Fred. He told me, "They're cooking Fred!" and I immediately began working on an article with that title.

This is proof that you can get plenty of ideas for your poems from everyday life. Bruce Springsteen said, "Well, they blew up the chicken man in Philly last night, and they blew up his house, too" and I'm saying, "Well, they cooked up the squirrel man in Bensalem last night, and they micro-waved Fred, too."

My artist friend moved away. No one has seen him in years. The squirrels aren't talking. I would conduct an investigation into what really happened to the artist but I don't need the hassle of installing aluminum window shades.

ZACH, THE LOVABLE COYOTE

Little Larry had a pet
Coyote, he called "Zach."
Who ate the rug and TV set
When Larry turned his back.
One day, his father asked for his
Report card and his grades.

Larry said, "Zach ate them.
You know he loves scrambled A's."
So, Larry's dad went down to school
To see if it were true.
Did Larry get all A's? Who knows?
Zach ate the classroom, too.

WHAT I PROBABLY MEANT TO SAY: Whenever possible, stick to your story.

I changed the last line to "Zach ate the classroom, too." Originally, it read "Zach ate the teacher, too" but I realized that gobbling up the teacher could be viewed as non-lovable. Additionally, I know from experience that teachers have a hard-enough time, without getting eaten by coyotes.

I once played a werewolf in a Jules Feiffer play who gobbled up his entire family ("It's the real me!") yet was still considered lovable. So, it is possible for Zach. I went full Stanislavsky into that werewolf role and practiced extra throaty wolf howls for weeks in my neighborhood. No one noticed.

IN A FOREST, SOMEWHERE ...
AND THE FIRST ROUND DRAFT PICK IS ...
(Imagine a polar bear with one leg in the air)
"I'm stretching my arms
And I'm lifting my legs.
I once was a very good hunter.
But this year I'm trying
To break into sports.
Do you know if the Bears need a punter?"

WHAT I PROBABLY MEANT TO SAY: Polar bears, while endangered, can kick.

WEIGHT WATCHER
(imagine a dancing pelican)
"5, 6, 7, 8;
I'm dancing here because you ate
All the crabmeat on your plate.
One of us should watch our weight!"

Seen here: one serving of stone crabs. I ate 3.5 servings.

WHAT I PROBABLY MEANT TO SAY: Don't over-eat crabs, like you're a pelican with no conscience. I didn't, until recently. I tried the all-you-can-eat stone crabs in Hollywood, Florida. (The stone crabs came from Key West.) They told me later, when I felt better, that I had consumed 18 of them. The good news is that I've gone to a semi-Paleo (caveman) diet since the crab-a-thon, as described in a 2018 poem about Florida on page 254.

I wrote the children's book *In Here, Somewhere* because I was constantly saying that to myself. It became an everyday expression for me, like jawn. And it's so elusive. I just had it. I know where I put it. How about it? Tell me, what is it? You can't put a finger on it. Admit it, we usually don't have any idea what it is. We just go on looking for it and accept the fact that the soda's hard to find beneath the fizz.

IN HERE, SOMEWHERE

It's in here, somewhere, yes, it is,
A story that you'll find
Cheerful and uplifting.
If you don't ... Well, I don't mind
Much.
Sometimes, people only read
What they believe is right.
To get through with new ideas,
I need to use a light

Touch.
Poetry, it seems to me,
Can make our learning fun
And help us ask more questions, like,
Today, what have I done?
They say no one is out there
Who cares to read, it's true.
I can't share this with anyone;
No one, that is, but you.

WHAT I PROBABLY MEANT TO SAY: As I ended my children's book, I was asking myself, "Today, what have I done?" I'll tell you what I had done that day. I had done gone to the beach and was feeling guilty. This poem from 1984 is a hard lesson in self-discovery. I now see what I was doing 36 years ago. I was bragging about my work ethic which was sporadic, at best.

"I work through holidays, like Isaac Asimov," I once told a friend. Well, I'm calling bullshit on myself in this case. Self-discovery sucks sometimes.

"In Here, Somewhere" started and ended with stories ("A Leprechaun Named Levity" and "In Here, Somewhere") told in verse. "Levity" was published as a stage play in the early 2000s and was performed by school kids across the U.S. The original children's poem is below, written in 1978, in verse, all in one night. The spark that ignited the creative cannonball was an aggravating phone call. I was sitting on the floor, pissed at my career's path, shouting at a friend, when I just hung up the phone and said out loud, to an empty room, "I'm taking this all too seriously."

I've gotten some of my best story ideas while sitting on the floor or standing in the shower. The shower is where I conjured up my TV series "When Angels Speak … They Argue" (all ten episodes of the first season; written with my finger on a steamy glass door) but this time I was sitting on the carpet on the floor of my apartment. As I looked at the phone leaning over on its side near the coffee table, I thought about the ramifications of taking things too seriously. What if some sensitive soul decided that he or she would stop taking things so darn seriously and not take anything seriously, ever. It would make sense, wouldn't it, to stop caring when all your caring and nurturing only resulted in the sound of your own heart breaking. It would be your survival instinct kicking in: "I'm numb. And I'm much happier now."

Wouldn't that person eventually see that there's a fine line between apathy and neurotic concern … and that there are some things you have to take seriously?

(1978)
A LEPRECHAUN NAMED LEVITY

In a town not very far from you;
On a day much like today,
A leprechaun named Levity
Asked, "Who else wants to play?"
No one gave an answer.
No one asked the elf his name.
No one here had time to greet
This stranger or play games.
Levity, who lived out where
The forest almost ends,
Walked along strange streets
And thought he'd try to make new
    friends.
Faces that he saw were pale
And looked a little worried.
No one's work was getting done
But everyone was hurried.
He asked around, about this town,
In his normal, carefree style.
Residents were more inclined
To whine at him than smile.
"I don't take things serious,"
He said to folks he met.
"You have highs and you have lows ...
But I have no regret.
What's so darn important, Folks?
What's the harm in telling jokes?
Be the best that you can be
Then say, 'So what?', like me."
No one seemed to trust him
With his "What's-the-difference?"
    smirk.
He's the kind of leprechaun
Who'd take a day off work.
The town folk took work serious
And covered up their ears.
No one had vacationed here
For seven hundred years!
So, Levity, uncaringly,
Moved on with nothing gained,

To sleep out in the forest
Since he didn't mind the rain.
"I don't take things serious,"
He said to trees he met.
"You have highs and you have lows ...
But I have no regret."
Well, one tree had a sweaty palm
And wrinkles in his bark.
He worried he'd go Timberrrrrrrr!
Then be benches in a park.
His friends got jobs as weapons,
Though they weren't mean at all.
Cut, then shaped to baseball bats
That crush the little ball.
The Tree said, "Trees would never
Hit a baseball – people do!
I'm antsy 'cause we trees
Deserve consideration, too."
"Don't take it so serious,"
Levity replied.
"Why upset your woodwork
Over games you haven't tried?
What's so darn important, Tree?
Why take it so seriously?
Be the best that you can be
Then say, 'So what?', like me."
The Tree soon felt uplifted.
His attitude improved.
He moved around and told the elf
'Bout jobs which he'd approved.
"I'd like to be a hospital –
A very helpful thing.
Or else a fine piano;
Maybe I could learn to sing.
I could dance to my own music
With the pedals and the keys.
Build appreciation
And respect for all us trees.
But if I'm just a toy I'll be
The best that I can be.

Giving from my roots because
I take things seriously."
Levity moved onwardly
And he didn't even care
If he should lose his way
Or if the turtle led the hare.
Well, soon Lev met a dog
Who was a ruler, so he claimed;
And since the day that he was born,
King has been his name.
"Why am I in charge?" King asked.
"I don't have time to sneeze."
"Digging, sniffing everywhere
And holding all these keys.
Governing is serious

To everyone I know.
I have highs and I have lows ...
And I have got to go!"
"Wait," Lev said, "don't you see?
You take your job too seriously.
Just be the best that you can be
And say, 'So what?', like me."
"So what?" King sneered. "Dumb elf,
I'd slap you if I weren't a prince.
Once I hit a boxer ...
And he hasn't battled since.
Naturally, dogs look to me
As leader of the pack.
I tell 'em when to miss a meal
And when to hit the sack.

But this responsibility
Has got me chewing claws.
I'm the judge and jury ...
And I don't know the laws!"
Shouts of, "King, get back!" made King
Run off; still serious.
Then in the sky, Lev saw some lights
That looked mysterious.
Suddenly, he saw a spaceship!
Landing ... on the grass!
An alien got out and mumbled weakly,
"Out of gas.
I tried to find a station
When I stopped off for a bite
Near Mercury, but golly gee,
My money's getting tight.
I didn't take it serious
That I was low on cash.
Lucky I had credit cards
Or else I would've crashed.
Maybe you can help me
With a temporary loan.
I need a little extra
To help repair my phone.
You see, the nearest spaceship shop
Is ten light years away.
I'd like to call them up
But they won't come if I can't pay."
"Sorry," said the leprechaun,
"But I don't have a cent."
"I live in the wilderness
And don't pay any rent.
What's so darn important, Friend?
How much money can you spend?
The richer things in life are free.
Just say, 'So what?', like me."
"All I need's a Geezorp
To fill my empty tank."
The Alien said, "I didn't come
This far to rob a bank.
A Geezorp is the money
That we spend throughout the stars.
I hope that I have better luck

Borrowing on Mars!"
Lev thought he might someday Like to
    travel out in space.
But there's a guy whose planet
Is too serious a place.
Lightening, thunder; everywhere
But Lev did not complain.
He found a cave while climbing;
Went inside, expecting rain ...
... That never came. He wondered why
The ground and leaves were dry.
An old man said, "You – droopy ears;
Would you like to try?"
"I'm the Weathermaker.
I take orders from the top,
To help the droughts in deserts
And help farmers grow their crops.
But I can't start a sprinkle.
This machine just won't respond.
Frightened fish are thinking
That the plug's pulled from their
    pond."
Lev said, "I don't take it serious
When it forgets to rain.
Don't let minor setbacks
Wash your good work down the drain.
Look at all the snow you've made
To play with and to ski.
Be the best that you can be
And say, 'So what?', like me."
"I, for one, am serious."
The Weathermaker said with pride.
"I hear trees asking, 'Where's the rain?'
By now, they're petrified."
"Trees can tell when something's
    wrong
With nature, right away."
Then the blame will fall on me –
I won't know what to say.
'The rain is late'? That's no excuse.
They'll think that I don't care.
I'd better think up something good
To tell the eight-foot bear!

He believes it's serious
When rivers aren't deep.
Rain improves his fishing
And he says it helps him sleep.
So, leave me now. You won't get wet
Until I fix what's stuck.
But don't go West because you'll find
A lot of angry ducks!"
Outside the cave, the angry ducks
Stood waiting, their arms folded.
"Couldn't you do anything?"
The angriest duck scolded.
Lev said, "The man apologized
Because the rain is late.
I'm sure he'll do his job
If we just let him concentrate."
Lev, the ducks and bears walked West;
Rain fell as they reached the sea.
Lev saw an Angel surfing in ....
She told him, "Come with me!"
He did not take serious
The next words that she said:
"Sorry, little fellow,
But, officially, you're dead!
You want to know what happened?
Well, I researched and I found
That what's-his-name made too much
      rain.
It says right here you drowned.
"I don't take it serious."
Lev said, "I'm not upset.
I had highs and I had lows
So I have no regret."
The Angel said, "You're wrong,
You didn't have the highs or lows.
You never frowned or smiled.
That's what all my research shows.
But I think you'll smile
When I tell you super news:
You've been good so you'll come back
Anytime you choose!"
"So what?" Lev said, "It's not so great
Being by myself.

No one takes me serious
Because I'm just an elf."
The Angel whispered, "That is why
You never felt a thing:
You numbed yourself to happiness
As well as suffering.
Now you'll have another chance
To see all that you've missed.
You will learn the difference
Between getting punched or kissed.
If no one took things serious,
None of us would feel
Friendship, love or decency;
The things that make us real."
Levity was crying now;
His heart was touched, at last.
Feeling those emotions
That he hid from in the past.
"I'm gonna take it serious,
No matter what the cost!
Dancing when I'm happy ...
And screaming when I'm lost."
"Even if I hear a couple
Words that hurt my pride,
I will still be comfortable
With what I have inside.
That's what's so important, Miss.
Watch me smile and unclench my fist.
I'll have a leprechaun's spirit with a
      lighthearted air
But be serious about problems all of
      us share."
And so they laughed and danced until
Lev's spirit was repaired.
 "Send me back to live my life –
I'm totally prepared.
I'll start from the beginning
In a second childhood,
To feel all those emotions
That I never understood."
The Angel told him, "Do your best,
Leprechaun Named Levity.
'Cause what's the use in being free

If you don't take it seriously?"
It's been some time since Levity
Got a second chance on Earth.
He's seen his loved ones growing old
And known the joys of birth.
He started taking serious
Everyone he met.
Now he has highs and he has lows ...
But he has no regret.
In a forest pretty close to you;
On a day much like today,

A Leprechaun Named Levity
Mixes work with play.
He knows that he will manage to
Rise up if he should fall.
He knows that he has made
Some special, new friends after all.
So, think about young Levity ...
Who's mainly feeling good
'Bout taking life more serious.
Sometimes, you know, you should.

WHAT I PROBABLY MEANT TO SAY: I am speaking directly to myself in this poem. Did I know it at the time? No. I'm saying don't take yourself too seriously and don't go to the other extreme and numb yourself into a dry pulp, like Levity and the character in my earlier poem, "A Decent Man."

If you care too much, you get burned. If you care too little, same thing. Levity inspired a spinoff poem. One of the characters (The Weathermaker) warned Levity about "A lot of angry ducks" in the area, so I "hired" those rain-loving ducks to tell their story in "I Wish That It Would Rain" (see it on page 143). It just happened; one of my characters in Levity suggested other characters in a different story. That's how automatic writing works, apparently.

You may be skeptical of my automatic writing theories. I can assure you that if someone had burned the original, handwritten copy of Levity that I wrote in verse all in one night, I would not have been able to replicate it the next day. I would've had to start from scratch and hope I remembered a verse or two.

Long before Levity was published and performed in schools, in 1980, someone read a copy and gave it to her friend in a hospital. This took place in L.A. so I assumed the friend had a nervous breakdown. (This was before anyone knew how to use microwaves to give people nervous breakdowns). I was told that it had cheered up the sick friend. That's the "Barton Fink" feeling of self-discovery, when you cheer up a sick friend with a poem. Try it sometime.

Your spirit will ascend.
You'll connect with all the good energy in the universe.
And you'll also save a ton of money on get-well cards.

I figure I've saved $500,000 by writing poems
instead of buying gifts for loved ones.
So I don't even have to make money from this book.

POEMS TO MY WIFE

Spouses deserve the best poems because they put up with the worst of our moods. (If you disagree, you've probably never been on a date.) That's why I suggest writing a love note to your spouse/partner on their next birthday. But what can you write that won't sound hokey? No one wants to get ridiculed for saying somethin' stupid like "I Love You."

People see me in Starbucks in Philadelphia and I often hear, "Don, our bathrooms are for customers only. Please leave. We just called the cops." (Luckily for me, the cops were asked to leave, too.) Being that I'm used to the brush offs (see poem on page 111, "Brush Me Off?") I stay and talk to people. They say things like, "Don, I'd like to save $200-$20,000 by giving my spouse a poem instead of a fancy gift. What can I write this year?" I tout them onto a sure winner: write about the day you met.

I've been writing poems to my wife, Marcia, several times a year since the day we met in 1991. Below is one of the poems I wrote to her about that special day.

March 3rd, 2015
ATLANTIC CITY
(Listen to Mumford & Dylan's "Kansas City")

Dear M:
The salt air freezes smack dab on your
    face;
That's how you know you're almost there.
In March it's such a quiet seaside place
But it's loud and clear 'bout all we've
    shared
Down here in Atlantic City.
And it seems so right
To take you here
And celebrate with this birthday tune
In the place we met
And fell in love;
Where we started this honeymoon.
Goin' to Atlantic City.

Jump in, the Jacuzzi warms your hands
    and feet.
You can use it as your swimming pool.
And then sit with me as the bubbles
    seep;
We'll look through the top of the tee-
    pee hole,
Sayin' thanks to Atlantic City.
And it seems so right
To take you here
And celebrate with this birthday kiss
In the place we met
And fell in love;
Where we started this wedding bliss.
Goin' to Atlantic City.
All my love on your birthday & forever,
D!

WHAT I PROBABLY MEANT TO SAY: There's an indoor pool at Harrah's Atlantic City that has a glass cover and is shaped like a teepee. We've spent many happy weekends there, in all four seasons. The teepee pool is a spiritual place for us. In this poem, I'm thanking the gritty town of Atlantic City for being so lucky in love for me.

> In the place we met
> And fell in love;
> Where we started this wedding bliss.

Not only did we meet in Atlantic City, we also honeymooned there. It was a modest honeymoon for sure, only an hour away by car and only three days in duration. Yes, we were by the ocean but the ocean temperature was about 35 degrees, much warmer than the air. We hung out with our parents and visiting relatives; almost all of them 75 or older. I can be seen on videotape during our honeymoon gushing about my new bride as the gale force winds almost blow me off the boardwalk in front of Caesar's. It was an inexpensive and old-fashioned honeymoon and it was the best week of my life, if that makes any sense. It was a honeymoon filled with love. It's not like we didn't have the resources to go on an extravagant excursion. We were both in our 40s so we had over 80 years between us to save up for a honeymoon.

You may be wondering: where is the poem I wrote to her about the night we first met in Atlantic City, when we found each other in the same club at 1 am. It's below, written 23 years earlier, in 1992. It's set to Leonard Cohen's, "Halleluiah," which became our wedding song. On our first dance as a married couple, we sang along, not to Leonard's edgy lyrics but to the words below.

January 10th, 1992

FIRST POEM TO MARCIA

(Listen to Leonard Cohen's, "Halleluiah.")

Dear Marcia:
I felt the first Autumnal breeze
While walking into Memories.
The end of summer changes tend to shape
    me.
You appeared, flashed warmth and grace.
Stuck your eyeballs in my face
But would you stick around to bioscape
    me?
Bioscape me, bioscape me
Bioscape me, bioscape me
A week had passed since we first met.
I transferred credit just to bet
But how and when I lost it all escapes me.
I was thinking, "She might leave."
You hid your charge cards in your sleeve
And dropped a hint you'd rather bioscape
    me.
Bioscape me, bioscape me
Bioscape me, bioscape me.
We drove down the avenue.

Rushed to a room without a view.
I stared and then I started to undrape
    you.
Even though the night was late,
I knew you'd get a second date
And with it came a chance to bioscape
    you.
Bioscape you, bioscape you
Bioscape you, bioscape you.
You live in a one room studio.
There's static on your radio.
When I get cold you take the quilt and
    crepe me.
But we don't need a large estate,
Just carbohydrates on our plate,
Sorbet, then for dessert, you bioscape
    me.
Bioscape me, bioscape me
Bioscape me, bioscape me.
I'll tell you what I'm feeling here.
I'm happy just to have you near,

So close you can emotionally scrape me.
But you bring out the good in me.
You're a woman made from quality.
I knew that first, before you bioscaped me.

WHAT I PROBABLY MEANT TO SAY: I wrote this about five months after we met, a re-telling of how we started chatting over drinks in a nightclub called Memories in Margate, NJ, on August 24th, 1991. Marcia sat next to me on a stool around a bar and, as we spoke, she put her face thisclose to mine. This is not what Americans expect from other Americans. I could almost feel her eyeballs on my face. It was like she trusted me from the first moment we met. In this poem, I'm telling my future wife that she brings out the best in me.

"Salt N Pepper."

I haven't written an advice piece since The Ogontz Outlet at Penn State University featured my "Dandy Don Predicts" column in 1975. But I strongly advise all of you to marry a special someone who brings out the best in you and/or someone you can't live without. Either one works.

Penn State Ogontz changed its name 30 years ago to Abington (the township where it's located, near Northeast Philadelphia, where I grew up) because the Native American name was deemed inappropriate. I guess giving Chief Ogontz and his tribe a raw deal, then chasing them out of Cranberry Place, their home for centuries, was appropriate and necessary but ... naming the campus after him was not.

The bioscape reference is an inside joke. It's a foam mattress that we put on a sofa bed to make it more comfortable. I'm talking about spending time in the sack.

People who knew us said we were an unlikely couple. So, I wrote this to her.

March 17th, 1993

Dear Marcia:
You're up in the morning and I'm up at
  night.
You sleep on the left side and I on the
  right.
You smooth things over; I like a good,
  clean fight.
An unlikely couple are we.
You like veggies and I like steak.
You like cleaning every hour you're
  awake.
I once caught you cleaning in your
  sleep, for goodness sake.
An unlikely couple are we.
I'm more creative; an accountant I'm not.
I drive a sports car and you walk a lot.
I can't really blame you with the legs that
  you've got.
An unlikely couple are we.
You've got brown hair while my hair is
  gray.
You're younger and I'm older – that's
  what you told me to say.
Our relationship spans the calendar;
  April and May.
An unlikely couple are we.
You're so Midwestern and I'm citified.
I'm more outgoing and you're pretty shy.
I couldn't do your aerobics if I tried.
An unlikely couple are we.
You clean the mess when I stir 15 pots.
I like the race track and you like the slots.

We both kind of like it when we come
  out on top.
An unlikely couple are we.
But we both care about people.
And appreciate the small yet important
  things in life.
What we share in our hearts far out-
  weighs differences in style.
And the longer we're together,
The more balanced we'll become
And the differences won't matter after
  a while.
No one would ever consider us as an
  unlikely couple if they would only
  stand
Between us when we're making love
  and felt what we felt.
But they would never stand between
  us for long
Because they'd melt.
Long ago it seemed unlikely that the
  sky would be blue
And the ocean would, too.
That grass would be green
And pictures would move on a screen.
That we'd walk on the moon
Or I'd be awake before noon.
It may be true there are couples more
  unlikely than me and you.
And I bet that they're happy, too.
You make me so happy, so happy
  birthday to you.
All My Love, D

WHAT I PROBABLY MEANT TO SAY: Even though we're opposites, we have the same values. You're my happiness, my muse … and you're hot! Parts of this poem (not the spicy parts) were read by the rabbi during our wedding service in 2000.

The line, "We both kind of like it when we come out on top" was changed from the original, "We both kind of like it when we cum on top."

It looks like both of us stayed too long in the Mexican sun.

February 14th, 1992

Dear Marcia:
In case the wind chill gets to minus 30.
And gale force winds do dances on your face.
When plants conspire to lock you out on the balcony ...
Remember – you can't get frostbite in a passionate embrace.

WHAT I PROBABLY MEANT TO SAY: I was reminiscing about the night we almost got locked out on the freezing balcony of my parents' high-rise NJ condo in January, while they were visiting Florida. The door was blocked by a window shade. I had to pull on the sliding door to un-jam it and ended up doing damage to the dry wall inside.

"Good news and bad news," I told Dad on the phone. "Good news is we didn't freeze to death. The bad news is you might need some plaster work inside your unit."

Later in the same poem from 1992, I found an oldie but goodie:

> I like when you're acting pretty bossy.
> I like when you try to order me around.
> Although I like it when you're bossy –
> I'd like it more if you stopped right now.

WHAT I PROBABLY MEANT TO SAY: Just line four (just like before).

Marcia and I had met at a seaside bar about nine months prior to my writing this next poem (written without any melody in mind) and I was already considering living together. I was a 36-year-old bachelor revealing to myself that my bachelorhood was coming to an end.

June 4th, 1992

Dear Marcia:
Everyone's askin' me – how do I feel?
'Bout issues I'm not even certain are real.
And my position could change any day.
But when I think of how I could position you,
There isn't a one you couldn't get me to do.
'Cause I'm hungry in a fat cat kind of way.
Now ... I know most fat cats have long lost their edge.
They won't go to great heights unless there's a ledge.
And a cat who's not hungry could stray.
You keep me hungry and satisfied, too;
Who can get bored when they're doin' somethin' new?
Yeah, I'm hungry in a fat cat kind of way.
So you're wonderin' what it'd be like if we moved in.
Like someone said, "Ok, let those games begin!"
I'd have to feel that I'd never move away.
Before any notion like that comes to front,
I know exactly just what I'd want –
I'd want to be hungry in a fat cat kind of way.

WHAT I PROBABLY MEANT TO SAY: Let's move in together. This poem reveals that Marcia brought up the subject first. I'm glad somebody did.

I was inspired to write this to my future wife in 1994, when she was about to move in with me, a year and a half after I wrote the "Fat Cat" poem above.

January 29th, 1994
MARCIA G
(Listen to Counting Crows', "Mr. Jones")

Dear Marcia G:
Tra la la la la la la
I was hangin' out on Arch Street, with
    an old-fashioned girl.
Marcia G; she had a friend named
    Otis,
Who was a bug eyed wealthy,
    homeless person.
You know, she's gonna move into my
    place.
It's gonna be wonderful
Maybe better than wonderful.
I'll leave if it's not wonderful.
We'll have much more time to do
    things together.
Tra la la la la la la la
We watch TV.
We're about to have 5 TV's.
Pass me the clicker, Marcia G.
She's moving in.
There's one thing I learned 'bout
    moving in.
I'd rather be the one who moves in.
Marcia G and me go to Saratoga
    Springs
And we laugh at the guy with the
    shovel;
There's our Travers horse, he's stickin'
    his tongue out at us.
It's been 29 months.
We're gonna be inseparable.

But if one of us acts poorly, they will
    live in the basement.
She's got a sense of humor;
We're always ad-libbing some funny
    routines.
Most of the jokes we tell
Are told very simultaneously.
One day I missed the turn to the
    stadium.
I didn't want her to walk in the pouring
    rain.
Then we saw a guy crossing I-95 on
    foot ...
So why should we complain?
Marcia G and me go to watch the
    Eagles' games;
In the winter they don't sell any coffee
    –
It's a rule they have –
And we leave when the rain turns to
    sleet.
We're so complimentary.
She's the best accountant I ever met.
But if one of us acts poorly
They will live in the basement.
They will live in the basement.
We all want an ideal mate.
We need to recognize true love
And have the awareness to act upon it.
For us, there's a lot of reasons to be
    optimistic.

We only get dressed up like this a few times a year. I'm wearing my Star Trek "Captain Picard" shirt under my sports jacket in this 2012 photo, which is impressive, I know, but not as impressive as Marcia's sparkling eyes.

If you live with me
Then ya gotta be flexible as lead can be
And I need a girl made of flexible lead.
Flexible lead. Flexible lead.
Marcia G and me, hopin' that we'll get along
When she tells me it's time to start cleaning
I'll put headphones on, then I'll go up and rewrite this song.
I wanna get her a Honda.
Marcia G, she wants a car as practical as cars can get.
I've got a feeling she's gonna be stubborn—
And I haven't mentioned the Honda to her yet.
Marcia G and me, we coulda moved to the main line zoo.
Do ya know how many nice people we'd meet if we moved there?
Maybe about one or two.
I can't wait till she moves in cause I'm good for her
And she's good for me.
When she moves in, I'm gonna get her a map that shows our house,
There in Montgomery county.
Marcia G and me, we're gonna make love often.
All My Love, D

WHAT I PROBABLY MEANT TO SAY: I was trying to tell Marcia how happy I was that she was moving in, because I was usually the one who moved in (so I could move out, if necessary). I poke fun at how we often talk at the same time. And I pay homage to the guy who shovels shit at Saratoga Race Track, again. (See "Saratoga" poem on page 31.) That shit-shoveler — a bald, middle age man I had always ridiculed — made me realize that if you love what you do, you'll be happy with the job, even if others think it's crappy. I'm also giving her fair warning that living with me means she must be flexible and made of lead, and that I'm high maintenance.

Years later, in 2002, I went back and re-wrote the "moving in" poem. I had more to say on the subject and wanted Marcia to know. Bob Dylan rewrote "Tangled Up In Blue" and Harry Chapin wrote a sequel to "Taxi" for the same reason.

I wrote this sequel eight years after Marcia had moved in and stayed … and married me. It was the first marriage for each of us. We were both past 35 when we met and in our 40s when we married in 2000. Why did I wait so long when it was clear, through my poems, that I loved her and couldn't live without her? I'll tell you why — because I was fucking broke!

March 3rd, 2002
MARCIA B
(Listen to Counting Crows', "Mr. Jones")
(Part Two; about eight years after I wrote Part One)

Dear Marcia B:
Tra la la la la la la, uh huh.
I'm here in Andalusia, with an old-fashioned girl –
Marcia B; she's made some friends on the golf course;
They're Canadian and they honk while flying.
You know, we went and got married in Y2k.
The idea, it just came to me.
On Muir beach, natural beauty got through to me.

Not marrying her seemed insane to me.
Now we've both signed on to a lifetime ketubah (Jewish marriage contract).
Tra la la la la la la la
We watch TV.
We've got 30 digital movie channels.
Pass me the clicker, Marcia B.
We're married, see.
The one thing I've learned 'bout married glee
Is that consideration is the key. Yeah.
Marcia B and me go to pet the thoroughbreds

And we cruise down the lake in the "Ha-
Ha."
There's our parasail; well, we'll fly when
the gale warning ends.
It's been 126 months.
She's the most essential cog
But if one of us acts poorly, they will live
with the ground hog.
She's got lots of stories;
She's always telling me some kind of
office tale.
Most of the tales that she tells
Are very, very trivial.
But, you know, I sit there and listen
When she vents 'bout an office clown or
knave,
I take her side of the mission,
Like she does for me when I start to rant
and rave.
Marcia B and me got our Eagles' SBL's.
We don't have any clue where we're
sitting.
It's a rule they have –
And our stocks rise and fall with our
coach.
We're right on the Delaware.
We watch tree branches outlined in the
fog.
But if one of us acts poorly
They will live with the ground hog.
We both could've married young.
Oh, we both had chances to make
mistakes.
It's a miracle that we found each other;
Ten lifetimes worth of lucky breaks.
Living here with you
Is like living with the angels up above.
And the rooms are filled with
unconditional love
Unconditional love, unconditional love,
yeah.
Marcia B and me, boy, she's really been
my muse.

Marcia's smile is the subject of many of
my poems to her.

She inspires me in all that I'm doing,
Chases off the blues, and with her in
my face I can't lose.
I want a 2003 Honda.
Marcia B, she's so practical, she'll want
a 2002.
She'll drop her glasses down low and
tell me, "Babe,
Here's the newsflash: new is new."
Marcia B and me, coulda moved near
the Evesham train.
Do ya know how many rivers or
swimming pools they got there?
None! And the squirrels aren't tame.
I'm so happy we're married now. I'm
always there for her
She's always there for me.
And it amazes me to know that because
of her
I'm now second favorite in my own
family.
Marcia B and me, our love is ever
blooming.
All my love on your birthday and for all
time, D

WHAT I PROBABLY MEANT TO SAY: Meeting her is equal to "Ten lifetimes worth of lucky breaks." The theme that keeps appearing is unconditional love and how it's manifest in our standing up for each other.

Notice that I call her "Marcia G" in the 1994 poem and "Marcia B" in the 2002 poem. She wasn't Marcia B. Grees anymore, she was Marcia B. Rutberg and I wanted her to know that it was the best thing that ever happened to me.

Here we are before the NFC championship game (Vikings at Eagles) in January, 2018. A drunken Viking fan referred to Marcia as "Grandma," nearly starting a riot (long story) outside of the stadium.

The concept of consideration being the key to a good marriage appears in the 2002 poem above. It was my Dad's theory. On my wedding day, Dad revealed on videotape that his secret to a long and happy marriage was consideration. He and Mom were married 56 years at the time so I couldn't really argue. At the end of this poem, I admit how I went from favorite child to second favorite child after my parents got to know Marcia. She leapfrogged me in my own family. Am I the only one who's been leapfrogged in love? Probably not. So how do we cope with this? Therapy? Start a Fund Me cause: Hugs for the Leapfrogged? How would we trademark that?

Have you ever trademarked something? I have, a children's book series called, "Did What?!" (In a rare event, "Satchel Paige ... Did What?!" was published as a stage play. "Neil Armstrong ... Did What?!" was never published, as I explained on page 134). A trademark costs between $750 and $75,000, depending on your lawyer. If you infringe on my trademark, I could sue you, but only if I had an extra $200,000 lying around to pay my lawyer to sue you.

Our boat ride on the Ha-Ha around Lake George was a déjà vu for me; like I had seen it in a past life. Then I realized I had seen it in a movie, "Last of the Mohicans."

Look closer and you'll see that getting "Leapfrogged in Love" within your own family is a blessing. It hurts at first, at any age (listen to the late Andrew Gold's, "Lonely Boy") but then it hits you that you've brought a complete stranger into the fold and magnified the all-around family love.

THEME ALERT! Love makes you unselfish. By the way, I'll be selling "Leapfrogged in Love" t-shirts in the lobby after the book is finished, assuming I can procure speaking gigs, and that's not very likely to happen since I've only had about two dozen speaking gigs in 40 years.

My Dad's theory about consideration being the key to a good marriage also appears in this next birthday poem I wrote to Marcia.

March 3rd, 1994

Dear Marcia G:
HOW YOU TREAT MY LOVE
(Listen to John Mellencamp's, "Human Wheels")

You're looking good, there in the sun.
Find other ways to have your fun.
You walk alone through murky, des-
    perate streets;
To danger, you're impervious.
You ski the mountain full speed
    through the trees
Then you say I'm too serious.
Careful now, how you treat my love.
You best start watchin' what you do.
Careful now, how you treat my love;
Don't you know my love is you.
You limp downtown to exercise.
It's pain that you romanticize.
A lonely woman has to stay in shape
Well, you're not lonely anymore.
You've got to learn to go easy on
    yourself,

Help us maintain esprit de corps.
Careful now, how you treat my love.
You best start watchin' what you do.
Careful now, how you treat my love;
Don't you know my love is you.
I take my chances constantly.
When I can't find them, they find me.
I'm not denying, I've had my share of
    thrills
Endangering my sanity and health.
Now all those joy rides affect you, too.
You're my protection from myself.
I'm careful now, how I treat your love
I have to watch me constantly.
I'm careful now, how I treat your love
Because I know your love is me.

WHAT I PROBABLY MEANT TO SAY: Marcia was about to move in with me and I loved her so much that I didn't want her hurting her knees or walking in downtown Philly at night or even getting a sunburn. I took the title line from my Dad (again) who would say be careful how you (meaning us) treat my love. He was saying take good care of yourselves, the people he loves. It was one of those lines that took years to figure out. Example: "How did we get front row seats to see the Supremes?" I asked Dad when I was a kid in the 1960s. He said, "Mr. Jackson got us in." Twenty years later, I took out a $20 bill and saw Jackson's face on the bill. He was the guy ($20 tip) who got us on the front row in a South Jersey hot spot to see the Supremes, where Diana Ross, I am not kidding, winked at me!

At that point in the late 1960s, I had touched a deer's nose in California and been winked at by Diana Ross, from close range. Life was a cabaret, filled with friendly wild animals and flirty pop stars. (They were two different groups back then.)

Front row at the Supremes concert in 1967, when I was 11 and Diana Ross winked at me. My older brother, Jeff, is with us.

In the "How You Treat My Love" poem above, I again use a French expression:

> A lonely woman has to stay in shape
> Well, you're not lonely anymore.
> You've got to learn to go easy on yourself,
> Help us maintain esprit de corps.

No one told me (this time) to change the line because it's French and supposedly no one would understand it, like when I used the word ingénue in my poem, "The Road" and the band members who were (drunkenly) recording the song didn't understand it and balked. So, don't let drunken, ex-convicts change your lyrics unless it's the ghost of Johnny Cash.

February 14th, 1997

LOVE ME, TONIGHT

(Listen to Bob Seger's, "Roll Me Away.")
Made a right off 13th Street, barely missed a homeless man.
Picked her up near the soup kitchen when the preacher moved his van.
Headed out on the Franklin bridge; hope to merge the best I can.
An hour later we were at the shore,
Man, those were some happy plants.
Bought a form and studied some more;
Then I decided to take a chance.
I held her in my arms on the balcony
As we watched the rushing tide.
I knew what she needed; I knew what she wanted.
"Oh, feed me tonight, won't you feed me the world tonight?
I need a meal and I need a show; I don't care if it's corny or trite."
I kissed her gently, squeezed her hard;
Put her mittens on just right.
And we drove,
To a buffet for a bite.
We stood in line an hour, smelling plastic flowers.
The salad bar looked good. I'd grab some if I could.
I finally found some roast beef; the server saved a rare piece. She wiped
    away a crumb. I said, "I'm still not done."
Held her hand by the pastry bar, feelin' just a little funny.
Strawberry shortcake, hot apple pie, it was all up to my own tummy.
I stopped and stared into her eyes and it was then I realized –
Marcia B. Grees, was all I wanted.
Oh, love me tonight, love me a million more of these nights.
Who needs buffets and 200 races?
If you love me then everything's right.
And whether it's Valentine's Day or just a winter's day of sleet.
The truth is: you make ... my life so sweet.

WHAT I PROBABLY MEANT TO SAY: Going on vacations is nice, but all I want is you. My message is simple: "If you love me then everything's right."

In the summertime during the 1990s, Marcia and I rented a house (shared by 10 adults, in five bedrooms) by the beach in Ventnor, NJ. I referred to the house earlier in this book on page 20, (in "For Ten Sweet Years") when I wrote about wanting to be alone with her right after we met but there were logistical problems with shared rooms. We had to go to a cluttered enclosed front porch (named "The PMS Room") for some smooching action. The neighbors could look right in so we had to stay low.

> Wanting you more
> On the PMS floor.
> Better stay low
> So the neighbors won't know.

I wrote a few other poems about the beach house, such as a parody of a Ricky Martin song. My version was called, "Live In A Casa Loca." I read it to my housemates (it was about them) and nobody understood it. They just watched the Ricky Martin video like they were in a trance. That pretty much sums up the 1990s.

I wrote this one below after noticing that Marcia was the one who kept the share house together.

August 30th, 1997

Dear Marcia:
You're the crazy glue who keeps this house in tether.
When the lazy do no housework, you say, "They'd better."
If the hazy dew brings clouds, you change the weather.
'Cause you're the crazy glue who keeps this house together.
You make peace when Sheila's voice sounds just like leather.
When it's too cold for Renee, you lend a sweater.
When my mouth is really dry, you make it wetter.
You're the crazy glue who keeps this house together.
When Eddie drives to kill, you say a prayer.
If someone breaks a rule, you say, "No fair!"
If Iris needs to barf in our car, you say, "We're almost there!"
You're the crazy glue who keeps this house together.
When Steve and Linda show up, you say, "What a welcome sight."
When Lloyd shows up, you ask, "What? No game tonight?"
You stop Honey from entering our room and turning off the light.
You're the crazy glue who keeps this house together.
You never walk around naked for "Fred" or Phil.
They've quietly offered thousands if you will.
Renee offered less for a perverted thrill.
(She's got tendencies, well, you know the drill.)
You're the crazy glue who keeps this house together.
You're a big sister to the young girls in our place.
By default, you won our last bicycle race.

You throw ringers, then you laugh in Eddie's face.
You're the crazy glue who keeps this house together.
You tell Merrill which slots to play and which are duds.
When Renee steps on a nail you stop the blood.
And if you can't, you stay and sweep away the flood.
You're the crazy glue who keeps this house together.
At restaurants you figure out the bill.
When bad Sci-Fi's on TV, you watch with Phil.
You'd watch with Sheila but you'd have to take a pill.
You're the crazy glue who keeps this house together.
You make newcomers "Fred" & Wilma feel at home.
You leave half your steak so Suzie can have the bone.
You're the best roommate that I have ever known.
You're the crazy glue who makes this house a home.
All my love, DR

WHAT I PROBABLY MEANT TO SAY: She keeps things (including us) together.

March 3rd, 1998
TAKE YOU AROUND
(Listen to Matchbox 20s, "Push")

Dear M:
You say you don't need something
    special for your birthday.
You're something special already;
Like a diamond, dazzling with your
    smile.
And there's no price too high for me
    to pay;
I'd even wrestle with Eddie
To make your lifestyle cushy for a
    while.
And I'm a little unsettled, well ...
It feels funny, on March third,
Not buying your present in a store.
All I give you are words of love.
You know, sometimes they mean more.
I want to take you around
To the stores, in the mall.
I want to take you around,

Colonial Downs, in the fall.
We want a trip to Bay Meadows.
We want to see Uncle Irving.
And we will.
They say all people really want is
    security.
Well, that's what we'll be sharing
When my wild fish come swimin' in.
And I need to have you in close prox-
    imity,
'Cause with a woman who's caring,
There's no earthly prize I couldn't win.
Though I'm a little slow starting, well ...
It feels funny, on March third,
Not buying your present in a mall.
All I give you are words of love.
But soon you'll have it all.
I want to take you around
To the stores, in the mall.

I want to take you around,
Colonial Downs, in the fall.
I want to take you to Europe.
We'll buy tix for Uncle Irving.
And we will.
Oh, I know your happiness
Depends not on gold.
But living is easier
When books are sold; lots sold.
You're my true lover. You're my life's
    partner.
I want to take you around
To the stores, for a fling.

I want to take you around,
Churchill Downs, in the spring.
I want to meet you in that aisle.
Yeah, you'll walk with mom and Uncle
    Irving.
Yes, you will. We will.
Sheila will take a pill.
Yes, she will.
She will. (She should.)
Yeah. I want to take you around.
Jump on your merry-go-round.
And I will!
All my love, forever! DPR

WHAT I PROBABLY MEANT TO SAY: In this poem, I'm pre-proposing marriage. I broach the subject, which is nice considering we'd already been dating and/or living together for six and a half years.

Mentioning your loved one's favorite relatives is always a good idea. In this case, I write about Marcia's Uncle Irving, the man who, two years later, would give away the bride at our wedding.

> I want to meet you in that aisle.
> Yeah, you'll walk with mom and Uncle Irving.
> Yes, you will. We will.

We did! That's where I saw the face of God in my Mom and Dad's smile. It was a great day, December 10th, 2000. The Philadelphia Eagles beat the Cleveland Browns that day, which I took as a good sign. (Other good signs were that I loved her more than anything and couldn't live without her.)

In the poem above, I'm apologizing for not being able to go out and spend a few thousand dollars on a nice gift for her. It'll happen soon, though, I tell her, even though there was no basis for it happening soon. It seems like I'm buying time in the poem: "Don't give up on me. I'll build you a dream house tomorrow." Didn't Lindsey Buckingham build his woman a dream house on a hill in "Big, Big Love?" Yes, he did. And she still left him! (Lindsey warned us, it's not "lookin' for love," it's "lookin'

OUT for love.") Anyway, it's been 21 years since I wrote the poem and Marcia still doesn't have the dream house I promised to build her last century. You can't have everything.

As the year 2000 approached, we were worried that computers would crash, lights would flicker, food would spoil, gasoline would be rationed and alcohol banned. Some of us went to the store and bought all the liquor we could carry or bury for later. But I didn't care about end of millennium problems. They were superfluous to me.

December 24th, 1999
100 MONTHS

(Listen to Steve Forbert's, "One More
Glass Of Beer")
Dear M:
All this talk of millennium;
Is superfluous; you see,
The only number relevant:
100 months of you and me.
It all started accidentally
With an intro from a guy
I hardly knew; he sat near you,
With a push from way up high.
Why was I so congenial
With a guy I hardly knew?
And why was it left up to strangers
To make miracles come true?
So now winter raises its curtain
And the millennium comes, too.
To me, it's just the first full day
Of my next 100 months with you.
Our values are the same; we stand
For love and equality, too.

We stand for hope, compassion, fun;
You stand for me; I stand for you.
These past 100 months have moved
So quickly, like a blur.
And every day, the prayer I say,
Is, "Thank you, Lord, for her."
Now it's far in the future;
The best 10,000 months I've ever
known.
Side by side with my Marcia, dear,
Wherever, whenever we've flown.
Forever, we're together
'Cause that's what we choose to do.
The months behind and those ahead
Are joyous romps with you.
Thank you for the first 100 months,
For the kindness you have shown.
And for all your unselfish, loving
deeds,
Small and large; unknown and known.
All my love for 10,000 months, D

WHAT I PROBABLY MEANT TO SAY: (THEME ALERT!)

- Our values are the same.
- We stand up for each other.

By the way, you can just write those two sentences to your loved ones and sign your name and get a big hug and kiss. Sure, actions mean more than words but it's nice to read a card that says, "I've got your back."

My millennium poem refers to the night eight years earlier when a near stranger fortuitously introduced us in a night club. I'm wondering why it's left up to strangers to make miracles come true. Think about miracles in your life. Have complete strangers played a part? Sure, they have. As Mr. Klein, the Eastern European Holocaust survivor and tailor used to say, "It's a lot to think about."

December 10th, 2001
Dear M:
These poems to you may be the most
Worthwhile words I'll ever write.
Loving you is like standing in
Unimaginably beautiful light.
All my love forever and ever, D

WHAT I PROBABLY MEANT TO SAY: I'm saying in lines one and two that my poems to her are the most heartfelt words I'll ever write (Wisdom From My Younger Self). In the second half of the poem, I'm telling her she lights up my life. No mention of how I was "Leapfrogged In Love."

There must have been rumblings of war in 2003 when I wrote this one below.

February 14th, 2003
(Listen to Bob Dylan's "You're Gonna Make Me Lonesome")

Dear M:
The president just made a speech
'Bout soldiers landing on the beach.
He's bombing kvetchy (angry) countries, large and small.
But I walk 'round with a happy face
When we're together in our cozy place.
I'm gonna love ya, baby, through it all.
The infidels want us void and null.
They call it religious ritual;
They gas the air, while in their caves, they crawl.
But we both know how we'll escape
With goalie pads and ducky tape.
I'm gonna love ya, baby, through it all.
The airport may be close to here

But we don't feel the rising fear
That burns our jets from here to Montreal.
We can always take a cool retreat
In Betsy Pearl, with cool-down seats.
I'm gonna love ya, baby, through it all.
We're gonna make it with a little mazel (luck).
Breathin' ain't so bad through dampened cloths.
It could be our chance to clean the closets,
When we're hidin' there with "King Korn" files and moths.
Oh, we've got a cell phone and a shore plan:
We'll breathe through straws under Ventnor's fine sand
When the bad guys throw their dirty fireball.
But when panic hits the streets from that scene,
We'll be holding hands – 'cause we're a real team.
I'm gonna love ya, baby, through it all.
Tough times are gonna make us even closer,
Under blankets, in the steam, in our shower stall,
Where we'll safely stay 'till the war is over
And we've given those dictators a good overhaul.
Oh, the times are strange, we can't deny it.
We're American Jews; our enemies won't buy it.
We may stagger but we're never gonna fall.
So go on, wipe away those tears,
They couldn't kill us, if we gave 'em another 5,000 years –
And I'm gonna love ya, baby, through it all.
With All My Love and Smiles on Valentine's Day, D

WHAT I PROBABLY MEANT TO SAY: Through all kinds of weather, we're a team.

What I'm doing in this poem is taking clichés like "thick and thin" and "you light up my life" and putting a personal spin on them. My Dad used to say, "Work isn't work when you're working to win." (I'm sending that line at once to the trademark office.) For aspiring poets, just take the "thick and thin" line, add a personal line or two from your own marriage, end it with spin or begin, and you've got a new anniversary poem. Your savings (some may call it not spending on gifts) will be $50-$25,000, depending on your budget.

Still having trouble rhyming? Then get yourself a rhyming dictionary to help you rhyme a line or two. It's on the Internet, or I can lend you

a paperback copy from 1985. Right on the front cover of my rhyming dictionary is a used clubhouse seat sticker from Saratoga Race Course, dated August 3rd, 2015. There's a 100% chance I wrote a poem to Marcia sometime that month. You may remember this one from earlier in the book. It has a theme of "I'm lucky in love" and starts like this:

August 24th, 2015
GONE TO SARATOGA

(Listen to Queen's, "Barcelona")
Dear M:
I had this lucky day.
In 1991.
It was August 24th.
The Travers was on TV
But no one there could find me
Because I was down the shore in surf and sun.

This poem (a full version appears on page 35) is a personal spin on the cliché, "I'm lucky in love." The Rolling Stones did it. The late, great Tom Petty did it. OK, Tom's ex-girlfriend got lucky, not him, but the takeaway is there's no law against using clichés if you put a personal spin on them.

Here's a theme that every family experiences: **Coming through the door after work.**

March 3rd, 2003 – (03/03/03!)
HERE SHE COMES, THROUGH THE DOOR

(Listen to Randy Newman's, "Baltimore")

Dear M:
Sittin' by the window;
Watch 'em plow the snow.
Ain't much light around here;
Nowhere I can go.
And the river, it's frozen;
Can't wave to no one on a tug.
Just me and my computer
And stuffed doggies on the rug.
Oh, Marcia B,
Here she comes, through the door.
Oh, Marcia B,
She's what I'm livin' for.
That's for sure.
Wearin' this ol' outfit
I wore in high school.
Lookin' from the clubhouse;
Moonless sky and empty pool.
No strangers do I dance with;

No drinks do I consume,
Till my baby makes her way back
From the ladies' room.
Oh, Marcia B,
Here she comes, to the bar.
Oh, Marcia B,
She's my own shining star.
My shining star.
Never had a best friend
Who's as loyal as you are.
Never thought I'd have one
Or an electric car.
Let's buzz out to the beach, babe,
And have some birthday fun.
As long as we're together,
I'm feelin' like I won.
Oh, Marcia B, You're the most loving
    wife.
Oh, Marcia B, You're the love of my life.

WHAT I PROBABLY MEANT TO SAY: You're extremely loyal. I'm driving an electric car. Life is good. (Again, this was before I started teaching in college.)

Below is another story about my spouse coming through the door after work for some laughter, love and hijinks.

February 14th, 2005
VALENTINE'S DAY DREAM
(Listen to Glen Campbell's, "By The Time I Get To Phoenix")

By the time I drink my coffee she'll be eating
The two-pronged tuna "samich" that I made.
She'll smile when she sees slices of sweet peppers
And she'll eat them in the Bellevue's esplanade.
By the time I read the paper she'll be searching
For the boss who's down at Starbucks or $elling jewels.
She'll orchestrate the secretaries' duties
While the secretaries desecrate the rules,
Like greedy fools.
By the time I take a shower she'll be commuting
Back to our little love-nest where we'll stay
Entwined throughout the evening, filled with laughter –
A Valentine's Day dream we live each day.
More in love each day.
That's her in the doorway.
Now it's time to play.
All my love on Valentine's Day and Every Day, D!

WHAT I PROBABLY MEANT TO SAY: Life is a dream. I'm also appreciating the fact that she has to wake up about six hours before I do and then commute to downtown Philadelphia to work with fools. At least I make her lunch. That's something, right?

Below is another poem about her coming through the door. It's a duet.

March 3rd, 2004
YOU MAKE IT ALL SO NICE
(Listen to The Kink's, "You Make It All Worthwhile")
Hello, Luv:
You look so cute in your mittens and scarf.
Here, let me hang up your coat so you can change clothes.
That's a good girl. Take the bag off your shoulder.
Don't poke yourself in the eye or bang your nose.
So, how have you been?
Go on, get into your comfy slippers and watch the flat screen.
All your favorite weathercasters are standing by.
By the way, how was your day at the office?
(Your part in italics)
I can't put up with secretaries at work.
Each one redefines the term, "Worthless jerk."
It's like their purpose is to drive me berserk.
With their pettiness and their selfish quirks.
But when you come home
You make it all so nice;
You make the salad
And I make the ice.
And after your hard day
Being so precise.
You make it all so nice.
Oh, I meant to tell ya, I made a shellfish, guacamole, Humus, tahini
    pizza for dinner. That OK?
(Your part in italics)
What? You know I don't like all those fancy, exotic toppings … and the extra, extra cheeses
    and spices and ….
All right. I'll make a plain cheese pizza.
And afterwards, I'll write a birthday poem about us.
You've got to rise above all that stuff.
You've tried your best and you have suffered enough.
Settle down while I make some fries,
There's a road map to a smile –
It goes through the town of Pizza Pie.
Oh, baby, I wanna see a birthday smile.
I know it's rough in concrete-land
But brooding ain't your style.

Yeah, honey, you know I'm not adverse to great wealth.
But I prefer to work at home by myself.
It's a boon to my emotional health.
And I know that soon, I'll take the pressure off you.
But when you come home
You make it all so nice;
I make spaghetti
Or you'll make some rice.
And after your hard day
Chasin' all the mice
You make it all so nice.
(Your part in italics)
Would you like some French Citron sponge cake for later?
Honey, that would be wonderful!
And when you come home
You make it all so nice.
You make me marvel
At your sage advice.
And, oh, how I'm grateful
For your sacrifice.
My words here can't suffice.
Come on, darlin'. Let's go clean the grill!
And when you come home
You make it all so nice
I made our pizza,
Let's have a slice.
Just having you with me,
It feels like paradise,
On your birthday, twice as nice.
All My Love, Luv, Eternally,

WHAT I PROBABLY MEANT TO SAY: Living with you is like paradise. Hallmark doesn't have the guts to write it on a card but I do.

Again, a cliché such as "Living with you is like paradise" can be personalized and used thematically in any poem to your spouse or loved one.

December 10th, 2005

Dear M:

Just like in the movie,
If a billionaire asked me if I loved you,
I'd say, "She's my life and everything in it."

GOOD THINGS HAPPEN ON DECEMBER 10TH

(Listen to Bruce Springsteen's, "From Small Things")
The postcard came from Caesar,
Asking if we'd like to stay
In his hotel-casino –
In the quiet time 'fore Xmas day.
I smiled at my anniversary baby;
To please her, I'd go to any length.
Besides, good things happen
On December 10th.

It was after noon, one Wednesday;
I drove in town to pick up my love.
It wasn't exactly December 10th
But for the sake of this song it was close enough.
We headed to Atlantic City;
For her, I'd drive to any site.
'Cause good things happen
When she holds me tight.
But the network was calling.
It was CNN.
The gang at Newsmakers,
Wanted me to appear again!
So, she speed-dialed Comcast
And asked for the VP, name of Buck Dopp.
She told him, "Bucky Boy,
We can't let all this good luck stop."
I smiled at my anniversary baby;
From her, I draw all my strength.
Besides, good things happen
On December 10th.
(guitar)
Well, we saw the marble at Caesars
And marveled at our suite.
I turned on the Jacuzzi
But she didn't have time to dip her feet.

She was busy making scrillions –
A string of luck in which nothing could intrude.
Then she took me to an Indian restaurant
Where a Spanish waiter served us Chinese food.
I smiled at my anniversary baby;
To please her, I'd go to any length.
Told ya, good things happen
On December 10th.
All My Love, Forever, Baby, D!

WHAT I PROBABLY MEANT TO SAY: I'll do anything to please you. That's a popular phrase in any relationship. Go with that line anytime. In this poem, I also refer to George Thorogood's song, "It Wasn't Me." George met "A German girl in England who was goin' to school in France" while we met a Spanish waiter in an Indian restaurant who served us Chinese food. Hey, you don't have to be as smooth as the songwriters you are humming along with. You are expressing thoughts specifically tailored to your loved one so don't worry about being smooth or slick, just be loving.

Buck Dopp was a producer at Comcast in Philadelphia who liked my 2004 book, "A Writer's First Aid Kit," and put me on TV to help promote it. I had my episode of "Comcast Newsmakers" transferred to my phone; in case anyone asks to see it. I'm guessing the next person who asks to see it will be the archeologist or the anthropologist who fishes it out of the flooded Delaware river basin near my apartment in 600 years and gets it restarted. How do I know the Delaware river will be flooded in 600 years? I'm betting that the climate changes we're seeing now (melting icebergs in the Arctic, etc.) will someday cause rivers to flood the land. The Delaware will expand so much that it will have a new name: the Delaware/Ohio river, nicknamed the D&O. And if climate change is worse than expected, in 600 years the river may taste a little salty. Try to adapt. If you don't, the insects win.

Archeology is the study of old things. Anthropology is the study of humans. (Author's note: middle aged people, baby boomers like me, should learn new things to keep their minds sharp.) I wonder if the archeologist or the anthropologist who finds or fishes out my phone in 600 years will really

189

be interested in me or my old photos or my "Comcast Newsmakers" video … or if they'll simply want to grind my bones into "Soylent Green" to feed the mutants. Food may be a little scarce. Try to adapt and be like the man in the old sci-fi movie who said, "That's good-eatin' rat." If you don't, and you starve to death, the insects win.

December 10th is again mentioned prominently in this anniversary-themed poem below.

December 10th, 2004
DECEMBER THE TEN
(Listen to Bob Dylan's, "The Man In The Long, Black Coat")

Winter is whistling
It's gray flannel tune.
The sun's looking weary
A few hours past noon.
We're bracing for weather
Only wild geese can love,
I'm thanking our
Lucky stars up above.
It's the best day on Earth –
December the ten;
It's the most loving day
'Cause you married me then.
I remember you standing
At the top of the stairs.
While a kind man stopped Mom
From tripping into the chairs.
Your family, on camera,
They kvelled (spoke lovingly) at your
    name,
While my family got up there
And … they did the same.
It's the best day in my life –
December the ten;

It's the most blessed day
'Cause you married me then.
It seems so surreal that it's been
Only four years.
It's like hearing 'bout K-Mart
Merging with Sears.
But none of those companies
Ever had our spark.
It's the most sacred date
Whether it's light out or dark.
There's oil in the river,
It won't take long to freeze.
But look in through the golf course,
Past the ground hogs and trees.
We're here in our love nest,
In great teamwork and cheer.
As our love for one another
Grows stronger each year.
It's the best day on Earth –
December the ten;
It's the most loving day
'Cause you married me then.
All My Love and (real) Tears of Joy,
D

WHAT I PROBABLY MEANT TO SAY: As far as I'm concerned, our anniversary, December 10th, is the best day on Earth! I mean, you can't beat that for drama. I was happy in February, 2018, when the Philadelphia Eagles finally won the Super Bowl but the best day on Earth was December 10th, 2000.

Sports fans: write your loved one a poem comparing your anniversary to the day his or her favorite team won the championship.
That will work every time; college or pro.

I was intrigued about K-Mart merging with Sears at that time. Not sure why.

The following dramatic poem has four acts. Poems like these can basically cover your presents for birthday, anniversary, Valentine's Day and Mother's/Father's Day. It's a grand slam that saves you $5,000; more or less, depending on your budget. These poems are about everyday events and the love that inhabits them.

March 3rd, 2006
PART ONE
COME ON, LET'S DANCE
(Listen to Al Stewart's, "Bedsitter Images")

The ground hog stretched his legs
  today
As squirrels went running past his way.
The geese drink from the putting
  greens;
Are they as clueless as they seem?
The river's colder than the air;
Is that the Edmund Fitzgerald there?
I'm so happy that today's March 3;
I jump around on this old balcony.

Come on, let's dance,
Take a chance
On a birthday night romance.
It's a stance that I take
When there's fire in my pants.
There's a bird flying North.
What's he got beneath his wing?

It's those March birthday messages
That welcome in the Spring.

PART TWO
COME DRIVE WITH ME
(Listen to Frank Sinatra's, "Come Fly With Me")

Marcia tries to fit in with some weird women but she's not quite weird enough for this carnival.

Come drive with me;
We'll roll down to the zoo.
In the monkey cage, we'll get on stage,
Eat a banana muffin for two.
Come on, drive with me, I'll go ape over
    you.
Once I get you in the car
Anywhere near a Wal-Mart
And get a cart
You'll know your part.
Once I get you in the car
Anywhere near Franklin Mills
You'll get some thrills
When you enter Johnny Rockets'
And say, "Keep 'em comin'!"
Well, March is here; your birthday wel-
    comes Spring.
Soon we'll be back home
Where our ring-a-phone
Sings the song from, "Twilight Zone."
It's an ideal day to celebrate this thing;
This thing called love – the love, the love –
That we share all year round!

PART THREE
I'VE GOT YOU BACK IN MY BIN
(Listen to Frank Sinatra's, "I've Got You Under My Skin")

I've got you back in my bin.
I've got you back in my middle drawer.
But how can you be there so clean
When I wore you the day before?
I've got you back in my bin.
I don't know where to begin.
I should start here by stating that I don't have
Your kind of discipline.
I just wear whatever I can find as long as it goes
With my moccasins.
I've got you back in my bin.

I don't take the tact I'll see you soon on my rack
If, in fact, I ever see you at all.
When I take off a shirt that's this dirty and stained
I just figure I'll see it next summer or fall.
Oh, you know, some clothes, are gettin' thin.
They're washed with authority,
Like clean is the priority.
And when they are pressed, I must now confess,
I get a rush of adrenaline.
'Cause I've got you back in my bin.
Well I don't have the proof but it could be the truth
That a genie works in this place
And she makes all the dirty stuff clean as a garment can be
And the pillowcase smooth on my face.
Oh, the dryer's rinsed and goin' to spin.
This load is just two hours old!
And now we've got towels to fold.
And with each towel I hold, I see your heart of gold,
And smile back with a fluff-and-stuff grin.
I'm gonna fold now, using my chin.

PART FOUR
IT'S MARCH THE THIRD

(Listen to Frank Sinatra's, "Fly Me To The Moon")

I wanna take you to the shore
And let you splash with all the clams.
Jet you off to Vegas-town
To see Mr. Hoover's dams.
It's March the third.
And my birthday gal
Is the greatest love;
The greatest pal. Yeah.
Join me as we walk
Along the corridors of time.
Some of them are level, dear,
While others, we must climb.
It's March the third.

And my birthday gal
Is the greatest love;
The greatest pal. Yeah.
I wanna thank you every night
I wanna tell you every day;
You're the one who gives me joy
And light, to find my way.
It's March the third.
You, birthday gal,
Are the greatest love;
The greatest pal. Yeah.

WHAT I PROBABLY MEANT TO SAY: Your birthday welcomes Spring. You've got a heart of gold. You're a great laundress. We're going to have ups and downs but we're such great friends that we can weather any storm.

Ten years later, in 2016, when Marcia was diagnosed with uterine cancer, we were in the storm's path. We got through it with help from God or God knows and He's not saying. (See the poem on page 83, "One More Thing I Have To Do.") Our family experienced a life-or-death situation that revealed our devotion to each other. When doctors gave my wife their diagnosis, we both started screaming and I swear I almost dove into a trashcan in the hospital's outdoor garden patio. The doctor, Elizabeth Burton at Abington Hospital near Philadelphia, asked if we needed time to calm down. She'd return in an hour. But there was no need for that. It wasn't like I was going to feel better about this in an hour. A few days later, Dr. Burton operated and saved Marcia.

How did we cope with the days of uncertainty; days when we didn't know if she was going to survive? I talked to my Mom every night and heard my Dad's voice in my head – "Stay positive." So, we did. We watched funny movies in the hospital room, like "Austin Powers" and "Dumb & Dumber." I hope the writers of those movies know that they are cheering up people in hospitals, like my Levity poem cheered up a patient 40 years ago. It's a true blessing to help the sick feel better by creating laughter and positive vibes. Remember that when you write your own get-well cards.

"Remember!" (It's what Spock told Dr. McCoy when he gave him a mind meld.)

Marcia told me she was kept alive by her desire to save me from a lonely life. I think that's more touching than anything I've ever written to her.

March 3rd, 2007

MISSY SUNSHINE

(Listen to Supertramp's, "Easy Does It" & "Sister Moonshine")

We're going to AC,
My birthday bride and me.
It's a March 3rd ritual.
It's a love affair that's mutual.
Now I can only guess
Which show we're seeing next.
It doesn't matter if it's "Buy" or "Rent."
All that matters is the sentiment.
And if you just wanna know,
Why I'm so psyched to see a show,
It's 'cause my love for you will
Take me anywhere.
So, if you wanna see a show,
I'll be telling you, "Come on, let's go."
No matter what, I'll say, "What a pretty,
     what a pretty, what a real, nice
     pear."
(Beat picks up)
A show about the weather?
Or about CSI-LV?
Will I get hit with another feather
Or with reality TV?
Oh, I wonder what we'll see.
Something altogether wholesome …
Or just corny?
Do you wanna see a concert?
Or a show with SPX?

Forever! D!

Will you wanna go for dinner
Afterwards, or go have sex?
Will I need an Imitrex?
I don't care as long as we're together
     …
I say, Hey, Missy Moo-shine,
You're synonymous with the sun.
I say, Hey, Missy Moo-shine,
I put you above everyone.
Who do we tip
For a seat near an aisle?
We gotta watch out for
Feathers in the eye.
If you want a comedy,
We can be our own troupe.
We'll paint ourselves a color
And become our own darn group!
If we see a circus,
Let it be the Circ de Hoop-Dee-Hoop.
If we see golden oldies,
Let it be the Whoop-Dee-Whoop-Dee
     Whoop.
What I'm trying here to say:
You bring joy to me each day.
I say, Hey, Missy Moo-shine,
You're synonymous with the sun.
I say, Hey, Missy Moo-shine,
I put you above everyone.
All My Love, My Darling Missy Moo,

WHAT I PROBABLY MEANT TO SAY: "You bring joy to me each day" is pretty clear.

Remember to weave pet names into your poems to loved ones. (If you skipped the first half of this book, my pet name for Marcia is "Missy-Moo.") You can choose a pet name for your soul mate that is easy to rhyme; names like dear, honey, cheeks and Flo. Cheeks rhymes with geeks, freaks, reeks, weeks … sneaks; the list goes on. (If you skipped the first half of this book, you missed mention of a rhyming dictionary to help you rhyme lines. It's on the Internet, and that's a good thing because I may have the only surviving paperback copy from 1985.)

The pear is a reference to "The Godfather" movie, when the struggling immigrant (Don Corleone) brings only a pear home for dinner yet his wife becomes very excited and runs to wash it and slice it. "What a nice pear!" she gushes and Don Corleone (played by Robert DeNiro) smiles to himself, knowing how lucky he is to have been blessed with an unspoiled wife.

In the Showtime series, "Billions," one of the characters is interested in dating a different kind of woman, one who orders $10,000 worth of caviar, as an appetizer! In your poems, tell your spouse that you appreciate how she or he is the unspoiled type who gushes about a simple pear for dinner.

This isn't the first time I used the pear story from "The Godfather" to tell Marcia that she's charmingly unspoiled. I mention the pear earlier, in my "Happily Wed" poem. What this means is that I was deeply moved by the pear-for-dinner scene in "The Godfather" and how Marcia reminded me of Don Corleone's wife.

I was also eating a pear in the waiting room of Abington Hospital when doctors told me they were pleasantly surprised with Marcia's surgery and that the cancer was contained and she would be all right. To this day, I keep the half-eaten pear wrapped in our freezer. And whenever I see a pear, I get emotional. I'm sure you understand.

Buy wait! One old guy at my pool didn't understand and actually mocked me for saving that pear I was eating in the hospital's waiting room when they told me my wife would survive. This guy was snickering about my attachment to the pear.

My reaction? The same as it was in the earlier poem, "Brush Me Off?"

> You know, I got used to the brush-offs.
> Some I'm proud of when I consider the source.

I was going for the "judge me by my enemies" feeling but then I thought no, that would be paying too much rent to the true idiots of the world. The better approach to life would be "judge me by my close friends."

Yes, I'm holding onto our lucky pear. Some couples freeze their eggs and sperm; we froze our lucky pear. When I see it in our freezer, it makes me smile more than any refrigerator magnet ever could.

In the next poem, "My Special Door," I tell Marcia that if I had to choose between fame and fortune or her love, I'd pick her.

December 10th, 2006
MY SPECIAL DOOR

(Listen to The Who's, "Real Good Lookin' Boy")
When I arrived in Southern California
And saw that golden corridor,
Right then I swore,
"I'm gonna go right through that door."
I saw myself as a special invitee
To all those Golden Globe Awards.
And thought, "Hey,
I'd love to go right through that door."
I reached out for those golden handles
And I pulled with all my strength and gambled
On finding success and maybe a chocolate box.
But instead I saw this man
Who said, "Try to understand this, if you can.
I'm your Kabala guide, son, hold onto your socks.
That is not your special door."
The guide explained, "This door's all wrong for you.
There's no lovin' for you here.
It's just a façade built by the shallow-squad.
You feel that draft?
That'll be you gettin' the shaft
From Mr. and Mrs. Insincere.
It only looks like a special door."
Guide Men said,
As he stood in the light,
"You'll know it, son,
When you find the door that's right."
Now I'm here with you, my love, on the jet plane
Holdin' hands on our way back home from Key West.
And I feel my soul and my spirit soar.
And my Kabala guide, I see him floating;
Eating a kosher meal way over there in first class,
And he tells me, "Marcia is what you were waiting for."

The guide gave me an invite
To something so pure and sweet.
He showed me your face
And he let me feel your never-ending heat.
God helped me choose the world's most blessed door.
All My Love Forever! D

WHAT I PROBABLY MEANT TO SAY: It's the same theme (love over material success) that I conveyed in my 46th birthday poem to myself in 2001. (See it on page 131; it's imaginatively called "46.")

I remember writing this poem on the plane ride back from Key West, Florida. The raw emotion pumped tears out of my eyes, down my face, onto my shirt and pants. (Crying while writing a poem is a great thing. It's a sign of purity and honesty.) Marcia, however, kept interrupting me to ask if I needed a bottle of water or a mint or a fucking sweater and I finally said through grinding teeth, "No! I'm writing you a love poem! Stop bugging me! Don't you see tears streaming down my face?"

She handed me a tissue.

December 10th, 2007
PLAYA TOWN

(Listen to Bruce Springsteen's, "Lucky Town.")
There's an iguana on our bed, looks like an old praline
And we're tellin' him exactly where to find some sardines.
"Will the owner of the Jaguar kindly move his skins?"
Keep walking past the mushroom farm - the raft ride begins.
We're going down to Playa Town.
Going down to Playa Town.
We're gonna do it Mayan-style
Down in Playa Town.
We're gonna go muy loco with some fine cuisine.
Don't need Haggan Diaz azucar or Starbucko's caffeine.
We know to say "Cantina" por for vor, not "Canteen."

We eat 8 meals a day but no eating in-between.
We're going down to Playa Town.
Down to Playa Town.
It couldn't be a more serene style
Here in Playa Town.
Water's got something in it and it's not fluorine.
Is that Elvis speaking Dutch over there on the mezzanine?
We drank everything they offered us but the Grenadine.
Only 79 degrees? Now, lady, that's obscene.
We met a Fort Knox colonel and a brave marine.
Wondering why we've traded gold for a little gasoline.
At 9 am, we'll all reconvene
On a beach bed looking out over the tequila scene.
We're going down to Playa Town.
Down to Playa Town.
I'll go to any earthly town
As long as I'm with you.
You bring out the best in me because you are the best.
All My Love on our 7th anniversary and forever! D

WHAT I PROBABLY MEANT TO SAY: Anywhere we go is fine, as long as we're together. This was written during our first vacation outside of the U.S. There was so much to write about. It was when I first became aware of the fact that whacky stuff happens on vacation. For example: I got up from my beach bed to swim in the ocean and when I returned, I found an iguana in bed with my wife! He was a celebrity iguana, posing for pictures with tourists for $20.

"Find your own girl!" I shouted, before I even dried off.

The iguana, who was already drier than dried off, looked me right in the eye, as if to say, "Hey, you got up to swim in the ocean, pal. The bed was wide open."

I respected him for that. Most celebrities wouldn't do that. They believe that because they're famous, they can just grab 'em by the tail.

Marcia and I share a moment with a very photogenic yet brazen iguana. I finally had to yell at him, "Find your own girl!"

The most honest line in this poem is: "We eat 8 meals a day but no eating in-between." Now who can't relate to that?

March 3rd, 2008
TAKE ME TO THE SCI-FI CHANNEL
(Listen to Duncan Browne's, "Wild Places.")

Dear M:
My birthday beauty, settled in her easy chair.
But she was focused, I knew it by her "Geez-Peas" stare.
She said, "These creepy movies don't make sense to me, I swear!"
I'd change the channel but a bug screamed, "Don't you dare!"
Out in the back, Comcast just cut Hot Wire's cord.
I'm on demand with them but truth be told I'm not on board.
And she went "Shush!" to me and then she checked cable guides:
"Please close the shades, 'The Blob' is on, and I don't wanna go outside."
And oh, baby, take me to the Sci-Fi channel,
I'll watch you squirm when ol' Godzilla drools.
If you want an American werewolf, I'll be unshaved in flannel;
Just give me a sec while I go check exacta pools.
The planes are landing or are they UFOs?

200

The boats outside are cruise ships, or are they spying for the Moon Group?
These answers – so complex that no one knows,
At least not till next week's episode debuts over the You Tube.
And she sighs, "Can I watch some stuff on DVR?
I taped old 'Twilight Zones' & reruns of 'My Mum, The Car.'
There's a time traveling film aboard the USS Nimitz
And brain transplanting on 'The Outer Limits.'"
And oh, baby, take me to the Sci-Fi channel,
I'll watch you squirm when ol' Godzilla drools.
If you want an American werewolf, I'll be unshaved in flannel;
Just give me a sec while I go check trifecta pools.
I hear her snoring, now she's the one who's droolin',
Sleeping in the big chair, her mouth wide open.
I put her breathe-right on and make sure the humidifier's coolin'
Back here in the bedroom, where I take her clothes off.
And I say, "Honey, show me that extended reach.
It's not a monster flick, it reminds me more of 'Bikini Beach!'"
And she says, "Wait a minute, is this 'Loch Ness Lagoon'?
Or do you want a preview of what surely will be coming soon!"
And oh, baby, take me to the Sci-Fi channel,
I'll watch you squirm when ol' Godzilla drools.
If you want an American werewolf, I'll be unshaved in flannel;
Just give me a sec while I go check superfecta pools.
One more time.
Oh, baby, take me to the Sci-Fi channel.
When I hold you in my arms, babe, you always make me drool.
All My Love. I hope this is the best birthday ever! D

WHAT I PROBABLY MEANT TO SAY: You know you're comfortable with your wife when you mention how she snores and drools. I poke fun at her taste in Sci-Fi movies and also flatter her with, "Didn't I see you in that movie, what's was it called, 'Bikini Beach?'" Good-natured kidding and over-the-top flattery are both effective tactics.

December 10th, 2008

Mrs. R

(Listen to Bob Dylan's, "Ballad Of A Thin Man")

Dear M:
We sit every morning
By the sand and the sea.
28 Celsius,
That's the way it should be.
Sitting on a beach bed
Is our main activity
Unless you count sauntering up to the
    bar.
And nothing is really happening here
But that's fine with you and me.
Ain't it, Mrs. R?
They're biking through Playa
With helmets and gears.
While our crowd throws mints
Past their mouths and their ears.
Who doesn't have 55
Mixed drinks while they're here?
One gets the feeling they won't be
    biking that far.
And nothing is really happening here
But that's fine with you and me
Ain't it, Mrs. R?
Joe's our protégé from Philly
Who has 55 drinks
And time travels in the bar stool
When he pauses or blinks.
I'm his mentor and I don't
Even know what he thinks
But he's been a fun guy to mentor so
    far.
And nothing is really happening here
But that's fine with you and me
Ain't it, Mrs. R?

Might wanna parasail
Or jet ski with you.
On second thought,
Let's try something safer to do.
Besides, as New Yorkers would say:
Whom would we sue?
And why would they think us bour-
    geois?
And nothing is really happening here
But that's fine with you and me
Ain't it, Mrs. R?
Take a peek at Cozumel;
Wonder what's there.
Looks so intriguing;
Wonder what they wear.
I'm thinking madras shirts
Are the rage everywhere
And the official uniform in the next
    coup d'état.
And nothing is really happening here
But that's fine with you and me
Ain't it, Mrs. R?
We saw all the photos of
The Mayan caves
Why have cave shit in our hair
For 12 or 14 days?
I have no love
For giant wasps, anyways.
But my love for you grows from here
    to Zanzibar.
And that's what's really happening
    here,
Superfine with you and me,
Ain't it, Mrs. R?
All My Love On Our Anniversary &
    Every Day, D

WHAT I PROBABLY MEANT TO SAY: The line about Zanzibar sums it up. I'm also telling Marcia that we were lazy and drunk for a week straight but it was a fantastic anniversary trip.

I really did bump my head in a silver mine cave and had cave shit in my hair for more than a week. The Mayans were short people, based on the way my scalp looked.

I say "12 or 14 days" because our Dutch friends loathed the number 13. And then their takeoff time from Cancun to Amsterdam was changed to 1:13 AM. They wouldn't leave. They just stayed in the lobby, drinking.

I also use some French words, which don't come naturally to me. (There's a possibility that I misuse French words in my poems and cards all the time.) But here I use bourgeois because I'm trying to say that it's bourgeois to think about suing people before you even take off on a balloon ride, like some New Yorkers did.

And then I used another French phrase, coup d'état. I used two French words in one poem. I had only done that once before, using ménage a trios and chaperone in a poem to an ex-girlfriend in Playa del Rey, California in 1981:

> She's kind of like the new year, never early, often late.
> If you want to spend time with her, you'll learn to love to wait.
> Confusion if her partner, so you'll never be alone.
> A ménage a trios when I'm around to act as chaperone.

It isn't what you expected, is it? You thought I was referring to an actual ménage a trois since it was the 1980s and it was set in an L.A. beach town. Nope. It was just me, her, and her confusion. Chaperone counts as a French word, too. Try to toss in a French word or expression once in a while. It's the language of love, so get on the bandwagon.

March 3rd, 2009

I LOVE YOU IN AN "I LOVE THE EARTH" WAY

(Listen to Don McLean's, "Crossroads")
There's something that I want to say. for your birthday.
You are #1. I love you in an "I love the Earth" way.
But you're much earthier than any planet;
So down-to-earth, like "Life on Mars."
And you're much lovelier than the sunrise
And much more brilliant than all the stars … up above.
You know, you multi-task so well.
You're kind of like a whirling dervish
You have a strong belief in self;
It's oh so Fran, Lilly and Uncle Irv-ish.
I see how other husbands live,
Both in real life and on the telly.
The home is cold, there is no joy
And no one tickles anyone's belly.
So, thank you for your joy and love;
For always lending me your hand
And making me the happiest
And luckiest kind of man.
All My Love, Always, D

WHAT I PROBABLY MEANT TO SAY: You bring me joy.

December 10th, 2009

WAVING ON THE BEACH

(Listen to Kingfish's, "Big Iron")
Dear M:
It was gettin' kinda windy in the middle of the dune.
The clock above read 6 am, then an hour later, noon.
I had rum right after breakfast mixed with pineapple and peach.
And I was smiling at the woman who was waving on the beach.
Waving on the beach.
I was 37 miles from the second oldest shul.
And had 37 minutes to get grades in to the school.
I had no more obligations, no more classes left to teach,
Only coaching from the woman who was waving on the beach.
Waving on the beach.
There were no rules to follow – that was the one and only rule.
As the band played Dire Straits and Freddy twisted by the pool.
Then we slipped into the pool bar, if there's etiquette, it's breached;

I saw her hands and realized that she held a drink in each.
Held a drink in each.
We taped a late day session in a bubbly whirlpool.
While the aloe man along the beach sang lovely cheers of Yule.
And that sound of someone shouting? It was more of a beseech.
Coming from the woman who was waving on the beach.
Waving on the beach.
I was hoping for a boat pull, maybe that wouldn't overreach.
Found a raft and sailed but soon my ride came halting to a screech
By the sound of someone shouting; she was practicing free speech.
And I was smiling at the woman who was waving on the beach.
Waving on the beach.
The raft ride was relaxing for every muscle and molecule.
I admit I touched the rope way out but how far past was miniscule.
Then I heard my name called out, your voice, it had that special reach.
And I was smiling at you baby, as you waved there on the beach.
Waved there on the beach.

The Caribbean Sea looks calm enough but Marcia
doesn't want me going in if the waves are more
than one foot high.

You were watching me so closely, like I was your prize, couldn't get away.
And I saw you waving lovingly and my heart felt the same way.
I paddled back to tell you you're the one I'm thinking of
Kinda like I'm careful about how I treat your love.
And my love is you.
These past 9 years were rough on some; not us, we cruised right through.
Because we put the other first in everything we do.
When we say our love is everything, we practice what we preach –
And that's what made me smile at you waving on the beach.
Waving on the beach.
All My Love On Our Anniversary And Forever and Ever! D

THEME ALERT! The theme of "We put the other first in everything we do" reappears in this love poem. Therefore, as a person who has saved over a half-million dollars by writing poems to loved ones, I suggest you use this theme abundantly.

WHAT I PROBABLY MEANT TO SAY: This vacation scene in Aruba was real. I went out a little too far on a raft and Marcia started screaming like the hotel was on fire. She feared a jet skier or shark or even a shark on a jet ski would run right over me. I paddled to shore to learn that my meditative raft ride was interrupted because I drifted one inch over the rope.

"That was my doctor's prescription bungalow I was riding out there," I told her.

She didn't remember the old Who song; she just wanted to keep me safe. My poem to her was really about her being protective of me.

When I say:

Kinda like I'm careful about how I treat your love.
And my love is you.

I'm referring to my 1994 poem about being "Careful How You Treat My Love." (It appears earlier in this book, on page 174.) So, you can use this time-traveling trick yourself. Write a poem about the poem you wrote 15 years ago.

In my opinion, writing poems to loved ones eliminates the need for a psychiatrist. You can be your own psychiatrist and grow as a person, while doting on loved ones and making them happy. Plus, you save money in the process.

March 3rd, 2010

JUST LIKE SPRINGTIME

(Listen to Meat Loaf's, "I'm Gonna Love Her For Both Of Us")
Dear M:
Is that the sun rising over the snow?
Or one of those mirages that the Lenapes would see every year.
Is that a pleasure jet or UFO?
Or a flying Toyota, I hope the pilot can steer.
I love you, baby, more than it shows and more every year
And much more than the law here allows.
More than Comcast needs a new image and
More than that San Simeon bull ... wanted one of those cows.
And on your birthday, it's time to review
What I've done and what I will do for you.
I handed over my heart
And now I give you my word
That I will love you after cows come home.
It's just like Springtime on March the third.
It's the most amazing day there ever, ever could be
It's just like Springtime on March the third.
God gave you life and you've made it all the more worth living for me.
Ain't it grand thinking 'bout the future, me and you, sexpot.
Driving through North America in a mobile home – stop in Vegas; why not?
Or we could head way down south near the Gulfstream Park in Hallandale.
Where we'd bump into friends during lulls in hurricanes and hail.
It's the most amazing day there ever could be
It's just like Springtime on March the third.
I give you my heart and my word,
It's just like Springtime on March the third.
(bridge) I can see us walking near the surf, on your birthday
Splashing around in the warmth of the semi-tropical sun.
And we're laughing and making plans for some kind of luau that evening.
I want to take you to places that make you smile
When you get there and when you stay there.
Baby, baby, I'm taking you there ...
Or maybe you'll take me.
All My Love Forever, D

WHAT I PROBABLY MEANT TO SAY: I'm predicting that we'll retire near Miami, Florida, and it's looking prophetic right about now. I'm also suggesting an RV trip. Not sure why.

I start off by mentioning the Lenape Indians, who lived on the land near Philadelphia where we live now. We're right on their burial grounds near the Delaware river. They could've shot the movie "Poltergeist" here. I refer to Native Americans in several poems, because deep down I'm not comfortable with the way we acquired land from them. No one gets out-negotiated that badly, all the time.

The Lenapes named the creek about 20 miles from where I live "Cranberry Place." That's the creek I jumped into as a teenager in the summer of 1972, when my Grand pop Lou died and I had so many feelings to express, and wrote one of my first poems. I'm still hoping to find the original version of that poem about Grand pop Lou. It may be in our apartment, in a box of memories, being pointed to frantically by friendly Lenape ghosts, if they can get to the third floor of our building. I'm not sure if ghosts can rise 30 feet off the ground, and I should know because I wrote a book called "Life After Death" that was never published. Not enough research, I guess.

Bob Marley's ghost, if there was one, would perform in Trench Town, Jamaica. We went to Jamaica to celebrate our 11th wedding anniversary so there was a 100% chance I'd set my lyrics to a Marley melody.

December 10th, 2011
CLIMBIN' THE ROCK SLIDE
(Listen to Bob Marley's, "Buffalo Soldier")

Dear M:
Oy oy oy, Naked as can be
Oy oy oy, On the balcony
Climbin' the rock slide,
Hope I got my shoes tied.
As the water rushes down the rocks.
I wish I'd brought some extra socks.
I'm thinking, "Yah, be clean, Mon.
That woman means everything."
Sure, we're American.
Now we act Jamaican, mon.
So glad I find her.
Always right behind her.

Climbin' the rock slide
Hope I got my shoes tied.
Climbin' the rock slide
I and my lovely bride.
As the water rushes down in sheets,
I wish I'd brought a pair of cleats.
I'm thinking, "Yah, be clean, Mon.
That woman means everything."
We're just climbin' the rock slide,
Hope we got our shoes tied.
Climbin' the rock slide,
I and my lovely bride.
All My Love Forever, D

We had just slid down a natural water slide at Dunn's River Falls near Ocho Rios, Jamaica, which was refreshing and exhilarating. This picture received many "likes" on Facebook, raising both of our dopamine levels.

WHAT I PROBABLY MEANT TO SAY: You mean everything to me.

This poem was written about a refreshing walk up Dunn's River Falls in Jamaica. Before we climbed on the rocks by the waterfall, I asked the guide if I should be in front of my wife, so I could pull her up, or stand behind her, so I could catch her if she slipped.

He answered right away: "Behind her. Always behind."

I didn't mean it that way. He didn't care. After our climb up the falls, a man with an old donkey tried to sell me a donkey ride and an earring. (Those two things don't usually go together.) I didn't accept either offer; I was wondering why the 100-year-old donkey was still working, still giving rides to kids. Hell, that donkey had gone blind 20 years before those kids were born. And there was also a personal connection; my friend Anthony (previously mentioned in my "Kentucky Mark" poem) told me to send his regards to the man who worked with the old donkey. So, I was supposed to exchange pleasantries with the sadistic earring salesman who was, as a side job, working the aged donkey like a rented mule. (Where's the oversight, Jamaica?) I didn't say a word to him because I knew the donkey, like the Lenapes, wasn't getting a fair deal.

I should write another children's book about saving endangered animals and here's the jawn (word): an old, blind donkey joins forces with the Lenape Indians to invent a word (jawn) and finally get a fair deal.

The word jawn, I'm told, is any noun. Some say this slang word for, really, any fucking noun in the English language originated in Philadelphia, PA and others say in Baltimore, MD. Using it in a sentence would look like this: "Pass me that jawn."

Do you know who else never gets a fair deal? Pandas! I saw pandas in the San Diego zoo one summer and those bears were badly overheated. They were passed out on tree branches, looking like overdone cookies. Also, I read about a zoo in China, where a fellow on his lunch (beer) break climbed over the fence and a panda bear bit him on the shoulder. Then the beer drinker bit the panda on his shoulder! It went back and forth, like in a "Three Stooges" movie. (In fact, the "Three Stooges" didn't get fair deals, either.) It was man against bear, standing nose to snout, one with beer muscles, the other with bear muscles, biting each other between their shoulder blades. It makes the scene from "The Revenant" seem tame.

To recap: my old professor, Jack Langguth, didn't get a fair deal when he was denied a Pulitzer Prize he deserved. The Lenapes didn't get a fair deal, nor did the pandas, nor did all "Three Stooges." Knowing Jack Langguth as I did, he'd probably be honored to be in such company.

In another poem about Jamaica, "Sweet 16" (see page 229), I recall our raft ride on the Martha Brae river, near the Dunn's River Falls. I advise you to write poems about things that excite you both. Marcia and I happen to like raft rides and water slides or anything around water, including running around on the beach, like a klutz.

December 10th, 2012
SHE'S GONNA BE ALL RIGHT
(Listen to Steve Forbert's, "Gotta Live Up To His Shoes")
Dear M:
Missy was a klutz, runnin' 'round on the beach.
She used to stumble in and out of the sea.
But lately she's been moving like she's in some kind of ballet
And she's a model of improved dexterity.
Missy walked into the ocean in Montego Bay,
All the band-aids on the island were on her toe.
But she was wearing beach shoes with, "No Problem" on the side
And that's made all the difference in the show.
So let her glide, let her glide real fast.
And let her slide, let her slide at last.
Walk some more
All over the ocean floor
'cause she's gonna be all right in those shoes.
I don't know when she picked up the pair.
It must have been early in the day.
Now all of a sudden, she's up to her hips
Outmaneuvering all sting rays.
So let her glide, let her glide real fast.
And let her slide, let her slide at last.
Walk some more
All over the ocean floor
'cause she's gonna be all right in those shoes.
Oh, she's so well-balanced
Among these folks, so well-heeled.
She's so down to earth,
Yet in the sea.
So let her glide, let her glide real fast.
And let her slide, let her slide at last.
Walk some more
All over the ocean floor
'cause she's gonna be all right in those shoes.
Now she moves so nice and gracefully along the coral reefs,
Exploring the sea at its edges
And then I saw her today with a camera in her hand,
Running with some peacocks and jumping over hedges.
So let her glide, let her glide real fast.
And let her slide, let her slide at last.
Walk some more
All over the ocean floor
'cause she's gonna be all right in those shoes.
All My Love & Respect Mon, Forever, D!

WHAT I PROBABLY MEANT TO SAY: You're down to Earth and your shoes look great. On this vacation, instead of running with the bulls, we jumped with the peacocks, over hedges. So that's a thing with us now. If you and your mate enjoy parasailing, for example, write a poem about the time you almost landed on the roof of the hotel or other hijinks that only the two of you can appreciate.

"Missy" is a shortened version of my pet name for her, "Missy Moo."

Below is another poem from the same (12th) anniversary trip to Jamaica. Writing two poems for the same anniversary is like giving your love a watch and a car.

December 10th, 2012
SWIMMIN' IN MONTEGO
(Listen to Steve Forbert's, "Goin' Down To Laurel")
Dear M:
Everybody there, at the salad bar,
They don't understand the salad's gone.
Why then am I here? I'm canvassing the line.
Waitin' for bananas due at dawn.
Glad to find some pork.
Eat it with my fork.
Glad to be back in Montego Town.
This sure is paradise, go in, the water's nice
But when you do, look twice and all around.
I'm swimmin' in Montego.
It's a dangerous, freakin' bay, mon.
But I'm not here lookin' for any pearl.
My dear wife, love of my life, don't want her to squish no fish,
So I'm in the water with sting rays, guardin' my girl.
It's another sunny day, feelin' in a Jamaican way,
Now we hear commotion from the shore.
What's happening with that man, sittin' on the lifeguard stand?
He's tellin' us to run in circles. Huh? What for?
And look at Alabama, couple feet away,
Snorkeling near what might just be a kite.
He really ought to bail, the kite, it's got a tail
And it's chasing him from here to the traffic light.

I'm swimmin' in Montego.
It's a dangerous, freakin' bay, mon.
But I'm not here lookin' for any pearl.
My dear wife, love of my life, don't want her to squish no fish,
So I'm in the water with sting rays, guardin' my girl.
Oh, what a Hobie sail. Maybe it's safer way out here.
Everybody knows but they won't tell me. Oh, I forgot …
Before vacation ends, I'll ask a lionfish
If he enjoys the food served here or not.
Please don't mention Sting.
Please don't talk of Rays.
Please don't mention hiding in the sand.
Before I even think about banana drinks
I've gotta get her safely to the land.
I'm swimmin' in Montego.
It's a dangerous, freakin' bay, mon.
But I'm not here lookin' for any pearl.
My dear wife, love of my life, don't want her to squish no fish,
So I'm in the water with sting rays, guardin' my girl.
All My Love & Respect Mon, Forever, D!

WHAT I PROBABLY MEANT TO SAY: I don't approve of the inherent risk involved when swimming with sting rays. We were just too close to them. And it was all our fault because this was their part of the bay, their domain for thousands of years until the hotel was built a few months earlier. It's another "Please be careful how you treat my love" poem. Montego is a dangerous, freakin' bay, mon. Go to Negril.

I wrote a poem about writing poems for loved ones. ("The Best Days Of My Life" appears below.) That's what's called art imitating art. It's like when I take a photo of you in front of the Wynnewood Walls near Miami, and then I give that photo to you as a birthday present. I theorized that writing these poems to loved ones was the best thing I had ever done and the process of writing them made me feel happier than anything else. (So, yes, I'm enjoying writing this book.)

Marcia posing at the Wynwood Walls near Miami.

March 3rd, 2013

THE BEST DAYS OF MY LIFE

(Listen to "Steve Forbert's Midsummer Night's Toast/Rainbow Dreams")

Dear M:

Here's to poems that I wrote at first romance.
"Halleluiah," then like a dream, our wedding dance.
Here's to poems written on Windsor's kitchen floor.
Careful how you treat my love as the draft came through the door.
Well I've been writing you poems since my first tooth.
It's the most loving way for me to express the truth.
And I'll tell you – the best days of my life
Are when I'm writing poems to you.
Here's to poems: Levity and lucky ducks,
Folks I met in NYC and other schmucks.
Here's to poems sayin' just relax, of course.
And wakin' up the raisins and a flying horse.
Well, I've been writing you poems since my first sneeze.
When I addressed the letter to Ms. Marcia Grees.
And I'll tell you – the best days of my life
Are when I'm writing poems to you.
Atlantic City on your birthday
Seems like we're always here, on vacation.
But to a location – you're a location!
It doesn't matter – my life is wherever you are.
Here's to poems that I wrote for B&B.
Until you got here, they were the ones who rescued me.
Here's to birthday wishes – all of 'em coming true.
It's funny how that works, my dear …
All your wishes are for me and all of mine are for you.
Well I've been writing you poems since my first air.
It's the most loving way to find you there.
And I'll tell you – the best days of my life
Are when I'm writing poems to you.
All My Love, D

DOUBLE THEME ALERT!

(1) We always put the other person first.
(2) The best days of my life are when I'm writing these poems to you.

My parents always put the other person first so theme #1 was passed down to me, like eye color. As for theme #2, the best days of my life are when I write these poems to my wife because when I write them, I take time to consciously feel the love we share. That's the key to writing poems to love ones. Take the time to feel the love. You probably take time out of your day to think about all the people who screwed you. (I haven't done that but I've seen it done.) Those thoughts create stress. Loving thoughts create more love. So, if it's between the flowers (loving thoughts) and the garbage (angry thoughts), where do you want to stand? It's like I told you earlier:

> The wisest all tell me I must take a side.
> In the flowers or garbage ... and I can't decide.
> Of course, relax.

WHAT I PROBABLY MEANT TO SAY: The poem describes how my poems to my wife are really checkpoints on the map of our love and marriage.

Also, in "The Best Days Of My Life," I rhymed ducks with schmucks:

> Here's to poems: Levity and lucky ducks,
> Folks I met in NYC and other schmucks.

By "other schmucks," I meant the folks I met in L.A.

I had rhymed Mercedes Benz with amends (so did Janis Joplin) but never rhymed ducks with schmucks. You can only do that once.

I'm comparing happy poems (Levity and the r ain-loving ducks) with unsettling stories set in NYC. (See "One More Stop" on page 26.) What was so dreadful about the town? Well, on one occasion, I gave my business card to an agent at a convention in NYC and told her I had a book published ("A Writer's First Aid Kit") and she yelled sarcastically and dismissively, "Congratulations" and threw the business card into my face, frisbee-style and with malice, just like "Odd-job" in Ian Fleming's "Goldfinger."

Marcia Grees was my wife's maiden name. She was Miss Grees and everyone called her that when she vacationed on a Greek cruise ship 15 years before we met.

"Miss Greece is on the ship!"

"Miss Greece is single. No chaperone!"

They thought she was a "Miss World" beauty pageant contestant. That was jumping to conclusions. Heck, the former Miss Grees doesn't even like olives. That's like someone with the last name of Maine not liking lobster.

When I say "But to a location — you're a location!" it's similar to the old joke I saw on a Rush music video: "To me, you're a genius. To a genius, you're no genius."

To me, she's a beauty pageant winner. To a beauty pageant winner, she's no beauty pageant winner.

But she knows I love her completely. She's read my poems.

December 10th, 2013
JUST LOOK AT HER SMILE

(Listen to Airborne Toxic Event's, "Sometime Around Midnight")
Dear M:
And the day begins at 10:30,
When we can all get our coffee, food, sugar and liquor fix.
And you know the room will still be dirty
'Cause the maids don't start cleaning any of the rooms until 6.
That's when I see her in her kimono dancing on the sands,
In a palm tree bikini with a mimosa and a noodle in her hands.
And I see that she's dancing with Mo-Mo,
The Jamaican girl in short-shorts,
These girls are really putting on a show.
And I hear the steel band drumming to the song "Matilda."
It's one of the few Jamaican songs that I know.
And we take out our cameras
And capture the beach scene on video.
While overhead, the pelican watches,
As she spreads out her wings like two sails and the blue heron waves.
And my heart and my soul start to soar as she smiles and shakes.
I even love a sun-tan line on her nose that her breathe-right makes.
And she leaves as the beach crowd applauds her.
She takes her noodle and mimosa,
Points to me and tells Mo-Mo, "Dance with him."
And it's so early and I'm so altered,
I don't know how I'll keep my wits.
And now Mo-Mo starts thrusting,
I thrust back and YouTube's got 2 million hits.

Then my love walks to the beach chair
And I follow her there as coconuts fall off the trees.
And she smiles and asks, "Would you like to play bocce with me?"
Just look at her smile. Just look at her smile.
Just look at her smile. Just look at her smile.
Just look at her smile.
You know that I'll be on her team.
Forever.
All My Love, D

WHAT I PROBABLY MEANT TO SAY: Dancing with the 18-year-old sports girl in tight shorts, Mo-Mo, was terrifying because it was early and I was altered and I can't fucking dance. And then Mo-Mo started thrusting, and I started thrusting back (still half-asleep) and, with the Euro gang recording the fun, YouTube would soon get two million hits (still less than the raccoon who climbed up 16 stories). The main point was the line I repeated five times: "Just look at her smile." (The repeated line by Airborne Toxic Event is "You Just Have To See Her.") Her smile is a major part of her charm and I tell her that in these love poems.

She's also a great teammate. That's why I'll always be on her team.

March 3rd, 2014
THE LADY IS FOR REAL
(Listen to "The Lady is a Tramp" by Sammy Davis, Jr.)
Dear M:
I've socialized in Malibu with beautiful jet-setters.
Been scrutinized in Hollywood by dutiful go-getters.
So I went looking for that lover with the touch of ingénue;
A girl who's like the greatest pal and perfect soul mate, too.
But how would I find the true love of my life?
I went to Margate in '91 to find me a wife.
She gets excited, boy can she talk.
Shows off her wingspan and soars like a hawk.
If they don't throw in a sunroof, she tells the salesman she'll walk.
That's why the lady is for real.
Doesn't need the Revel, the Claridge is fine.
Feeds the meter for me, that's a really good sign.
Just a little impressed that Lewis Jaffe is a friend of mine.
That's why the lady is for real.
She's quite a Pisces,

Swimming both ways, a fish
That's so delish.
Headstrong – not wrong!
Loves the Travel Channel and she loves a great deal.
That's why the lady is for real.
(Ladies & Gentlemen, Marcia, Emma & Michael!) Yeah!
Hates losing luggage,
Asks if they make it in teal.
That's why my lady is for real.
She's got that co-co-
Nut kimono untied.
I'm lookin' inside.
She's built – full tilt.
Loves Saratoga,
Only adds to her appeal.
That's why my lady is for real.
Happy Birthday
All My Love Forever, D

WHAT I PROBABLY MEANT TO SAY: You're a woman of high character.

When we first met, Marcia would take the elevator down to Arch Street in center city Philadelphia and feed my parking meter while I slept. That was a really good sign and made a great early impression.

"Marcia, Emma & Michael!" refers to a Jamaican vacation where Marcia and her British girlfriend, Emma, danced with a Michael Jackson imitator on stage. Emma's husband told me minutes earlier that Emma would never get up on stage in front of strangers. I knew that was about to change. A minute later, we saw Emma on stage, dancing with Marcia and a Jamaican Michael Jackson. Marcia had a loosening-up effect on Emma (and so did alcohol). I admire that quality and let Marcia know about it in this poem.

"She's got that co-co-nut kimono untied. I'm lookin' inside" means she turns me on. This is a good thing to say to your spouse at any age. It's also the second time in a row I rave about how good she looks in a kimono. We were both over 60 so it's never too late to say you're attracted to your honey.

I use a French word, ingénue, like I did in "The Road" (see it on page 107) to indicate I was looking for a happy-go-lucky, fresh and innocent gal. I must love Marcia's ingénue (and ingenuity) because I mention it to her a lot.

"Shows off her wingspan and soars like a hawk" refers to a photo I took of her on our first long drive together, to New Hope, PA in 1992. There were black hawks flying above and she posed hawk-ishly for the camera, with her long arms extended.

In a poem from March 3rd, 1996 (see it on page 10) I wrote:

> And I love spending these birthdays with Marcia Grees,
> On the way to New Hope, soaring like black hawks.

Since that day in 1992, I get very sentimental when I see a black hawk in the sky. So yes, I cry in malls (where my parents walked with their fingers entwined) and in delis (where they served soup to my parents on no-soup days) and whenever I see a black hawk in the sky or a pear in the supermarket. Steely Dan cried when they wrote their song, "Deacon Blues." So, sue me if I cry too long. (As the middle child of the Baby Boomers, I feel it's only right to cite Steely Dan at least once per book.)

Also, Lewis Jaffe is a very popular friend of mine. He's on social media more than most. Marcia is just slightly impressed that he has a thousand friends on Facebook. But I think it's great. He's a social influencer, making him the closest thing I have to a publicist.

December 10th, 2014
WHAT I'M LIVIN' FOR
(Listen to 10cc's, "Baron Samedi")

Dear M:
I've seen Brazilian girls in thongs
And don't look twice.
Don't look twice.
Don't look twice.
I don't look twice.
They wink and drop their beach
    sarongs
And I don't blink twice.
Don't blink twice.
Don't blink twice.
I don't blink twice.
I've seen bikinis made of strings
And don't look up.
Don't look up.
Don't look up.
I don't look up.
Been called a playboy and a few more
    things
But I don't hook up
Don't hook up
Don't hook up
I don't hook up

Trust me.
Girls will offer me key chains
And lots of Vodka made from French
    grains.
They ask me if I wear plain Hanes.
I get some knee scrapes and grass
    stains.
Run from women who are young
    Danes.
To meet me later, they take great
    pains.
But I just wave them away.
Tell you why I don't need their plea-
    sure.
You are my life and its greatest trea-
    sure.
Your love means the world to me.
Your curves are the only ones I see.
To bring you joy, that's what I'm livin'
    for.
Your love always has me wanting
    more.
I can't wait for what's in store.
It's our 14th anniversary.
And I'll tell you what it means to me.
It's a daily dose of ecstasy!
All My Love Forever, D

This key chain was a gift from a young Canadian woman. Other parts of the poem, like girls offering me vodka made from French grains or asking if I wear plain Hanes or getting knee scrapes and grass stains running from women who were young Danes are totally made up.

WHAT I PROBABLY MEANT TO SAY: This is a version of "I Only Have Eyes For You" or "I Fooled Around And Fell In Love." What I'm saying to Marcia is that I'm picky and I picked you. I don't think twice when Canadian girls give me key chains. You're my daily dose of ecstasy.

Below is a second poem with the same date. Apparently, I was doubly inspired by her daily dose of ecstasy.

December 10th, 2014
30 DAYS
(Listen to 10cc's, "Hotel")

Dear M:
Going to our sunny island,
Where the mountains are so blue.
14th loving anniversary,
Look up, thank God for you.
Let's sell the Birds' tix.
Let's sell 'em all.
We'll pre-plan our 12/10 vacation
Every season in the Fall.
Let's sell the Birds' tix.
They're stocks, after all.
We'll give the profits to Riu
And come down here and have a ball.
Oh, it's a great big hassle when we go
To the stadium
Where they pat down my balls on the side,
And they ask me what kind of booze I hide,
And they say your wallet's a bit too wide,
And they won't change our seats, though Lurie tried.
We'll sell 'em all and come down here.
Sunny vacations every year.
We'll watch the games on TV,
If there's nothing else to do.
We'll see the scroll on ESPN2.
Super Bowl, we'll get our tix someday.
Let's sell 'em for 10k! Hey!
Stay 30 days? Stay 30 days?
We'll sell 'em all and come down here.
Sunny vacations every year.
Going to our sunny island,
Where the water is so blue.

14th loving anniversary,
Hold hands, thank God for you.
Let's sell the Birds' tix.
Let's sell 'em all.
We'll pre-plan our 12/10 vacation
Every season in the Fall.
Let's sell the Birds' tix.
Give Rick's Café a try.
We'll feed mosquitoes to the fish
And we'll chat with the Rasta guy.
Oh, it's a great big hassle when we go
To the stadium
Where they pat down my buns on the side,
And they ask me what kind of bombs I hide,
And they question the way that your shoelace is tied,
And they won't change our seats, though Lurie tried.
Lurie tried. Lurie tried.
We'll sell 'em all and come down here.
Exciting love-fests every year.
All My Love Forever, D

WHAT I PROBABLY MEANT TO SAY: Here is another poem about the fun we had on a Jamaican all-inclusive vacation, how it was subsidized by selling Philadelphia Eagles' tickets and how the team owner, Jeffrey Lurie, got involved in helping us (eventually) change our seat locations. I predict an eventual Eagles' Super Bowl triumph, which was more like a prayer since they hadn't won the Super Bowl in the 50 years that I cheered them on in person, usually in freezing weather. (The Eagles finally won the Super Bowl three years later.) And I talk about staying for extended periods in a warm, sunny spot in winter, which we're finally doing.

WRITING TIP: You can always go with the "brevity is the soul of wit" approach and keep your version of this poem down to a few words, such as:

Look up, thank God for you.
Hold hands, thank God for you.

Your poem is almost finished. Now, add a shared experience, like this:

We'll feed mosquitoes to the fish
And we'll chat with the Rasta guy.

Just plug in your shared experiences, which should be even more fascinating than feeding mosquitoes to fish. (The Rasta guy showed us a pond on the hotel grounds that was straight out of "Swamp Thing." He bred mosquito-eating fish in that pond.) But even if they're not super fascinating, these happy or silly or poignant moments are unique to your love affair. These experiences tell the story of your life and your love. Expect to hear a lot of "ooohs" and "aaahs" when your loved ones read these poems. Expect a lot of romance, too. (See below).

December 10th, 2015
HOT SEX AT 60 PLUS

(Listen to Bruce Springsteen's, "Held Up, Without A Gun")
Dear M:
I was a newlywed at the turn of the century
And I knew it was love and it was meant to be.
But there's one thing a bride and groom do not discuss:
(Is there)
Hot sex at 60 plus.
There are so many things in marriage you don't wanna lose.
In a perfect world you'd like to hang on to.
And for me, one of those important things is lust.
(Is there)
Hot sex at 60 plus.
Well, we've been half-naked here for a week and a half.
And I can't wait to grab your thigh or your calf.
Might not be like this for everyone but it is for us.
Hot sex at 60 plus.
All My Love Forever,
D!

WHAT I PROBABLY MEANT TO SAY: Thank you for staying so sexy.

As an added feature, when you give your loved one a poem thanking her or him for staying so sexy, you'll probably get some loving that night. You can skip right past the fancy downtown dinner, saving you hundreds.

December 10th, 2015

IF I HAD A DOLPHIN

(Listen to Peter, Paul & Mary's, "If I
Had A Hammer")

Dear M:
If I had a raft here,
I'd ride it in the ocean,
I'd ride it in the pool by
The faux waterfall.
I'd take a few pics, dear,
With my underwater camera.
But then I'd think about what makes
    my life worth living
And think of you.
If I had a dolphin
I'd ride him down the river.
I'd take him on the beach where
He'd ride horseback with me.
I'd ask a few fence guys
To save us some beach chairs,
But then I'd think about what makes

my life worth living
And think of you.
If I had a bobsled
I'd ride it down the mountain.
I'd ride it on the zip line
And up Dunn's River Falls.
I'd ride it to Scotchies.
I wouldn't pay cab fare.
But then I'd think about what makes
    my life worth living
And think of you.
Now I'm in the ocean
And the day's getting late.
And my mind's relaxed
In a near-perfect state.
I see the sun and the moon,
I see the sky, the land and sea.
I see the things I need just to live
And think of you.

All My Love Forever, D!

WHAT I PROBABLY MEANT TO SAY: The chorus rings out about how I can't live without her. For all the whimsy in this poem (like taking a dolphin friend horseback riding) it's rather serious. I'm telling her she's my air to breathe.

"If I Had A Dolphin" is another adventure story; how we risked our lives taking gypsy cab rides to a chicken grille called Scotchie's in Montego Bay, Jamaica. We were in Jamaica for the fifth time, at an all-inclusive hotel. There was no need to leave the hotel. It was also very dangerous to leave the hotel. You had to be out of your mind to leave, really, unless you were going to the airport. (Celebrating Christmas with the locals, we were told by hotel staffers, was the most dangerous thing we could do.) For some reason, our group of eight wanted to leave the hotel and take a cab to get authentically grilled jerk chicken at Scotchie's. When I signed out of the complex, I was happy to know that there would at least be some proof of my whereabouts in the hours before I went missing. The girls were skipping along the street like Dorothy and her friends in "The Wizard of Oz." And then this group of drunks didn't want to pay for a cab. (I wasn't drinking alcohol.) They wanted to hire a low-cost gypsy cab. (I wanted to pay for a real cab.) Let's be clear: this was not an Uber Prestige ride. It was a ride that had a 50-50 chance of ending with our kidnapping. Sure, it was hysterically funny and the chicken was great (made in fire pits, on metal plates) but it was risky and we shouldn't have done it. That's what I meant to say about gypsy cab rides: we're not doing that again!

THEME ALERT! It's the same theme as "Swimmin' In Montego," when I revealed my desire to stop taking silly chances in foreign countries. It's another "Please be careful how you treat my love" poem. Jamaica is a dangerous place, mon. Go to Aruba.

We wore life vests in Aruba on our catamaran sail. It wasn't as dangerous as it looks.

March 3rd, 2016

YOU'RE AS YOUNG AS CAN BE

(Listen to Gordon Lightfoot's, "Summertime Dream")

Dear M:
When it's time for payin'
At the Tor-res-dale train.
You can pay just 85 p.
Quite nice, they lowered the price
But to me you're as young as can be.
Well, you look well-toned
On this milestone.
You can choose Medicare A or B.
You just ooze vitality.
That's why you're as young as can be.
You'll be getting all those discounts
On bikinis and lacy things.
We'll join the Bowl-a-Rama
And we'll winter in Palm Springs.
And if you want more,
At the Super Fresh store,
5% discount looks good to me.
You look even better than that
Because you're as young as can be.

We'll be joining different walking clubs
And yoga by the sea.
Your slot play will be subsidized
By the folks at A.A.R.P.
We'll have dinner at 3
And go to markets of flea.
And travel audaciously.
You're known for your high energy,
You keep me as young as can be.
You'll be getting all those discounts
On bikinis and lacy things.
We'll join the Bowl-a-Rama
And we'll make love in Palm Springs.
You look so sweet
In your birthday suite.
I live for that smile I see.
It's a date to celebrate
Our love that's as strong as can be.
All My Love Forever & Ever!
D!

WHAT I PROBABLY MEANT TO SAY: Your smile is what I live for. Our love is strong. It needed to be strong. Later in the month, Marcia needed lifesaving surgery. She survived uterine cancer because she was very lucky. It was contained, her doctors at Abington Hospital near Philadelphia were great and she was otherwise in good health. So, she really was as young and strong as can be.

In the summer of 2016, Marcia completed chemotherapy, went back to work for a few months, then happily retired at the end of the year. In January of 2017, Marcia and I went on an anniversary/retirement vacation to Jamaica, where they asked her how long she'd been retired and she replied, "Twelve hours!" It was also where I wrote our 16th anniversary poem.

January 15th, 2017
SWEET 16
(Listen to Lou Reed's, "Dirty Boulevard")
We're back on the North coast of Jamaica,
Celebrating our anniversary, sweet 16.
For as long as anyone can remember
There used to be a nude beach here.
It's hard to say if that makes it more or less serene.
There are a lot of nude ghosts runnin' around this place.
You can see 'em if you have enough French martinis and beer.
We're thinking about climbing up Dunn's River Falls
But we've had enough obstacles to overcome this year.
We're gonna run
On the ex-nudie beach.
We're havin' fun
On the ex-nudie beach.
We're drinkin' rum
On the ex-nudie beach.
If you want to overcome obstacles
There's an obstacle course here.
I was feeling, let's say up for the task
So I put on Speedo beach shoes and my old Eagles' cap
And took a French martini in a flask.
I did the zip line, the log roll … and tried not to get caught
In the net they put a mile out of reach.
My baby's crackin' up as my tendons try not to tear
And I'm wondering what's goin' on at the beach.
We're goin' back
To the ex-nudie beach.
Oh, my back
On the ex-nudie beach.
Need a nap
On the ex-nudie beach.
Goin' back.
We took a slow ride on a bamboo raft
Down the legendary Martha Brae river.
Martha was a Taino Indian kind of a witch
And she knew where all the treasure was hidden.
The Spaniards invaded the island and looked Martha up.
They tortured her but she didn't shiver.
Oh, she told 'em where the treasure was hidden, all right
And then the ol' gal changed the course of the river.

Back at the coastline, I want to play in the sea.
But there are rocks all over the ocean floor.
I can't rearrange the rocks or change the course of the sea
But I can be with the woman I'm living for.
Just her and me
On the ex-nudie beach.
Love in the breeze
On the ex-nudie beach.
Sweet 16
On the ex-nudie beach.

WHAT I PROBABLY MEANT TO SAY: I'm grateful to God she survived a year filled with obstacles. I felt like writing "To The Stars Through Difficulties" but that's already been written and is the state motto of Kansas.

The slow ride down the Martha Brae river on a bamboo raft was surreal. Why? First, the weather changed five or six times, in 90 minutes. Then the raft guide encouraged me to light up a smoke, since pot was legal

Riding a raft down the Martha Brae river in Jamaica. I was singing, "Proud Mary" ("Rollin' down the river") while Marcia, for some reason, was singing the theme to "Rawhide." ("Rollin,' rollin,' rollin.' Get them doggies rollin.'") Afterwards, we bought a mini-raft souvenir and some Jamaican "cigars." ("Cigars" not shown.)

and I was holding onto a cartoonishly oversized joint. It felt like we were in a parallel universe.

The legend of Martha Brae was fascinating to me (even more so than K-Mart merging with Sears or the Bloomingdale's choir being purged). Martha was a Taino Indian witch who changed the course of a river to save her country's fortune. In my poem, I'm saying that I can't do something so awesome or inspiring but I can kiss my wife every night and that's all I need.

March 3rd, 2017
"EARLY RETIREMENT"
(Listen to Joan Jett's "Bad Reputation")
Dear M:
What's this I hear about your early retirement?
Thought "work till you're 90" was a Baby Boom requirement.
But it's making America Great again,
So I gotta say I'm all in.
And I'm so glad you opted for early retirement.
Oh yes. I am.
How much have ya got for your early retirement?
Here are some ideas for an income supplement.
Never get high on your own supply
And gamble only when you win.
So ya don't have to work in your early retirement.
Oh no, not you.
Whatcha gonna do in your new-found retirement?
What's the wild plan you're all set to implement?
We'll win another trophy as "The Band Aids" in
The "Ball & Chain" bowling league.
And I'm so glad you opted for early retirement.
Oh yes, I am.
Roll it, girl!

Whatcha ever do to deserve your retirement?
At such an early age, is it a social experiment?
Sure, you worked really hard for 45 years
And survived surgery.
I think we all agree you deserve your retirement.
A l'il bit.
Oh yes. You do.

Who ya gonna hang with in your early retirement?
Let it be the guy you showed what desire meant.
And the guy who's been so lucky to experience
Your precious kind of love.
And I know who you'll hang with in your new-found retirement.
With me. That's right.
With me. With me.
All My Love Forever, D

WHAT I PROBABLY MEANT TO SAY: Like all my poems since my wife's recovery from cancer, it's about gratitude. I'm "The guy who's been so lucky to experience your precious kind of love" and I'm so thankful I didn't lose her precious love. It's a spiritual poem, like most bowling poems or movies ("The Big Lebowski," for example, was considered spiritual). Sometimes they come out that way.

August 24th, 2017 (26 years since we met!)
HIEROGLYPHICS

(Listen to Joan Baez', "Diamonds And Rust")
Well, here we are, we've gone back in time again,
At old Saratoga,
Where we celebrate the anniversary of the day we became a pair.
Just look around, nothing but horses to see,
And some thousand-year-old trees.
The ghost of Jim Dandy, could be, grazing just over there.
They say there are sacred carvings hidden in these trees,
Called Hieroglyphics, they came
Way before the Revolutionary War
That took place down the road.
I just wanted to carve my sense of gratitude
To spirits that abound here,
And to God up in heaven
For blessing us so.
Then you say you think you know who you're betting.
You like the three horse, cousin Phyllis' friend's horse,
Lifetime record, 2-3.
"He's rested now, had a good workout last week.
Looks like his performance will peak.
His name's "Hieroglyphics." Bet him in superfectas for me."
And I jump up and say, "That's gotta be the hunch of the millennium.
I was just thinking about the trees' sacred carvings and making up some.

I'm amazed that he's still on the board at a hefty 7-1."
Like Levon, "Up On Cripple Creek," don't ya know that nag came in and
  won.

After we stood in line, paying our tax fee,
We went back to the old trees,
Thinking about fate and the Hieroglyphics of yore.
I'm just so glad that the love of my life has gotten healthy,
That we took a selfie
And posted it on Facebook, a sacred carving, for sure.
All My Love Forever, D

WHAT I PROBABLY MEANT TO SAY: The meaning of these August anniversaries, recently, is how grateful we are to be together. This is another poem set during the summer racing season at Saratoga Springs, NY. We have always celebrated the anniversary of the night we met in A.C. by visiting Saratoga, except for August of 2016, when Marcia was going through chemo. I flip from serious ("carve my sense of gratitude") to silly ("Who are we betting on?") in this poem. We cry, then laugh together.

"Hieroglyphics" is worth one-hanky. The following poem is a two-hanky affair.

January 10th, 2018
ORANJESTAD
(Listen to Michelle Shocked's, "Anchorage")
Dear M:
I saw some lounge chairs blown into the pool
From Florida, all the way to Cuba.
I said, "We're not goin' to Hollywood or Havana;
We're goin' to Oranjestad, Aruba."
Let's go.
Hey babe, look around this white beach,
It's the same sand that we stood on seven years ago,
When you grabbed that starfish up with your feet
And waved frantically to me on a raft "near Venezuela."
Hey babe, it's so great to be celebrating
Our 17th anniversary,
Anywhere
Where there aren't any hurricanes.
And we're graceful in Oranjestad.

Could be, that time has made us both less bold.
We'll say "no" to that trampoline ride 500 yards out to sea,
And that hover-surfboard, with the 10-foot high, vacuum hose
Looks sketchy to me.
At least now we have smart phones.
We took the plunge and got smart phones.
Oranjestad. Tasteful in Oranjestad.
No way we'll risk goin' up for a parasail.
Don't know what will happen if there's a wind shift or gale.
Don't want to wind up in Vermont when you start to parasail here.
That's no trip for the retired.
(Or the nearly retired.)
Hey, babe.
Walk down these streets with me,
Hand in hand, lips on lips, still gives me thrills,
Dazzle me with your emerald eyes and negotiation skills.
Our spirit guides are at our table.
Our spirit guides know our love.
Our spirit guides surround us.
Let's get them Aruba tee shirts
Or One Happy Island sweatshirts.
Hey babe, it's so great to be celebrating
Our 17th anniversary,
Anywhere
That we're together.
And we're grateful in Oranjestad.
Oh, Oranjestad. Grateful in Oranjestad.
All My Love Forever, D

WHAT I PROBABLY MEANT TO SAY: This is an anniversary poem partly about past anniversary poems written to her. Like Bob Seger said, we're "a lot less bolder" than we used to be. But we're making up for it by being more grateful about what we have. Again, I go swap-flip-a-roo, from silly ("Dazzle me with your emerald eyes and negotiation skills") to serious ("Our spirit guides are at our table"). I find that the silliness breaks up the tension caused by being so serious. It provides balance. For example, check out the scene in "One Flew Over The Cuckoo's Nest" when the serious meeting with Nurse Ratched is interrupted by a pants-on-fire hot-foot.

I go full Ouija board by referring to our spirit guides. It's clear I was feeling buddy-buddy with them in January, 2018. But eighteen months earlier, when my life was in chaos, I wrote:

> I couldn't get any counsel
> From my so-called spirit guides.

Maybe I've been a fickle friend to my spirit guides. At least I believe in them. So that's something.

I had to double-check the date of this poem because it was written only a few years ago, surprising me, the poem's author. I thought it was an older poem. That's what happens when it takes 40 years to write a book.

I FOUND MY ORIGINAL POEM TO GRAND POP LOU!

The chances of me finding a handwritten copy of a poem I had written in 1972 were minuscule. There were only two copies; the original draft and a neater version for passing around to family members who may have shared some interest in why Grand pop shot himself in the head.

I was looking through old family photos and saw a tablet, by Penmate. It had 90 tear-out sheets, 8 x 10½. It was made in Garden City, NY, which, for some reason, was printed plainly on the front cover, along with the zip code: 11530. Cost: 59 cents.

I looked through it with great anticipation and recognized it as my diary from the summer of 1972, when I was a waiter/dishwasher at camp. It was also the summer when Grand pop died. In the middle of the tablet was a list I'd compiled about every song from the Who's rock opera, "Tommy." My bunkmates had voted on which song they liked better on the original version versus the new, orchestral version. "New Tommy" got more total votes than the original "Tommy" but the old album garnered a winning consensus in the final song, "Not Gonna Take It," in case you're a Who fan, keeping score. (My bunkmates played a lot of Derek and the Dominos that summer. I heard "Layla" so many times that I can't listen to it anymore.)

At the end of the tablet are notes for attending my first classes at Penn State University, written a year later, in 1973. But in between the Who's song list and my PSU things-to-do-in-my-Freshman-year list, there it was — my original, handwritten poem to Grand pop Lou. I had taken the tablet to camp so I could write every day. I would spend more time lifting weights and competing in sports and beer drinking contests than I spent on writing but not many 16-year-olds back then were into journaling all summer. (You would've been labeled a kook.) I'm pleased my younger self desired an outlet for creativity. As it turned out, it was also an outlet for my grief.

(August 3rd,1972 – just after Grand Pop Lou's suicide)
My Grand pop was someone who, throughout the years,
Taught me what's wrong and what's right.
And when he got sick, I asked myself why
He didn't even put up a fight.
He told of respect and how much he got
And other things that can't be bought.
Well, he taught my parents and then they taught me,
So he just got back what he taught.
I was saddened and maddened by what he had done.
The family was broken apart.
And could I forgive him for what he had done,
Broken my grandmother's heart.
Just how much pain can one man take?
Somewhere a line must be drawn.
But man did it hurt when a relative said,
"The great one, our buddy, is gone."
His wife was his partner and also a friend,
And even a chambermaid, too.
Doctors are wrong, miracles happen you know;
What he did, he didn't have to do.
He could've been sicker, more depressed than we thought.
Only his conscience could tell.
I cried when I heard it. I still do: in fact,
He had broken my heart, as well.
He'd say almost nothing, he kept it inside.
"What's wrong? Well, it's just 'things.'"
And as the rabbi said on that very sad day,
God will keep him in his wings.
Oh, how I'll miss him as I look back on his life,
One that was sweet and not tart.
And as for the heartbreak I mentioned before,
I give him that piece of my heart.
Goodbye, Gramps.
Your loving grandson, Don

WHAT I PROBABLY MEANT TO SAY: You broke everybody's fucking heart, Grand pop! You were from a family of professional fighters; why didn't you show a little fight? My Grand Mom Lil did. She pounded on the casket, at the graveside, yelling, "Lou, you idiot!" Bob Dylan wrote about a sudden death in "The Man In The Long Black Coat" and insisted

Grand pop Lou, early in his career, walking the beat as a traffic cop. He once threatened to break a senator's ribs with his night stick if the senator didn't have his driver move the limousine that was blocking traffic around Philadelphia's city hall.

This is the notebook with the original poem I wrote to Grand pop Lou after his suicide in 1972. Here's the hand-written first draft of the poem.

that folks were just beating a dead horse. Grand mom was beating a pine box. It was beyond traumatic because no one suspected that anything was (physically) wrong with him. The man swam around Steel Pier in Atlantic City, way out in the ocean, in his mid-60s. He was a physical fitness nut. So, I wrote to him, "Why did you have to do it?"

Grand pop Lou went to synagogue, or shul, every evening, at least when he stayed in our house. He'd come home, walk straight to our liquor cabinet, and drink a few shots of rye whiskey. My Dad would never do that in front of his kids. I had to look at old photos from Dad's office Christmas parties to see him looking a little altered. My Dad would take drinks out of my hand at family weddings, so I wouldn't get bombed and embarrass the family name. But wait a minute. I've hardly ever been bombed on alcohol (it gives me migraines), maybe five times in my life, so back then I'd feel confused and uncomfortable when he did that. I'd usually take a half of a Quaalude to calm down.

But Grand pop Lou, my Mom's father, drank openly and smoked cigars. He quoted from the bible, just like "The Man In The Long Black Coat."

"You mustn't fight with your good friend," Grand pop told me on audio tape during a 1964 recording session of a family celebration. It was odd that he often spoke like a peaceful, religious man but argued with everybody, about everything. The only

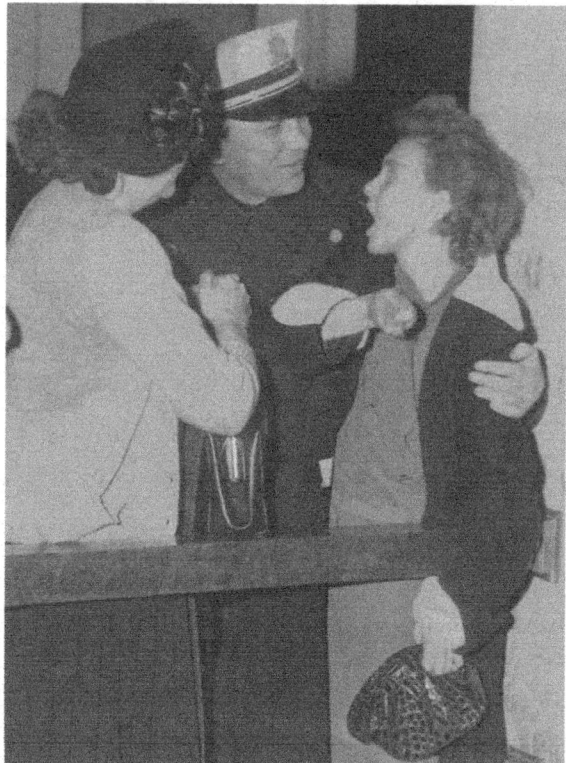

Grand pop Lou in the unfamiliar position of being a peacemaker.

Grand mom Lil with Grand Pop Lou and me at age 7. Notice the vase in the old picture? It's still with me, 57 years later. The vase was a lamp when it was new, back in the 19th century. Also notice that Grand Mom Lil is sticking out her tongue playfully, and it looks like we're all about to crack up laughing.

proof that he ever broke up a fight is a strange photo taken in the 1940s. Grand pop is in his police uniform and he's clearly playing peacemaker. He's seen calming down an irate woman. It's strange because he was normally the antagonist. His family, most of whom were born in Romania, were contrarians. When you said "It's a nice day," they said it was cloudy and damp. They were proud to be called, "The Whacky Wagners."

The family adopted the name Wagner from Gimbelovich when they arrived in the U.S. about 1900. (Grand pop Lou was born in Philadelphia in 1905.) We went to a Wagner family reunion in 2000. My Dad and I talked to Wagners who disagreed with us no matter what we said. It was a game where the winner had to goad someone named Wagner into agreeing to something, anything. There were no winners.

At this reunion, I asked a "Whacky Wagner" cousin how they chose their name. This cousin said, "Because in the old country, Romania, our fathers and grandfathers all drove buggies or wagons and sold things to eke out a living."

So … I could've been born in a wagon of a traveling show, like Cher. I could've sold bootleg booze out of the back. At least now I know why I always root for gypsies in the movies. My maternal family took the name Wagner because they had been Wagon-ers. No one in the family could argue that point. (Some did anyway.)

So why would a man of faith like Grand pop Lou blow his brains out? Why couldn't he have left a note explaining why he went to a hospital, leaned against the emergency room door and shot himself in the head. (He did leave a short note, written with a very shaky hand minutes before his suicide. It explained little beyond his request that his money go to Israel, not Grand mom Lil. Why did he leave nothing to his own widow? My guess is that Lou knew my Dad would take care of Lil.) Grand pop Lou always preached consideration. He sang, "Ya gotta give a little, take a little" to me (more like at me) whenever I didn't get my way. When he sang that song, it was always at a low point in my young life. I'd go over and punch him in the arm out of frustration and he'd give me an airplane spin and we'd both end up laughing out loud.

Was his final move at all considerate? No. Breaking everybody's heart never is. I guess he gave a little and couldn't take any more. The truth is, the feelings I expressed in this 1972 poem (such as compassion) are exactly the same today as the day I wrote it. He broke my heart ... and he can have that piece of my heart. Come back in another 47 years and I'll feel the same way.

If I wrote a poem to him today, almost 50 years after his suicide, it would look like this sequel below.

June 28th, 2019
GRAND POP WAS AN OFFICER
(Listen to John Prine's, "Grandpa Was A Carpenter")

Grand pop had a gun
Strapped onto his sock.
We hoped that he didn't shoot some-
    one
When we drove him around the block.
Broke his nose, so many times
From being quarrelsome.
Beat up other kids in the neighbor-
    hood
So he'd sell all the gum.
Grand pop was an officer
In the Philadelphia P.D.
Started before the Depression hit
And retired in '63.
He made it to detective.
He was really hard to fool.
Drank a shot of rye whiskey
When he came home from shul.
I went with Grand pop to the pool
    when I was four.
He taught me how to dive.
He threw me in head first and said,
"Tuck your head if you wanna stay
    alive."
He liked to go unshaven
And rub his beard across my face.

Loved to bet on ponies –
The 2nd favorite in every race.
Grand pop was an officer
In the Philadelphia P.D.
His night stick still has blood on it
From the 19th century.
He liked to chew on lemons;
Carried one with him as a rule.
And drank a shot of rye whiskey
When he came home from shul.
Grand mom had two kitchens.
Grand pop only ate in one.
Grand pop told her that his sisters
Meant more to him than anyone.
He towered over Grand mom.
You could hardly see her by his side.
She took way too much Thorazine
After Grand pop's suicide.
Grand pop was an officer
In the Philadelphia P.D.
His night stick still has blood on it
From the 19th century.
He made it to detective.
He was really hard to fool.
Drank a shot of rye whiskey
When he came home from shul.

WHAT I PROBABLY MEANT TO SAY: This poem to Grand Pop Lou is about compassion; not just for him, for his survivors.

This is an homage to my Grand Mom Lil and how she put up with all kinds of crap from her detective hubby with barely a complaint, only to have his suicide ruin her. For some ghastly reason, in 1978, a doctor treated her depression with Thorazine. I was living in Los Angeles but my Dad said she was popping Thorazine like M&Ms and zoning out on our living room sofa. Dad had to rip the bottle of pills out of her 73-year-old hands, like in an arm-wrestling contest. She was a zombie, with exceptionally strong hands, even for a zombie.

My Mom with Grand mom Lil in a park in South Philladelphia

In this poem, I'm strongly advising against taking Thorazine, even if the doctor prescribes it for you after a family tragedy, like what happened to Grand mom Lil. I'd like to ask everyone with suicidal feelings: "Do you want to turn your loved ones into zombies after you're gone?"

Suicide prevention classes, I believe, should include details about the survivors' struggles. I remember being angry at the whole situation but wondered who was really to blame. Was the world so cruel that it wasn't any one person's fault? It wasn't Grand mom Lil's fault. Even the Wagners agreed on that and they didn't like her much; they deemed her not good enough for Grand pop Lou (who, after all, was the son of a wagon driver in Romania.)

What was he thinking in his last days? It had to be thoughts of hopelessness. My best bet is that he was concerned with the government in Israel, and whether or not they could have used an almost 70-year-old American man for important missions. Maybe the Mossad never called him back. Dad said the Israeli government told Grand pop Lou in a letter to stay home and "send the grandchildren." Ouch!

And that's the story of how I was almost recruited by the Israeli government when I was a child. (The Israeli government, I'm guessing, has even more rules than the Masons, so I doubt it would've worked out.)

When I say:

Grand pop had a gun, Strapped onto his sock

It was a fact. He had been cornered once while off-duty by a gang of criminals and promised himself that he'd forever carry a gun. One time, my Dad let the family out of the car in front of an Atlantic City restaurant and told Grand Pop Lou to go inside. When Dad drove away solo, he was nearly involved in a road rage incident. Later, Dad told me, "If your grandfather was still in the car, he would've shot the guy. And probably gotten away with it because he knew all the Atlantic City cops."

The entire poem is based on real events. Grand Pop's brother, the boxer, Eddie "The Kid" Wagner, threw a brick at his nose and broke it more than once. The brothers would sell gum and candy at the Philadelphia train station in the 1920s and, God-forbid, if an Irish kid or an Italian kid also wanted the concession, they'd send a soon-to-be professional boxer, uncle Eddie, to beat them up and chase them away.

Another tidbit about Grand pop Lou's brother, Eddie, is that in later years he was punch drunk and habitually drunk. Being enshrined in the Philadelphia Boxing Hall Of Fame didn't sober him up. My Dad said the family had to whisk away women and children from the holiday table when Eddie went on a Rosh Hashanah rant.

Grand Pop got the job as a cop because his older brother, Abe, owned the flower stand at Philadelphia City Hall and knew all the politicians. He's the one I referred to as "Heshe" in "The Sopranos" earlier in this book. The story behind the story is that Abe's wife was from a very successful side of the family, not related to me by blood. I heard they sold some kind of a bottled product. Not sure if they used wagons.

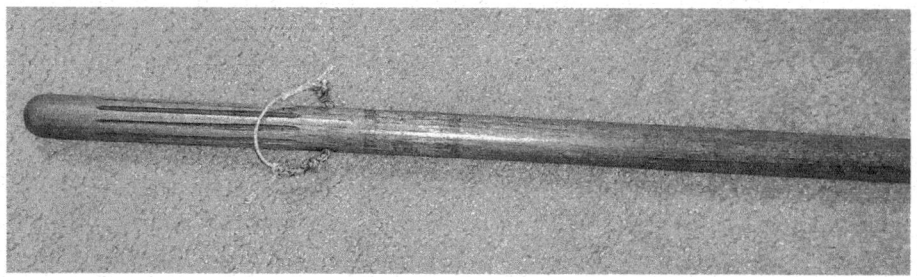

Grand pop Lou's night stick is about 120 years old. It still works!

Grand Pop Lou's policeman's night stick is in my living room; in Bubba Cila's (Grand mom Lil's mother) umbrella stand. It was heavily used from years of service when he got it in 1929, making it even older than my heirloom beach towels with the nautical designs. The night stick really does have blood on it from the 19th century. (With modern DNA testing, I could probably solve half of the cold cases from 1880-1960.) I'm surprised he didn't leave me his gladiator's shield.

The theme of both my poems to Grand Pop Lou is forgiveness. Everybody forgives you, Gramps, and there is quite a lot to forgive.

I once wrote a poem to my Mom about the framed picture of Lou and Lil Wagner. These two grandparents gave me almost no genetic material. I take after my Dad's maternal family, the Greinemans, of Vilna. (That family produced more than a few famous rabbis in Israel, none of whom were recruited by the Mossad, as far as I know.) All I got from the Wagners, I wrote to Mom, was a respect for gypsies, hair color and a pantomime. But I ended the poem by asking Mom, "How can I ever thank them for giving me the greatest mother of all time?"

Grand Pop Lou and Grand Mom Lil's wedding photo. November, 1922

FINAL THOUGHTS (PART ONE)

You know you're getting older and down to some final thoughts when you start writing love poems about financial planning.

March 3rd, 2018

HOPE THAT JERRY GETS OUR MAIL TODAY

(Listen to Tom Waits', "Hope I Don't Fall In Love With You")
Dear M:
Well, I hope that Jerry gets our mail today.
Because it contains a chunk of our IRA.
And we won't trust some sycophant to keep us safe and warm.
We need a guy with a keen, rich eye to clear us from a storm.
And I hope that Jerry gets our mail today.
Well, I hope that Jerry gets to Schwab ok
Because the money that he earns we'll need someday,
To drive up to the waterfall near the playhouse in New Hope.
And buy a hummus-veggie plate and a bar of Swedish soap.
Well, I hope that Jerry gets to Schwab ok.
Well, I think that Jerry got our mail today.
So we can go on a Bed, Bath & Beyond foray.
And walk through malls, fingers entwined,
We'll get ice cream – coffee buzz-buzz.
We order what the other likes best,
Ain't it funny what true love does.
Well, I hope that Jerry gets to Schwab ok.
Looking at family mementoes and photos in our place.

Seeing you with your arm around
Dad takes 1st place.
It could be a little thing, Mom's
serving plate,
You know it doesn't matter,
It's sharing our love that makes us
happy,
Not if our Schwab account gets fatter.
And they loved you just as much as
me.
It's your birthday, you've made
another healthy spin round the
sun.

I'm so grateful for all the angels have done.
But here on Earth, the stock market is volatile
And could burn us in a hurry.
And there is no way I want you to be exposed
To financial or other worry.
I think we should meet with Jerry right away.
Maybe Jerry couldn't reach Schwab so late in the day.
Yes, we met with Jerry just the other day.
Thanked him for making us 14% in the stock market fray.
Just before I ordered the indigestible lobster bisque,
Jerry said, "You're totally intolerant of any financial risk."
And I think that Jerry heard what we were there to say.
And we took the mail back from his hands today.
And I think our 3% will be ok.
All My Love Forever, D

WHAT I PROBABLY MEANT TO SAY: After hitting middle age, some people write poems about saving for retirement. In this one, I'm talking about spending in retirement, which is inherently more fun. It also refers to an earlier poem (on page 38) about my parents and how they walked through malls when they were well into their 80s, fingers lovingly entwined.

(From the earlier poem, "For 67 Years"):

Hey, look at the plaques upon the wall,
Some just for walkin' through the mall,
Fingers entwined there.

When I walk through a mall, holding hands with my wife, I think of my parents doing the same thing in retirement, many years earlier. I hum the above words to myself, start crying, then Marcia hands me a tissue. Every time I go to a mall with her, I spend $3 on tissues. I just can't afford to go to malls anymore, unless they have a dollar store.

You can write your own version of the "Jerry" poem above. Just ask yourself: what do we talk about most often? Kids? Food? Vacations? Bad relatives? Well, don't write poems about bad relatives. I admit I've done it and may do it again. But don't expend negative energy on that.

Also, try not to write poems about lizard people, even though that's one of the themes in the poem below. It was written by me for … me. It's an "I told you so" tale.

It's also an "I told you so" tail. (But it has nothing to do with the Mexican iguana I found on a beach bed with my wife. He was an ok fellow who looked me right in the eye.) It's about humans who act like reptiles.

November 6th, 2017 (my 62nd birthday)
IT WAS TIME TO LEAVE L.A.

(Listen to Coldplay's, "When I Ruled The World")
It was time to leave L.A.
When they pumped sludge into Playa del Rey.
But I just held my nose
And lived for years with the cons and pros.
I crafted children's scripts and they cheered up kids in hospital beds.
I submitted them to publishing links,
And publishers said, "Who cares about helping sick kids? Don't over-
    think."
One day, I poked my head next door;
They were making my script they'd rejected a week before.
And then they'd wonder, "Why you mad, bro?"
Hey, if you have to ask, you'll never know
Anyone wearing a skirt had to hike 'em.
For (insert name of Hollywood predator) and people just like him.
I heard a voice whisper in my ear
If you ever have a daughter, please don't send her here.
Racist cops that didn't try to hide it
I'd go up and say to them, "Hey,
Alabama's the other way."
It was time to leave L.A.
My agent got new office space;
It gave her more room to run while being chased.
I watched them shooting scenes in the movie, "Scarface."
Just what the town needed, more chazzers who didn't fly straight.
Then my agent tried to pimp me out
To a lady VP at Paramount.
And though I didn't want to fail,
I swear this chick had a tail.
I was a mile away when John Belushi expired.
I was in the valley eating sushi when Richard Pryor caught fire.
Once, at a party, I rolled a joint too tight;
I lost a sit-com writing job that night.
And yes, you can say it was sour grapes
But nothing in the world leaves this bad a taste.
No one asked if I enjoyed my stay.

It was time to leave L.A.
Oh oh oh oh oh
I went there to meet Charles Bukowski and Hunter Thompson.
All I met were the Bionic Woman and Gary Coleman.
I thought it'd be fun playing tarot card games.
But I sat there at USC with Charley Manson's old flames.
What kind of a place nurtures such sinful excess?
And where there's no such thing as savory success.
It's been 33 years to the day
When it was time to leave L.A.

WHAT I PROBABLY MEANT TO SAY: In this sad-but-true counter-punch, I wonder why no one in the L.A. movie biz bothered to ask if I enjoyed my stay? The answer is provided, however, in the verse about people having tails.

For the record:

- They did pump sludge into the ocean by Playa del Rey, California. It was sludge from Marina del Rey, right next door. The workers told me to go away when I asked why they were poisoning everybody on the beach, including me. I bet they're still doing it, so the yachts can go faster.

- Publishers, to me, did not seem interested in helping sick kids. They actually said I was over-thinking.

- A television studio, in 1983, produced a pilot episode of a TV series I had co-written; the same one they had recently rejected. We got no money or credit. My co-writer worked as an assistant director on a popular sitcom right next door to the sound stage where it was filmed. They had that much chutzpah.

- The L.A. cops said some racist things to me and didn't even try to hide it. Their comments just made my jaw drop.

- I really did watch them shooting scenes of the movie, "Scarface," at a car lot on Wilshire Boulevard. I love the line in that movie when the Porsche salesman asks Tony Montana if he wants to add a gun rack to the car.

- Yes, my agent did try to pimp me out to a lady VP at a major studio. (My agent knew I had a girlfriend; she was my girlfriend!) The lady VP was a cold-blooded demon but I never checked to see if she had a tail. Maybe she did.
- I was a mile away when John Belushi expired. I heard the ambulance go by.
- I was not far away when Richard Pryor mishandled his crack pipe and ran down the street, on fire.
- Once, at a party, I passed a joint that was rolled too tight and believe I lost a sit-com writing job that night. Later at that same party, my date danced with Squiggy from "Laverne & Shirley." As Sting would say, "It was a humiliating kick in the crotch."
- I met the "Bionic Woman" and Gary Coleman. (Gary was a nice kid. I didn't mention to him that child stars usually went broke by 30.) I met the original TV "Batman," Adam West. I also met Al Stewart, who wrote some great songs. I told him I loved a certain song and he said it was "trash". He hated his own song, one I loved. The rumor is that Tom Petty hated his own song, "Zombie Zoo." (He hated that song?) At Al Stewart's party, I met the guys from the 1970s band, Poco. They said I was the best pinball player they'd ever seen. I told them I loved their songs but I couldn't think of one on the spot, which was awkward. No one was thinking clearly that night in 1984. In fact, that particular party was the inspiration for my poem that started:

> There's gonna be a riot up in Hollywood tonight.
> My shoes are red, my sleeves are cut, my armpits smell just right.
> There's nothing I will do or say I'll ever recollect.
> So I'm driving slow and waiting for the drugs to take effect.

But when I look deeper into "It was time to leave L.A.," my poem about lizard people in Hollywood, I see how this is a gratitude poem, too. You see, I am grateful to L.A. — for not killing me. It's a back-handed thank you for the consolation prize called "At least it didn't kill me."

An even deeper look reveals that after all these years, I am still traumatized by my 1979 visit to Charles Manson's old house, with the naked redheads painted on the walls. I recall that after some scary woman (not as scary as Wanda in the camp kitchen) read my Tarot cards, my car wouldn't start when I tried to drive away. It felt like I was at "Hotel California" and I could never fucking leave. My date was a young lady I had met at USC (at the food truck where I worked) who had been declared legally dead for a few minutes after a car accident had knocked her eyeball across the street. (They later re-inserted it.) This was not a Los Angeles "Chamber of Commerce" moment. I would've taken the Watts riots over this. My date jiggled the steering wheel and then I could start the car. I drove away as fast as I could.

I wrote another driving away from L.A. poem, in the late 1970s, 40 years before I wrote "It Was Time To Leave L.A." It's about driving during an earthquake.

> The Earth is shaking; freeway's crammed.
> My car's electric window's jammed.
> What I feel as lanes collide,
> Is motion-sickness, side to side.
> Now I'm in Hawaii; volcano!
> The gas tank in my car's on "low."
> I shout out as the Earth gets hot,
> "Horace Greely, thanks a lot!"

WHAT I PROBABLY MEANT TO SAY: Horace Greely wrote, "Go West Young Man" and I was thinking he meant, "Go Home Young Man," which I did after seven years in L.A. Going farther west, to Hawaii, for example, was a bad idea as far as I was concerned. Nowadays, I won't even drive to west Philly.

Go west, young man; go home, young man. It became moot because the years flew by and I wasn't young anymore. (See my earlier poem, "Youth That's Gone Astray," on page 135.) I was middle age and I noticed that was the best age. Why? Because it's harder for people to screw you as you get into your 30s, 40s and 50s. And you only get screwed by your contemporaries. It's a buffer between very old and very young — ages when we're most vulnerable and most likely to get a raw deal. Middle age is not too old. It's the time to do anything we like. Freedom reigns. The middle of middle age is the most comfortable.

Steve Forbert wrote about middle age. I changed the words and made it about my new favorite place to go in middle age, South Florida.

Goofing around at Gulfstream Park. Marcia is clearly channeling my Grand Mom Lil by sticking out her tongue playfully. This kind of physical comedy must have skipped a generation because my Mom would've never fooled around like that.

March 23rd, 2018
FLORIDA

(Listen to Steve Forbert's, "Middle Age")
Florida has got us, in its grapefruit smile.
Haven't been here since RFK campaigned
So you know it's been a while.
Florida sure feels like, a burgeoning romance.
We've been here a week or two
And we'd move here if we got half a chance.
Florida. Florida. To us, it's a new state of euphoria.
Florida's got Gulfstream Park and the weather isn't bad.

Strolling down the boardwalk is how we'd like to turn into Mom and Dad.
Florida's got an ocean. Didn't know water could be so clear.
You know I'm really younger than most of the people here.
Florida. Florida. To us, it's a new state of euphoria.
Wait for us, Florida.
We can drive down to the keys and stop in Kokomo.
I've been here about a month and now I'm eating Paleo.
Florida. Florida. To us, it's a new state of euphoria.
Florida's been typecast, like it's heaven's waiting room.
But for us, it's "Get outta the way and give us a little skating room!"
Guess I'll get new windows, and for Dolphins I will cheer.
From Hollywood to South Beach, I can see our future from here.
Florida. Florida. To us, it's a new state of euphoria.
Wait for us, Florida.
We're loading up the bus, Florida.

WHAT I PROBABLY MEANT TO SAY: We'll be snowbirds and fly south every winter or just move to Florida soon. It's a hint that we're turning into our parents, in good ways. We'll enjoy the Florida sun in winter, stay active, eat healthy meals and go to Gulfstream Park for horse racing. We'll find amazing deals in flea markets, like a real NFL team parka for $7, thanks to Marcia's negotiation skills. (A manager at a car dealership recently called my wife, "The best professional negotiator" he had ever seen.)

Just like my parents did in the previous century, we'll walk on the boardwalk, fingers entwined; the main difference is that we'll be listening to The Who's, "Tommy" (orchestral version) on our smartphones and Mom and Dad did not have smartphones in the 90s. They had Sinatra on cassette tape. Even that technology was advanced for them. Dad always marveled about the home use of electricity.

Keep in mind, some of your poems will make you look like a swami. I predicted these Florida activities two years earlier (2016), in "You're As Young As Can Be":

> We'll have dinner at 3,
> And go to markets of flea.
> And travel audaciously.

I hadn't driven to Florida since my college years, the 1970s, when we would stop at toll booths to collect money for our next meal. Back then, I wrote:

> I'm drivin' with no license, go no money to exist.
> I'll pick up all those quarters at the toll booths, where they've missed.

It's like "Homeless Otis" explained to me years later from his crate outside of the Wawa convenience store: "If it falls on the street, I own it. I live here."

Otis owned a ton of magazines that literally fell off trucks. I collected coins.

In late 2019, I was mentally preparing for the December drive to south Florida when I wrote this next poem, just before our 19th wedding anniversary.

November 6th, 2019
DRIVIN' TO MIAMI
(listen to The Mamas and the Papas', "California Dreamin'")

Cruising 95,
On this Thanksgiving Day.
We are a-heading way down south.
Goin' all the way.
You know what we're both thinkin'
But never have to say.
Drivin' to Miami
To see the Eagles play.
Stopped to see a game
In Washington, D.C.
Well, the home team went and lost,
But now they draft at 3.

Saw the Falcons drop days later,
In Atlanta, GA.
Drivin' to Miami
To see the Eagles play.
Just got into town.
Missed the game today.
But it's really nice down here.
So I think we'll stay.
Super Bowl is right here
60 days from today.
Stayin' in Miami
To see the Eagles play.

WHAT I PROBABLY MEANT TO SAY: We're snowbirds.

THEME ALERT! The theme for our 19th wedding anniversary poem below is "something we did together." We drove to Florida for the first time. And though I looked for coin collection baskets at the toll booths, I couldn't find any. I found plenty of whacky moments to write about, though; plenty of loving feelings to convey.

December 1st, 2019
IT'S FLORIDA OR BUST
(listen to Puddles' version of, "Its Friday, I'm in Love")

Pack the car up in PA.
Winter time, no need to stay.
Cruisin' past Delaware Bay.
It's Florida or bust.
There's Camden yards in Baltimore.
No time now for baseball lore.
Washington; what's this circle for?
It's Florida or bust.
Welcome to VA!
Home of the Squires of the old ABA.
Folks here remember Dr. J.
Rush through Richmond if I could.
Traffic jams the neighbor-hood.
Petersburg never looked so good.
It's Florida or bust.
Stop for gas in Rocky Mount.
Like a movie set of a Southern town.
But it's rain, not snow that's coming
    down.
It's Florida or bust.
Welcome to SC!
The Carolinas look just fine to me.
But all I know is I gotta pee.

My baby wants to stop
And get out of the car.
So we eat at Ruby Tuesday's salad bar.
They've got dozens of treats,
Including pickled beets.
The anniversary feast is complete
With wasabi peas.
But now Savannah's in sight.
I say, "Let's drive all night."
And that leads to a close-range pillow
    fight.
But when she goes, "Ding! Ding!
    Ding!"
I brake for anything.
It's Florida or bust.
In a Jacksonville bar at kickoff time.
The Eagles team is so sublime.
Yet they lose to Miami,
Who's 2-9.
It's Hollywood or bust.
Driving past the Dania pier.
Sounds of waves inside our ears.
Celebrating 19 years
In the sunshine with my love.

Blending in to the Florida scene

WHAT I PROBABLY MEANT TO SAY: I'm telling her she's my sunshine and my love. And even though the trip was grueling and featured pillow fights, we survived. Now we're finally here, in warm weather, in winter. I had always promised Marcia I'd take her away from the cold winters. And as I look deeper into this whimsical poem (raving about wasabi peas at a salad bar) I see it's about gratitude and joy because our long-time dream has come to fruition.

March 3rd, 2020
THE GIRL ON THE BOCCE COURT
(listen to Bruce Springsteen's, "The Girls In Their Summer Clothes")

You learn to look both ways
When you walk across the Broadwalk
   here,
To get on Hollywood beach
With all of my bocce gear.
Bicyclists power through;
Some doing wheelies
To the sky.
And the daredevil rabbis
With babies in their hands
Fly by.
And the girl on the bocce court
Smoothing out the sand.
The girl on the bocce court
Caught my eye.
Palm trees on the sand,
Where the Europeans sit in groups.
One crew has only men,
While the other features
Female troops.
The ocean's wild today;
White caps out as far as I can see.
I figure out the odds
Of survivability.
And the girl on the bocce court
Smoothing out the sand.
The girl on the bocce court
Caught my eye.

Now she's bending over.
Putting on a pre-game show.
She's trying to distract me,
I know.
Get me out of my rhythmic flow.
A good luck kiss
To start this Flip-Flop bocce match.
I toss a tennis ball
For her to catch.
And she just bats the ball away
Like a ... tiger cub.
Today is her birthday
So I'm thinking maybe,
"Let her win."
But if I think she won't notice
Then I belong inside a
Loony bin.
And as the skaters fly by
With different kinds of show dogs in
   their hands,
I look to the sky
And thank the Lord for
These days in the Florida sands.
And the girl on the bocce court,
Smiling at me in the sun.
The girl on the bocce court
Saved my life.

WHAT I PROBABLY MEANT TO SAY: The inference is that she saved me from a life much like Charles Bukowski's (lonely, hanging out at the track) — minus his literary success. So the poem isn't about bocce or daredevil rabbis who ride their bikes at high speeds on the broadwalk – with babies in their hands! (I admit I was surprised by that. I thought Orthodox Jews liked babies.) I'm telling her that I love her competitive nature and companionship and beauty. When you write a poem to your loved one, you'll discover that you don't start out writing about those things. You write about moments and how you felt as you lived them. Put those thoughts to paper. Example: In that moment, I admired her competitive nature. A good emotional memory helps. You don't want to possess a super-great emotional memory. That would haunt you. The best example would be Paul Simon's character in the song, "The Boxer."

Much like Paul Simon's character, I remember every bump on the emotional roller-coaster. It leads to moodiness, if I'm lucky. For example, it leaves me low when the Post Office worker or the librarian treat me like a criminal, like I'm in a Larry David show. But there's a new library policy that uplifts me. I wrote a poem about it.

The record I took from the library was due 32 years ago, last Fall.
But now libraries have rescinded all late fees, which means I'm innocent, after all.
It's a burden I no longer have to carry, once I return the album by Talking Heads.
My worst affront to society – forgiven by the Feds.
So now you can't call me delinquent, uncivilized or a hoarder.
It's like they took me to the river and dropped me in the water.

"The Girl on the Bocce Court" and other Florida poems burst with over-the-top enthusiasm, which cannot be faked. The 2012 poem below is another example.

March 3rd, 2012

I GO OUTTA MY MIND

(Listen to any version of, "Kicks")

Dear M:

So, you thought you'd go to Harrah's
For a little extra birthday fun.
Seems like all through the inlet,
It's a birthday for everyone.
And then she licks her lips, I go outta my mind.
But it's her buoyant outlook on life
That's keepin' us young.
All My Love & Respect Mon, Forever, D!

WHAT I PROBABLY MEANT TO SAY: Her buoyant outlook on life is what's keeping us spry and she's a great kisser. The line: "And I've learned, in love, consideration is the key" is an homage to my Dad, who said on camera on our wedding day that consideration was the key to a successful marriage.

It's not the first or last time I'll quote my Dad. In fact, I'll quote family members in my poems to the very same family members! If nothing else, it shows I listen to them.

This one below is from 1977, when I was 21. I had just arrived in Los Angeles, in a 1972 Pontiac Grande Ville that slept seven. I put the entire poem on my business card, trying to make a statement, or something.

COMMERCIALITY

I've got commerciality.
Don't rhyme with originality
But it sounds like opportunity.
If it reads just like MASH
Then it could bring some cash.
When my villain gets killed
They'll put me
(Don Rutberg, phone #, address)
In the guild.
Oh, commerciality.
How 'bout a man and his horse?
That's too creative.
Let's be imitative
Let the love scenes pay for my Porsche.
'Cause commerciality
Undeniably
Comes to the tube

And a theater near you.
Think you can control it?
Your idea, well they just stole it.
But it ended with a scene
You saw in Rocky II, yeah.
Yours, they said, lacked artistry.
Evoked antipathy.
Wouldn't get to network chiefs
If you were Proctor or Gamble, or both.
So, move up in the industry,
Bring back all the imagery
You've seen with regularity
On late night TV.
Remember commerciality.
Forget all the misery
You used to feel,
Along with passion and growth.

COMMERCIALITY. I'VE GOT COMMERCIALITY. DON'T RHYME WITH ORIGINALITY BUT IT SOUNDS LIKE OPPORTUNITY

IF IT READS JUST LIKE M*A*S*H THEN IT COULD BRING SOME C*A*S*H. WHEN MY VILLAIN GETS KILLED THEY'LL PUT ME. DON RUTBERG. 6505 PACIFIC AVE., PLAYA DEL REY, CA. 90291. (213) 822-5488. IN THE GUILD

COMMERCIALITY? HOW ABOUT A MAN AND HIS HORSE? NO. THAT'S TOO CREATIVE. I'LL BE IMITATIVE. — LET THE LOVE SCENES PAY FOR MY PORSCHE. 'CAUSE COMMERCIALITY. UNDENIABLY. COMES TO THE TUBE

- SCREENPLAYS
- TELEVISION SCRIPTS
- NOVELS
- SHORT STORIES
- ARTICLES
- LETTERS TO UNWELCOME RELATIVES
- THREATENING MEMOS
- DESPERATE POEMS
- BIDS ON GOVERNMENT PROJECTS

WHAT I PROBABLY MEANT TO SAY: Don't be a sell-out.

If I were to write a sequel to "Commerciality," I'd call it "Simplicity," and it would begin like this:
> One word should suffice.
> Name your NARC saga Vice.
> That Alaskan adventure,
> Simply call Ice.

WHAT I WOULD PROBABLY MEAN TO SAY: Don't be a sell-out and don't dumb things down to appeal to the masses.

A publisher in California asked me to dumb down my "Life After Death" book, a book they had commissioned me to write. They said it was "too interesting" and wanted it to be all textbook-ish and dry. I said "No" because I didn't want to give my friends a copy of my book if the book wasn't interesting. I didn't want to get into awkward conversations with neighbors that would go like this: "Hey, Brian. Here's my new book. I removed all the interesting parts."

FIND THOSE OLD
LOVE NOTES IN BOXES

I've got old poems and stories in boxes labeled "Originals from 1977-1990," all typed on an electronic typewriter. (When I got my first computer in the mid '80s, I kept new work on discs.) What's in those boxes? Believe it or not, I don't know. I haven't looked! Those 30-year-old stories will be part of my next book, called "Wisdom From My Younger Self That Was Stored In Boxes I Haven't looked At In 30 Years."

The poem below is from the 1980s and has been in my head all these years. Now it's a bit different because I recently added Part Two.

1982 (Part One)
I Drew The Line
(Listen to any version of "I Fought The Law")
Breakin' rocks in the hot sun.
I drew the line and the line won.
I drew the line and the line won.
I needed money so I embezzled some.
I drew the line and the line won.
I drew the line and the line won.
I miss my baby and I miss my car.
They sure were loads of fun.
But I sold everything I ever had.
I drew the line and the line won.
I drew the line and the line won.

2019 (Part Two)
The party ended; I was not done.
I drew the line and the line won.
I drew the line and the line won.
My friends all bugged me;
    soon there were none.
I drew the line and the line won.
I drew the line and the line won.
I miss my baby and I miss my car.
They sure were loads of fun.
But I sold everything I ever had.
I drew the line and the line won.
I drew the line and the line won.

WHAT I PROBABLY MEANT TO SAY: Don't do drugs.

I wrote the first half of "I Drew The Line" in 1982, then wrote the second half 37 years later, in 2019. Not sure why it took so long.

Sometime in the late 1980s ...

1200 FILES

(Listen to The Proclaimers', "500 Miles")
My computer, at last has gone stone dead on me
And now I'm tellin' you I don't know what to think.
I'm no brooder but it linked me to society.
Now that it's gone it's gone and broken my last link.
And I just wrote 1200 files and I might write 1200 more.
When I get a new computer, I'll write "Love you" poems by the score.
Nah, nah, nah,
Nah nah nah,
Nah nah nah nah nah nah nah nah nah nah nah
All my grammar, well it used to be so bad
But my new software package knows to fix itself.
I used to stammer; my confidence was pretty sad.
This new computer has done wonders for my health.
And I just wrote 1200 files and I might write 1200 more.
If I work through breakfast, lunch and tea,
I'll have a novel done by four.
Nah, nah, nah, Nah nah nah,
Nah nah nah nah nah nah nah nah nah nah nah
And I just wrote 1200 files
And I might write 1200 more.
I can print them out in just a sec
If I buy inkjet at the store.

WHAT I PROBABLY MEANT TO SAY: At the dawn of the computer age, which was in the late 1980s (for me), I was much like Will Smith's character in Isaac Asimov's, "I, Robot"; very distrustful of technology. Then my Epson computer froze. I had almost no backup disks. It was a panicky situation since virtually all my work was on the hard drive. A 19-year-old tech guy at a computer store near the Delaware River in Bucks County, PA, stuck an oversized screwdriver into the hard drive to fix it and saved two of my novels, including "Superfan" that was later adapted into a comic book and nationally distributed.

"I taught Epson how to do it," the 19-year-old tech told me.

The hard drive story could've very easily been a hard luck story if not for the innovative teenager. The helpless feeling that kicked me in the gut back then lingers in my soul. I'm not technically inclined so I must depend on computer geeks to save my work in case of technical disasters. That's unsettling so I wrote a poem about it and yes, that did help me feel a little better.

"Superfan" never caught on as a comic book but, had it become a hit, and then a big budget, summer movie, I would've gone on TV talk shows and praised the 19-year-old tech (he'd be 50 now) to no end. He deserved it.

Speaking of using irony in your poems, like when a novel is saved by a screwdriver, I used irony in the next poem, too, about things happening when you least expect it.

I wrote the poem while listening to "The Highwayman" and like that famous old song, it's a little haunted.

January, 2005
THE RIDE
(Listen to any version of "The Highwayman")

I was a poet then.
I worked my feelings into verse
And took the blessing with the curse.
I wrote about the joy that love can bring our way
And sadness that would shriek, "Oh, Lord, please, not today."
About our heroes getting banned from the parade.
But poems still pervade.
I was a screenwriter
On the California coast,
With William Faulkner's drunken ghost.
Meeting starlets on the streets of Hollywood.
I swear, I did my share of writing when I could.
My agent kissed me off in the Fall of '84
But I'll just write some more.
I wrote for children.
Pairs of bears and butterflies;
Got paid with the wonder in their eyes.
When I spoke to youths in "low percentile" ranks,

They hugged me 'round the kneecaps just to tell me, "Thanks."
I haven't sold that many children's books or vids
But I still write for kids.
You know, I'll always write for kids.
I wrote textbooks
All about the writing life –
Showed 'em mostly to my wife.
Could be the ride will have to keep me satisfied;
Could be I'll sell a stage play with another try.
Or, I'll write a movie 'bout my reading this to you.
And watch the business it will do.

WHAT I PROBABLY MEANT TO SAY: This is my life story, and I'm sticking to it.

Similar to a line in Frank Sinatra's, "It Was A Very Good Year," when he was 35 and rode in limousines, I'm telling myself that I'm meeting starlets, and working at writing when I can get around to it, instead of the other way around. And I'm getting romantically involved with co-workers, a lot. Those things all happened, and I wanted to confess, cleanse my soul like the guy in the Airborne Toxic Event song who admitted to being a courtesan. (French words spice up any poem, as Leonard Cohen knew.) But there were no computers or space cameras back then so it all went unrecorded. There was hardly any evidence of my smart-alecky behavior. Actually, the only evidence of that is embedded in my own poems! That's almost as ironic as when a novel is saved by a screwdriver.

The ending to the above poem from January, 2005 (it's one of my only January poems) is my prediction that something totally ridiculous will make me a successful writer, years or even decades after I have completely lost interest in being a successful writer. That would be right about now so stay tuned.

But I already knew what was important in 1980 (25 years earlier) when I wrote this poem and put it on the wall of my L.A. beach apartment:

Up with loves and challenges.
Down with confusion and loss of pride.
Go up slowly, down quickly.
Be happy with the ride.

MAIN THEMES SO FAR:

(1) Stick up for each other.

(2) Be grateful.

(3) Be happy with the ride.

For me, loving relationships have only grown stronger while my ambition has grown dim; so dim that's it way past time to check the batteries (like my Dad and his pacemaker's batteries). For others, the opposite could be true and burning ambition could outlast the love (similar to behavior exhibited by some of my ex-girlfriends). I believe we get whatever it is we want most and it definitely is "In Here, Somewhere."

If the previously mentioned theory behind "In Here, Somewhere" is correct and, yes, we do attract the things we've got, it means we attract love and we attract problems, so our problems are our own fault. If we've got a problem, we are the magnets that have pulled its sorry ass over to our door and onto our shoulders.

An example would be my old cowboy hat. It was a gift. I wore it to a party in the late 1970s near Pacific Palisades, never thinking it would attract the wrong people. (I'm a Philly guy, not a cowboy.) As I mingled in this house that was built on an ancient Indian burial ground, a beautiful, older (26) blonde women who could've been a Playboy bunny chatted and drank with me all night. She asked for my number and promised to call. No way, right? But she called the next day! She came to my place at the beach, saw I was a Philly intellectual, not a cowboy, and left in ten minutes.

I wore the cowboy hat to Las Vegas a few months later, never thinking it would attract the wrong people because I was in Nevada, for crying out loud. About one hour after I arrived at The Stardust Hotel on the Las Vegas Strip, a young woman grabbed me and said she loved my hat. The next thing I knew, she had lost a fortune gambling, blamed me, and then put sugar in my gas tank to get revenge. (See my earlier poem on page 109, "I'll See That Girl Real Soon — A Trip To Las Vegas.")

The woman was friendly with an NBA owner of a team I couldn't stand, which was not a good sign. After we argued in the casino, she ran over to a security guard and said I beat her up, stole important documents and set something of hers on fire. The guard looked at me, made a confused emoji face 25 years before the confused emoji face was invented, and asked her, "This guy did all that?" My only crime was pointing out her gambling problem. I still can't root for that unnamed team (Lakers).

My car was fuel-injected, which was very high-tech in those days. Sugar in the gas tank was and still is bad for fuel-injected cars, which I learned while trying to drive through the Mojave Desert and isolated sections of Death Valley. I threw away the cowboy hat outside of Baker, California, on a 120-degree day. Baker has the world's biggest thermometer, and, on that day, it had one extra cowboy hat.

"How do you take this heat?" I asked the young gas station attendant in Baker.

The young man replied, "You just do."

I think about his answer from time to time. In any crisis, it's appropriate.

It was the second time I almost perished in the Mojave Desert. A year earlier, while driving from L.A. to Las Vegas, I was running out of gas on a 20-degree night. I had no coat and was wondering which coyote would actually eat me. Then, I saw a flickering gasoline sign off of Route 15. The old attendant in the station was sleeping in a rocking chair when I walked in, a sleeping bloodhound by his side. I was saved.

I told my friends about the gas station in the desert that prevented me from running out of gas right near "Coyotes 'R Us." They asked me to point out the station when we drove by a few months later. I looked for it, and couldn't find it. I never saw it again. It was like being in a "Twilight Zone" episode. It was the story of me being saved by an oil company. Now isn't that ironic, like when a novel is saved by a screwdriver? Not many people can say they were saved by an oil company. But I was saved by the phantom gas station and truck stop, just like Tom Waits in "Big Joe And Phantom 309."

Sometimes, you want to write a poem about a sad moment, like I did for Grand pop Lou after his suicide in 1972. I wrote and delivered the speech below after the passing of my favorite aunt, my Dad's sister, Esther. My sadness was offset by fun memories of some truly bizarre events in Esther's world. For example, she was saved by a defibrillator in 1951!

The doctor who invented it was operating on another patient two floors up when Esther's heart stopped during a hysterectomy so he ran and got his new device and saved her. The doctor had once been a professional wrestler. (It must be true — who could make that up?) Esther survived but was not herself for two weeks. Basically, she woke up after the operation, was in some kind of trance, then woke up weeks later and snapped out of her trance, in mid-sentence about Jessie's cinnamon buns, which no one had ever heard of! She didn't remember anything about her near-death experience. No one even told her for months. They had to tell her something so they said she had a collapsed lung. But women would see her in the supermarket and say, "Esther, we heard you were dead for a few minutes." She didn't know what they were talking about. She was a medical marvel who wanted to be a gossip columnist. There aren't many of those people running around.

October 4th, 2002
To My Dear Aunt Esther:

Whenever my phone would ring, I didn't think, "This could be aunt Esther." I
thought, "It is aunt Esther!"
I'd tuck Marcia in bed and she'd say, "Goodnight Don. Goodnight aunt Esther."
People would ask me, "How many times a day does she call you? Three? Four?"
And I would lie and say, "Yeah."

Remember the Hanukah story, where the oil miraculously lasted 8 days? Well, that was nothing compared to how her phone lasted 5 years. Aunt Esther was undeterred. She didn't just blow caution to the wind, she called it a "dummy!" I asked her to go to China with me tonight. She started packing. It took her 20 minutes to walk up a flight of steps but she'd say the whole time that the steps, "Weren't so bad."

When people get older, their families have to take away their cars, for their own protection and the safety of others. We had to take away her microwave oven.

Only once was she overly cautious. We were driving her home from Atlantic City when it started pouring on the highway. It was the worst thunderstorm of the summer and the car was getting bombarded by teeming rain. The car was totally silent — that really worried me. I could deal with zero visibility, screaming winds and flood conditions but not total silence from aunt Esther. I turned around to see what she was doing in the back seat and she was putting on her rain bonnet!

I said, "The rain can't reach you in the back seat of the car."

She said, "I know" and tied the rain bonnet tighter under her chin.

No one is here from the "Daughters of Lithuania" club. That was the only group to which aunt Esther did not have an affiliation.

I don't want to overstate how much aunt Esther traveled by air at discounted rates in her lifetime but an airline mentioned Esther by name in its bankruptcy papers.

I would never screen her calls and just let the answering machine take a message ... yet I was the only one she ever accused of doing that!

"Nobody answers the phone anymore!" she once yelled at me. I told her that Marcia had gotten the flu while working at a function that night and I had to go pick her up; that's why I wasn't home to take her call. So, she forgave me.

Aunt Esther was at her best just after she was caught passing along bad information. She would act like a sweet little girl and say, "Is that right?" But it was more important to her to provide information than it was to be accurate. This was a function of her trying to be helpful. I've known many reporters, including award winning New York Times journalists and aunt Esther had more passion for reporting the news than any of them. Many times, maybe even hundreds of times, I would fake that I hadn't heard something just to give her the excitement of telling me fresh news.

When she asked me, "What's doin'?" I would tell her I was grilling steak or going to the shore or buying sneakers. Her response was usually, "It's nice to have a rich nephew." One time, Marcia and I visited her in a nicer, bigger apartment at a retirement home. "Wow, this is a fancier apartment than the last one," I told her. "You even have a river view."

And before she could answer, Marcia and I both blurted out, "It's nice to have a rich aunt!" and all three of us cracked up.

Over the years, I wrote a few birthday poems for her:

No grandchild of yours can say they're not adored.
So what if you have more grandchildren than you can afford.
It's true that you've had trouble with gadgets, newfangled.
We're waiting to see if your cordless phone will get tangled.

It doesn't surprise me that she passed away during hurricane season. In the early 1990s, when she was about 75, I wrote this to her:

You're always energetic but you almost never scold.
Whether it's kindness or information; there's nothing you withhold
And just like any hurricane, at times you're uncontrolled.
But there's something special about Hurricane Esther
Because your heart is gold.

WHAT I PROBABLY MEANT TO SAY: Sometimes in my life, I've grieved over lost relatives while they were still alive; bad relations with bad relations, in other words. That wasn't the case with aunt Esther. She was a gem. I think of her and quote her once a week. Writing about her passing or any sad topic (eventually) makes me feel lighter and better. I get things off my chest and discover something in the process; something I probably knew all along.

Snooper as a nimble 1-year-old and Snooper as a super senior, posing with me and Dad on our street in Philadelphia. In her youth, Snooper would race me down that same street, even in ice and snow. There were some close races.

PET POEMS

People come up to me in Starbucks and, just before I'm arrested for loitering, ask, "Is it ok to write poems to beloved pets?" I tell them, "Is your pet's picture in front of you right now, or is it on your phone? If it is, then yes, you can write a poem to your pet." After all, Mr. Bojangles grieved for his doggie for at least 20 years. I'm going past 40 years. It's true, I still feel heartbroken about the passing of my childhood pet, a female basset hound named Snooper. Her pictures from the 1960s and 1970s are next to my computer and keyboard.

It was a few years after Grand pop Lou's suicide when his wife, my Grand mom Lil, passed away, and so did Snooper. I was in Los Angeles at the time (1979) and my Dad, who was born in 1920 and lived through The Great Depression and WWII, told me that putting 14-year-old Snooper down was the hardest thing he ever had to do. I wrote a poem for her right after she passed in the summer of 1979. It was one of the most emotional poems I ever wrote and one of the hardest things I ever had to do.

(Summer, 1979)
Snooper

We were once both puppies
With wet snouts and sensitive ears.
Your eyes were more bloodshot.
So, after 14 years of friendship,
Why is it that you're old and I'm not?
We loved to sprint up the driveway.
You always beat me to the lot
Or dragged me to a subtle scent.
And stayed until I promised a chop.
But what can I promise you now
That you're old and I'm not?
A bone? You wouldn't see me.
A prayer? You wouldn't hear me.
Your senses were so sharp,

New Jersey was in earshot.
You celebrated July 4th under the new sofa
And every other day on it.
But I sat with you.
I'm still young and you're not.
Remember that Olympic jump
From the moving car?
Mom was going to the store,
Not the vet. You forgot?
And you forgot to get off the kitchen table,
Where we left the roast.
Why are you old and I'm not?

You liked Frank Sinatra.
And chewed his albums to prove it.
The corner next to the heater was your
  spot
Until I got cold or you got hungry.
No one else had such a loyal mascot
Unless they fed you.
And now we're older
But I'm still young and you're not.
I'm not better than you
And no different.
We both knew exactly when Dad
  would be home
But you hadn't spoken to him on the
  phone.
You never taught me that trick
And you hardly learned any
Except for turning your chain into a
  knot

And howling for dinner before lunch.
I'm looking at your snapshot:
You're beautiful but old
So why am I not?
You can't hear my heart breaking now.
You used to hear brother Jeff break a
  milk bone
Two blocks away.
You can't see my tears or feel my fears
Or read this sad forget-me-not.
Snooper, my girl, I guess I love you too
  much
To know why you're old and I'm not.
I pray for your senses to return.
I pray you could live forever.
But I guess what I'm really trying to
  say is
I wish we'd have grown old together.

WHAT I PROBABLY MEANT TO SAY: Snooper was a wonderful dog; the reason why I pull over while driving so I can park, get out of the car, and roll around on the lawn with any basset hound I see walking down the street. They all remind me of her.

I don't get this dog years concept. It's not fair to dogs. It's animal cruelty, if you ask me. But when you love somebody or a pet or anything, you don't understand why you lost it. You're blinded by love. After my grand mom Sarah passed away in 1961, my Grand pop Ike said, "Why did she have to die? I would've taken care of her." It's one of the most beautiful things I've ever heard, along with my wife Marcia saying she had to survive cancer to keep me from having a lonely life.

FINAL THOUGHTS (PART TWO)

WHAT TO WORK ON NEXT

Suppose you never had a pet? Suppose you have writer's block? I suggest you use the think system, like Professor Harold Hill devised in "The Music Man." Think about what you want to say to a loved one, then dig deeper into the emotions. Hill worked with music. We're dealing with poems. But it's the same think system.

Maybe we should all try to be like Robert Browning who thought a man's reach should exceed his grasp and who was undaunted by failure. Of course, Browning was married to someone famous (the writer, Elizabeth) making it easier to grasp shit, survive failure and get your kids into a top university.

I got accepted to grad school at USC on my own. It sounds crazy now but that was considered normal back then. It wasn't that difficult. I already had a year of grad school under my belt at Cal State Northridge — as a theater major. The midterm involved having a girl sit on my lap in a Eugene O'Neil play and the final was about my howling like a wolf in a Jules Feiffer play. My grade point average was very high. An exchange student from Australia could've gotten a degree in theater, even if that student happened to be a kangaroo. Then I completed USC's MFA program in nine months, writing a bunch of screenplays, TV shows and novels, which, for me, was a lot of fun. I got to adapt "Star Trek" short stories and write dialogue for Mr. Spock! The classes were filled with beautiful, artistic women and one student even brought a pet. (I had never seen a pet in a college class back East.) I had dates with virtually every attractive female in those classes, except for the poodle. For some reason, it took nine more months for the university (that would also produce O.J. Simpson) to figure out I had passed all the requirements and mail my diploma to my parents. I hear O.J. got his Heisman Trophy right away. So, yeah, I'm still pissed.

If you have writer's block or if you can't get the hang of it, keep trying. Listen to an old, favorite song (not "Mr. Bojangles," unless you're a dog lover) for a rhythm or theme. Or find a new, favorite song, like I did with Nathaniel Rateliff's, "Hey, Mama." That one reminds me of a Robert Burns poem, not the one about the "Best Laid Plans Of Mice And Men" and not "Auld Lange Syne." It reminds me of Burns' "To The Louse" where he says what a gift it would be to see ourselves as others see us. Although I like that theme, I say no fucking way to that gift. Can you imagine having that gift? You'd hear what your family and friends really think of you. That wouldn't end well, unless you have a friend like Kentucky Mark who will always think highly of you because you wrote them a nice poem once. So, if you ever have that gift of knowing what people really think of you, take my advice and Auld Lange Syne it.

Similar to the Burns' concept from "To The Louse," in "Hey, Mama," Nathaniel Rateliff quotes his mother as she tells him what she really sees in him:

"You ain't gone far enough to say, 'At least I tried.'
You ain't worked hard enough to say, 'Well, I've done mine.'
You ain't run far enough to say, 'My legs have failed....'"

I'm taking Nathaniel Rateliff's Mama's advice to keep trying, which undoubtedly is a common theme for all of us. I've got plenty of notes for new poems and love letters. For example, my wife enjoys bowling so I plan to write something personalized to a Lindsey Buckingham song called "Big love." Buckingham tells his woman in that song that he bought her that house on the hill, so why isn't she happy? I would say something like "Didn't I take you, to bowl at T-bird lanes? ... Ooh, ah."

I've been listening to Tom Waits' "Downtown Train" and The Killers "From Here On Out" so I could write a little ditty to match the rhyme schemes of those songs. ("From Here On Out" could be called "For 18 Years.") Bruce Springsteen wrote "Radio Nowhere" and I plan to write my own version to Marcia soon. Springsteen wrote, "I just want to feel some rhythm." I'm asking myself: what do I want to say in that chorus? I just want to ... what? I want to get her port out and get an all-clear report from the doctors, if you want to know the truth. So, I'll write something like that. The poem's half written. (Now it's finished and appears later in this book, on page 282).

Remember the old song "California Sun" by the Rivieras, and later by the Ramones? They were "Out there havin' fun, in the warm California sun." We could be out there seeking (fill in the blank) in the warm Saratoga (fill in the blank). Fun/sun? Cash/dash? Once I get the rhyme scheme settled, that poem will be set.

Here is what I've tried to do in this book, as revealed in my early notes:

(1) Compile poems.

(2) Find best stories about the poems.

(3) Narrate the stories behind each love poem I've written.

(4) Categorize all the best poems; some for B&B, myself, general, for Marcia.

But as I'm finishing up, I think I know what I have to do. I have to reverse engineer the book. Reverse engineering works like this: I wrote it, now I have to figure out what I meant to say in order to fully understand it. It's just like diving before you know how to dive, or climbing monkey bars without using your hands or eating a lemon like it's an orange. You do it first, then try to figure out what happened and how to do it better, like Grand pop Lou tried to explain to me when I was a boy.

In the 1960s, kids on our Northeast Philly street would hang out in the driveway, playing hockey or football. I can still see my Grand pop Lou walking Snooper toward the empty lot a block away. Snooper would stop, sniff me to say hello, then dash toward the grassy lot. And as Grand pop Lou was being dragged away, he would shout to my friends, "I don't wanna hear about any of you smokin' banana peels!" I learned later that hobos in the 1930s would smoke dried banana peels to get high. My Dad said stew bums in those days would drink rubbing alcohol to get high. Then they'd take turns punching the drain pipes until their hands bled.

My question is: didn't they have hockey and football in the old days?

WHAT HAPPENS IF YOUR POEM ISN'T FINISHED ON TIME?

You explain to your sweety that you need a few more days. That strategy always elicits an extension.

On the 27th anniversary of the day we met (August 24th, 1991) I wanted to create a loving, poignant poem for Marcia. It was either that or go out and spend a ton of money on gifts.

I just heard Van Morrison singing "Why must I always explain?" Then I heard Steve Forbert singing "If you have to ask, you'll never know." Point taken, guys. But when I went back and heard Van Morrison's, "Real, Real Gone," I knew I had my rhythm and my chorus.

8/24/18
I'M ALL IN
(Listen to Van Morrison's, "Real, Real Gone")

Dear M:
I'm so all in.
I dove right into your ocean.
And found the true emotion.
Yeah, I'm so all in.
I'm all in.
Like I'm a Siamese twin.
Attached at the lip and chin.
Yeah, I'm so all in.
It's no common thing
Being Geez-Peas with everything.
Such best friends; some people claim
That's dysfunctional.
I'll tell you what's functional;
When you call me to the bedroom,
Baby, I'll always be punctual.
I'm so all in.

I won't field any bawdy offers.
Won't stream those lofty coffers.
You're my other half.
Yeah, I'm so all in.
Now, it's been 27 years of loving.
I can still feel the ocean air
And your bewitching boardwalk stare,
Like here's the other half.
And I'm so all in.

I'm so all yours.
I dove right into your ocean.
And found the true emotion.
You're my other half.
And I'm so all in.
All My Love Forever, D

WHAT I PROBABLY MEANT TO SAY: In the poem above, I repeat the theme of "you're my other half and you complete me." Use this theme gratuitously, especially if you don't know what to write and the clock is ticking on your loved one's big birthday or your anniversary or whatever it is that's going to distract you from the big game.

I'm also saying that 27 years have sped by since the night we met, when her friends told me candidly that if I mistreated Marcia, they would use witchcraft on my male parts. I never mentioned that story in any of my poems to Marcia. That's one of those things men don't joke about, like politics and religion.

Four months after writing "I'm All In" to celebrate the anniversary of the day we met, I wrote a poem to celebrate the anniversary of the day we married and I used the same Van Morrison song for the background melody and rhythm. Instead of "I'm All In," now "I'm Real Cheap."

12/10/18
I'M REAL CHEAP
(Listen to Van Morrison's, "Real, Real Gone")

Dear M:
I'm real, real cheap.
Can't let things just go to waste.
I pride myself on my modest taste.
Gonna start today.
Yeah, I'm real, real cheap.
I'm real, real cheap.
I won't spend unless I need to.
Shop for deals on booze and weed,
    too.
'Cause I'm real, real cheap.
We've got all this wealth,
In terms of love and spirit and health.
We don't skimp on things that shine
    like that.
But part of taking care of you, well, it
    clearly involves
Keeping the nest and eggs intact.
I'll be real, real cheap.

I won't order 18 stone crabs.
Or matching Michael Kors' bags.
Gonna start today.
I'll be real, real cheap.
Now it's been 18 years of marriage.
I won't skimp on giving you loving
    attention
While aiming for capital retention
For our silver years.
Yeah, I'm real, real cheap.

I'm real, real cheap.
Time to tighten up my belt.
Put it in the bank – that Hanukkah gelt
    (money).
For our golden years.
Yeah, I'm real, real cheap.
All My Love Forever, D

WHAT I PROBABLY MEANT TO SAY: Since I had already told her that she's my other half, I thought I'd make her happy by saying that I won't go out and spend all of our savings in the first few months of retirement. Women, traditionally, like security so if you're writing a love note to a woman, exploit this theme whenever possible.

When you're using positive themes like security and loyalty, try to avoid provocative themes like politics and religion. Sometimes, though, you need all four.

You know my motto: "If I Haven't Offended You In This Book, I Didn't Do It On Purpose." So, I feel it's only right that I set an example of just not caring if I offend someone while exploring the subjects of politics and religion. One jawn (example) is "Elijah's Back!" — my Young Adult story about the return of the biblical prophet. It was rejected by religious publishers for being "too irreverent" and by mainstream publishers for being "too religious." (It was too much in the middle between fun and serious, I guess.) But even that's better than losing a book deal because the book is "too interesting."

Having poked fun at religion and needing to research the bible to do it (fact check: can someone tell me for sure that Elijah will not return to Earth someday?) I couldn't help but poke fun at another provocative subject, politics, in the poem below.

8/31/18
I'M NOT LIKE FOX AND ALL THEIR FRIENDS
(Listen to The Kinks', "I'm Not Like Everybody Else")

I don't want to dig for uranium
In Utah state parks where kids used to swim.
And I don't want a tariff on aluminum.
And I sure don't want a war in Jerusalem.
'Cause I'm not like Fox and all their friends.
And I don't want to kill giraffes like Fox and all their friends.
And I won't mock the sick for laughs like Fox and all their friends.
Don't want Medicare cut in half like Fox and all their friends.
I'm not like Fox and all their friends.
I'm not gonna march with no hooligan,
Or follow social norms from before the flood began.
What's this, a new Civil War, or the start of it?

Let's make damn sure the free press is part of it.
And I don't want Joe McCarthy back like Fox and all their friends.
And I don't want Puerto Rico sacked like Fox and all their friends.
And I won't call a lie a fact like Fox and all their friends.
I'm not like Fox and all their friends.

WHAT I PROBABLY MEANT TO SAY: Don't believe what you
see on TV or any other source of news. As my USC professor, Stephen
Longstreet, told me in 1978, "There is no such thing as an unemployed
source."

Longstreet, whose job it was to keep William Faulkner sober in
Los Angeles in the late 1940s, told me first-hand stories about Ernest
Hemingway. He was hanging around with Hemingway and Gertrude
Stein in Paris in the 1920s. Me? I was with no one in particular at the
Algonquin Hotel in New York City in 1977. That had been the closest I
got to the literary giants of the early 20th century, until I met Longstreet.

"Hemingway's plane crashed and they sent a rescue airplane to pick
him up," Longstreet told me years ago in his Beverly Hills home.

"Then the rescue plane crashed! He banged his head again. He would
get into fights every day and kept getting punched. Then a ceiling fell on
his head in Paris. He had no sense left at the end. His mother sent him
the gun that his father used to commit suicide and Hemingway used it on
himself."

If you come across the gun that my Grand Pop Lou used to kill himself
in 1972, please do not send it to me. I've got his policeman's night stick,
which is bad enough.

Here is something more cheerful than a mother sending her son guns
through the mail or a French ceiling falling on a literary giant's head.
Below is my poem (which I thought about subconsciously for weeks) about
Marcia being completely healthy for more than two years and getting her
port out.

9/17/18
A LITTLE HELP HERE
(Listen to Bruce Springsteen's, "Radio Nowhere")
I was right outside my front door,
Saw a hundred hungry wasps flyin' around.
They were searchin' for cicadas.
Goin' for every single one in the ground.
Can I get a little help here?
Lord, I'm really hopin' you'll watch over them.
So, the summertime's about to go.
Waitin' for cicadas to put on a show.
And now I hear 'em on the leaves at night,
Singin' with all of their might.
Yeah, they got a little help there.
Lord, I'm really happy you watch over them.
Now they're gonna get their song out.
Now they're gonna get their song out.
I was waitin' for a phone call.
The minutes felt like a year.
Hopin' the doctor tells us
Her ctscan's all clear.
Can we get a little help here?
Lord, I'm really hopin' you'll watch over her.
I can tell by the happy look on her face.
And the way she's dancin' all over the place.
That her ctscan's lookin' just fine.
They're gonna take the port out this time.
We're so grateful for the help here.
Lord, I'm really happy you watch over her.
Now she's gonna get her port out.
(cicadas sing)

WHAT I PROBABLY MEANT TO SAY: My former USC professor, Stephen Longstreet, who told me every source was biased in some way, also claimed that life was for living, not for writing books or working at a job for 50 years. So, in this poem, I'm saying that I'm living my life, helping my wife recover from cancer and also saving cicadas from hungry wasps. I'm also saving a ton of cash on gifts, which is nice.

Let's finish on a silly/happy note. It helps to know that Marcia's maiden name was Grees. No, she wasn't Miss Greece, as was rumored on the Greek cruise line a few decades ago but she was always "Super Grees."

Marcia and her mother, Frances Grees, playing slots in Atlantic City, NJ

3/3/19
SUPER GREES

(Listen to Rick James', "Super Freak")

Dear M:

She's an independent girl.
Who likes to play slots with her mother.
And she takes care of my every need
Once I get her off the seat.
She likes to dance in the sand
In a kimono near the shore line.
But when she's bargaining at swap meets, she's all business;
Makes the swap meet hustlers sweat.
The girl is super sexy.
She's a Super Grees.
The kind of girl you dream about
When you're in little league.
She's all heart.
I'll take care of her forever. Yeah.
She's a Super Grees, Super Grees.
She's Super Greesy. Yow.
She likes to go to the gym.
Rides the bike for 9 plus miles.
I'm gonna take her to the deli for a bagel,
Once I get her off the seat.
She plans our Hollywood vacations.
Pokes her head in people's condos.
And she gets a super deal with charm and guile.
And gets WIFI thrown in for free.
The girl is super sexy.
She's a Super Grees.
The kind of girl you dream about
When you're in little league.
She's an independent girl.
Who likes to play slots on her birthday.
And I cherish every moment that I'm with her
Since she swept me off my feet.
All My Love Forever, D

WHAT I PROBABLY MEANT TO SAY: She's got charm and skills and looks great in a kimono, and it's not the first time I mention the kimono. I love her liveliness. They called my Dad "A Lively Fellow" in his 1934 junior high school yearbook. Through these poems, it's clear that I love lively people.

My Dad was called "Lively" at age 14

March 3rd, 2021

PORSCHE FOR MARCIA
(Listen to any version of "Guantanamera")

Dear M:
Porsche for Marcia.
Don't need a Porsche for Marcia.
Porsche for Marcia.
Don't need a Porsche for Marcia.

My love is having a birthday
And we are spending it together,
Down here in Seaside, Florida
In all this fabulous weather.
The only question is why does it have to be
Just a pandemic fantasy?
Porsche for Marcia.

Don't need a Porsche for Marcia.
Porsche for Marcia.
Don't need a Porsche for Marcia.

We're staying home for her birthday.
Maybe we'll go out and start up our non-Porsche ride.
Wipe the snow off the windshield
And remember what March is like in Seaside.
Just like in a Lewis Carroll story,
We'll try to navigate down this rabbit hole.

She says she's happy to stay safe and stay put.
Not a big risk taker, oh no.
And she'll never ask for a birthday dinner at the Waldorf;
She'll ask me to make her a Waldorf salad at home.
She likes the tartest of apples
But please go light on the salt and mayo.
(Someone yells, "Pecans!")

Porsche for Marcia.
Don't need a Porsche for Marcia.
Porsche for Marcia.
Don't need a Porsche for Marcia.

We take a walk around the river.
If you like snow, go ahead, take a fistful,
As the Canada geese squawk behind us;
They're not far enough south and look wistful.
While we're just loving each other
In a lifestyle that's quite simple but successful.

(Spanish Guitar)
(Someone yells, "My favorite senorita!")
(More Spanish Guitar)

Now the days start to get longer;
When the ice melts, the tug boats get through.
I take three pairs of gloves off
And feel grateful for time spent with you.
It may feel just like "Wonderland"
But I'm always grounded by my "Missy Moo."

Porsche for Marcia.
Don't need a Porsche for Marcia.
Porsche for Marcia.

Don't need a Porsche for Marcia.

Some years are tougher than others
But birthdays are all so sweet.
This year, for your birthday I'm taking you to Giant food stores
To pick up anything you want to eat.
We wipe down celery with wet ones.
But we do it with love that's so replete.

Porsche for Marcia.
Don't need a Porsche for Marcia.
Porsche for Marcia.
Don't need a Porsche for Marcia.

No, she won't be getting a Porsche this year.
We'll lease some other car one summer day
Or whenever it's safe to go inside a dealership.
We always get what I want anyway.
Besides, she doesn't even like to drive.
She just guides and says, "Watch the bumps," and I do.
I'll watch 'em, my love,
As long as I'm riding with you.

Porsche for Marcia.
Don't need a Porsche for Marcia.
Porsche for Marcia.
Don't need a Porsche for Marcia.

All My Love Forever! D

WHAT I PROBABLY MEANT TO SAY:

- I'm grateful to my wife for being so unspoiled and unselfish.
- I appreciate how she grounds me and takes such good care of me.
- We can navigate through tough times because we stick together as a team.
- We sometimes do silly things but can laugh about them.

Rotate these themes into your own poems to loved ones. My go-to writing move is making fun of silly things that happen, making me more like Jerry Springer than Arthur Miller. Even so, I recommend (1) good-natured kidding, followed by (2) over-the-top flattery. Then you rinse and repeat. Also keep in mind, the themes mentioned in the above "Porsche For Marcia" poem will resonate with most people involved in loving relationships. I didn't just make them up. And neither did the spirit guides who helped me write the poem. Spirit guides don't just make stuff up.

So, go ahead, try writing your own love poems. Practice. As the great Allen Iverson once said, and to this day, no one is sure what he meant, "We're talkin' about practice." I'll tell you what he meant: everyone except for him should practice in order to improve.

Of course, it will take some practice. But look at it this way: the poems will be family heirlooms in about 40 years. Besides, there are songs and poems in your head that you just have to write, whether you realize it or not.

> There are songs that I sing in my head for no reason.
> And they're always in synch with my mood and the season.
> Of course; relax!

Anyone can write poems and cards to loved ones. And even though I can't help you make $500,000, I can help you save that amount. Now it's up to $501,000 for my lifetime. So what's stopping you? Money?

THE END